PRAISE FOR
MY MOTHER IN HAVANA

"*My Mother in Havana* lifts the veil between the living and the dead and makes believers of us all. This story of a mother's absence and a daughter's need is written with a lyricism that filled my heart with beauty while also making it ache for loved ones lost. This is a stunning debut." —**Lee Martin**, author of the Pulitzer Prize Finalist *The Bright Forever*

"In Huntman's soul-stirring memoir, the author invites us to experience moments unbound from our accepted divisions of physical and spiritual worlds. With a pilgrim's devotion, and a grieving daughter's heart, Huntman takes us with her to places where, if we open ourselves fully, 'one could simply lift one's palm and brush the heavens.'" —**Brenda Miller**, *A Braided Heart: Essays on Writing and Form*

"*My Mother in Havana* invites us to understand ourselves not as solitary beings making our way alone in the world, but as part of a greater web of ancestors who watch over us and are always a breath away. A reminder, in an increasingly polarized world, of the interconnectedness of all life, material and spiritual. With language that is as energetic, transfixing, and sensuous as the batá drums that keep the rhythms of the spirits, Huntman's cadences conjure the divine spark that unites and animates us all." —**Richard Blanco**, Presidential Inaugural Poet, author of *The Prince of Los Cocuyos: A Miami Childhood*

"Spiritually rich and unabashedly passionate, this memoir is a feast for the soul . . . Huntman's deep love and respect for Cuba, and the Afro-Cuban traditions that permeate the culture, are abundantly clear in the writing." —*Kirkus Reviews*

"Journeying to Cuba, the ever generous island with a huge spiritual heart, Rebe Huntman receives the gift of healing offered by Ochún, the goddess of love, reconciling with the mother that she lost too soon. A profound quest that reveals the beauty and possibility of bridges to Cuba." —**Ruth Behar**, author of *Across So Many Seas* and *Letters from Cuba*

"More than a memoir, *My Mother in Havana* is a window to the spirituality of Cuba; Huntman's deep research and engagement with the rituals, specialists, and devotees of Afro-Cuban religion reflect her in-depth knowledge of these practices as both an observer and a participant." —**Grete Viddal, PhD**, Department of African and African-American Studies and Anthropology, Harvard University

"Rebe Huntman's *My Mother in Havana* does what all good memoirs should: travails a life with wisdom and insight, born of intimacy and vulnerability. Like the Trinity, *My Mother in Havana* is three things in one: an engaging travel narrative, a moving grief excavation, and an awe-inducing spiritual journey. Unlike the Trinity, Huntman's memoir defies the container of a single religious tradition. Huntman embraces multiple spiritual paths with humility and respect, seeking not just a mother beyond the grave, but a holy maternal energy long suppressed by mainstream traditions. *My Mother in Havana* is deeply feminist and fascinating—a profound depiction of one woman's spiritual quest for wholeness and healing." —**Heather Lanier**, author of *Raising a Rare Girl* and *Psalms of Unknowing*

"*My Mother in Havana* is full of ceremony and ritual, movement and music, miracle and myth. This evocative memoir takes us along on the writer's quest 'to call the ancestors and listen for their answer.' On this remarkable journey, the veil between the spirit world and this world, between past and present, between who we were and who we are—'the thin scrim that separates this moment from what's to come'—nearly dissolves before our eyes. I closed this book believing more than ever that the people we love, including the people we've been, never really leave us." —**Maggie Smith**, *New York Times* bestselling author of *You Could Make This Place Beautiful*

"In language pulsing with rhythm and ritual, Huntman leaves room for us to imagine what we might be looking for in our own lives, how we might need to mother and be mothered as we open to the messy wholeness of our own stories. What a gift." —**Jill Christman**, author of *If This Were Fiction: A Love Story in Essays*

"*My Mother in Havana* belongs on every bookshelf—right between *Loving Pedro Infante* by Denise Chavez and *Suttree* by Cormac McCarthy, with wrinkles on the cover from holding it and spending a quiet time reading it again and again." —**Edward Vidaurre**, author of *By Throat, By Miracle: New & Selected Poems*

"*My Mother in Havana* chronicles Rebe Huntman's journey to find maternal sources of healing, belonging, and becoming in Cuba. Moving from one end of the island to the other, the orichas, the Virgin Mary, and the dead guide her towards self-discovery and a powerful spiritual awakening rooted in intergenerational memories." —**Solimar Otero**, Director of Latino Studies & Professor of Folklore and Gender Studies, Indiana University, Bloomington

MY MOTHER IN HAVANA

A MEMOIR OF MAGIC & MIRACLE

REBE HUNTMAN

Monkfish Book Publishing Company
Rhinebeck, New York

Paperback ISBN 978-1-958972-55-7
eBook ISBN 978-1-958972-56-4

Library of Congress Cataloging-in-Publication Data

Names: Huntman, Rebe, author.
Title: My mother in Havana : a memoir of magic & miracle / Rebe Huntman.
Description: Rhinebeck, New York : Monkfish Book Publishing Company, [2025]
Identifiers: LCCN 2024020159 (print) | LCCN 2024020160 (ebook) | ISBN
    9781958972557 (paperback) | ISBN 9781958972564 (ebook)
Subjects: LCSH: Black people--Cuba--Religion. | Folklore--Cuba. |
    Mothers--Cuba.
Classification: LCC BL2530.C9 H76 2025 (print) | LCC BL2530.C9 (ebook) |
    DDC 200.896/0721--dc23/eng/20241025
LC record available at https://lccn.loc.gov/2024020159
LC ebook record available at https://lccn.loc.gov/2024020160

Front cover art: "Anunciación, la gran ofrenda". Óleo, acrílico, monedas cubanas, cerámica policromada sobre lienzo. (Oil, acrylic, Cuban coins, polychrome ceramic on canvas) 100 x 90 CM. 2022. Adrián Gómez Sancho
Line drawings by Adrián Gómez Sancho
Book and cover design by Colin Rolfe

Monkfish Book Publishing Company
22 East Market Street, Suite 304
Rhinebeck, New York 12572
(845) 876-4861
monkfishpublishing.com

For my mother, Mimi,
who gave me
her story,

& for my son, Alejandro,
to whom I offer mine.

CONTENTS

My mother I behold you
My mother is wonderful
A strong water
The one who is everywhere
Follow me.

PRAISE SONG FOR OCHÚN

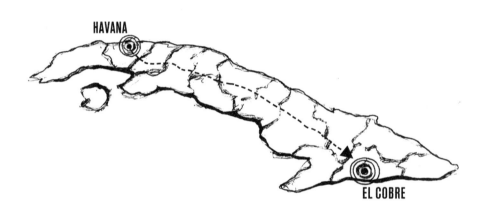

PROLOGUE

"**W**HAT HAVE YOU COME for?" Madelaine asks. And there it is, the question I've been circling ever since I first heard of a Spiritist in the small mountain town of El Cobre who talks with the dead.

With friends and family, I'd hardly dared speak of Madelaine. When I had, I'd treated the possibility of this visit as a lark, exaggerating the more salacious details: the telepathy; the raising of the dead. Omitting the part I kept secret even to myself—that I'd come not as observer but participant. That I wanted desperately to talk to my mother.

It had been decades since I'd heard her voice, the sound of it filling our house with scales and arpeggios as she washed the dishes. Pouring out the front door to call me in from a game of flashlight tag in the cul-de-sac. "Beeeeeecki, it's time to come in for diiiinner."

The last time I'd spoken with her, I was a sophomore in college, and she was dying in a hospital bed in St. Louis. She was fifty-nine.

Thirty years later, I have come to Cuba in search of her and that has led me to the house of Madelaine. In his sixties, he looks almost preppy in a striped shirt and shorts. His gray hair is cropped short to his head, and he has a neatly trimmed mustache.

An *espiritista cruzado*, he calls on both African and Catholic gods to help him cross the threshold and speak with the dead. His reputation had made its way to me where I live in Ohio. It was said that in his sessions the spirits overtook Madelaine so completely, speaking through him in a mix of Spanish and Bozal, an almost extinct language of enslaved Africans that his wife, Záhilys, needed to be present in order to translate.

Now, on a break from her job at the post office, Záhilys slips through the door of Madelaine's workroom and joins us at one of three wooden chairs he's placed at the center of the room. Her face is kind and round, her gray hair pulled back in a long braid. Around us every surface of Madelaine's workroom spills over with the objects that bridge this space with the realm of the spirits: statues of saints clustered near jars of feathers and stones. Water goblets filled with photographs of the dead. Bells and maracas; Buddhas and cigars.

I look across at Madelaine. With his neatly cropped hair and sparkling eyes, he defies any portrait I had in my head of the sort of man who might live among such things.

"The real deal," the people of El Cobre call Madelaine. As a child he could see things no one else could. Spirits looking through windows, shaking his bed at night.

"Mamá, close the curtains," he'd told his mother, who couldn't see what he did. "There are dead people looking at us."

"I want to talk to my mother," I tell Madelaine. My voice is barely a whisper. "Can we do it?"

Madelaine wrinkles his brow. "Have you brought anything?" he asks. He's referring to the offerings that normally accompany a Spiritist *misa* like the one we're about to attempt—a photograph of the deceased; her favorite flowers; an object she once touched. I think of the few things I'd kept of my mother's—a turquoise bracelet; a wooden spoon she used when baking Christmas cookies and birthday cakes. A note she wrote two months before she died: *Be my valentine in August, Becki. Because I love you always.* I hadn't thought to bring any of it with me, not even a photograph.

"It would be easier if we had something that belonged to her," Madelaine tells me. "Something that held her *aché*. But I'll try."

He fumbles through piles of candles. Plucks a slip of paper and pencil from a bowl filled with beads, and asks me to write my mother's name.

"Write it carefully," he says, "so I can read it."

I form the letters slowly, smiling as I print her first name. *Mimi.* Her parents had named her Mabelle, but at two years old my mother had insisted her name could not be something so silly, so irrelevant, so imprecise. She was not Mabelle. She was "Me."

"Me! Me!" she'd pointed, red-faced and insistent, at her own self until her parents drove to the county office and changed her birth certificate to Mimi.

Now I savor each letter as my mother's name springs to life beneath my pencil.

Mimi Meyers Huntman, Madelaine reads back to me. His voice trips over the guttural German sounds. When he finishes, he reaches for a goblet and fills it with water. "The medium through which we talk with the dead," he announces as he drops the slip of paper into the glass and my mother's name sinks to the bottom.

Madelaine then turns his attention to the preparations he hopes will entice my mother into the room. He lights a candle inside the upturned bowl of a hollow gourd, passes a bottle of cologne water around the circle, instructs his wife and me to christen our hands and head with the pungent scent he says will protect us from mischievous spirits that may try to attach themselves to us if we manage the break between worlds.

"Start singing and praying," he tells Záhilys, "as if it were a Mass." He joins her in the singing, and I expect to hear the Lucumí songs I've grown accustomed to among Santeros, but the two of them fill the room with Catholic hymns, both familiar and strange in their Spanish iterations. Madelaine's voice rumbles like water breaking over stone. Záhilys's rises clear and strong above it.

Time passes as one hymn makes way for another. From time to time, Madelaine pauses to fill a cup from the rum bottle he keeps near his feet. "It helps me get over myself," he smiles, passing the cup to me, "so

I can make room for El Cimarrón." He is referring to the Maroon, an eighteenth-century runaway slave who speaks through him when he is in trance—the very spirit who, if we are successful, will help Madelaine communicate with my mother. I take a swig and feel the hard liquor rocket to my gut and head. Still, it's hard for me to get over myself. I want so badly for this misa to work. I search my memory for any spiritual practice that might connect me with the traditions at work in the room. When my son Alex was young, I'd taken him to a Unitarian church where ministers spoke in hushed tones about a god they wouldn't name. Tired of all that ambiguity, I'd run to a Pentecostal church where pastors stomped and shouted for our salvation. Most recently, I'd begun attending a Buddhist center where we meditated quietly on cushions.

I squeeze my eyes shut, lay my hands, palms up, on my lap.

"You're trying too hard," Madelaine chides me. "Whenever foreigners come, they think they have to strike some sort of official pose." What he wants is for me to relax. Open my throat. Enter the chorus that he and Záhilys are weaving through the room.

The closest I'd come to their hymns was in the Congregational Church of my childhood. A crucifix gleamed at the front altar. The choir created pageantry as they filed in, not from the back of the church like the rest of us, but from the front, emerging as if from a secret chamber. Many sang in that choir, but it's hard to remember them because it is always my mother's figure, her face, her voice that I recall. She was in her forties then. Neither particularly tall nor large, but with a presence that seemed to fill every atom of space around her. As she sang, the light would stream through stained glass onto the hymnal she held open at her chest, her red and gold robes falling from her shoulders like wings. Her pure, strong voice—professionally trained as an operatic soprano— could rise as effortlessly as a bird taking flight. Its fullness announced that this is what she had come to do. Everything she had given her attention to throughout the week—her family, her sewing projects and her students, our house on Marvilla Lane—all funneled into this one moment. Everything she was made of was held in these notes she offered.

When the congregation joined in, I'd strain to listen past my father's voice, gruff and off key, and tune my voice to hers. But I was as tone deaf as my father, my sisters told me, and so I'd move my lips as if I were singing, hoping no one would notice I was only pretending.

In Madelaine's workroom, I find myself again going through the motions, joining when I can in Spanish, other times in English, always keeping my voice low enough to escape being heard. I'm ashamed for the Spiritist and his wife to hear my voice, afraid that they, who can summon such beauty from inside themselves, will discover that I'm tone deaf. Not just in song, but at my core.

But Madelaine is insistent. "We have to hold the energy of this space together if we're going to get your mother in the room," he tells me. And so, I try. I make up words, push myself to hum along. Still, I'm in my head, worried more about the quality of the sound I might make than the act of making it. Madelaine drops his head into his hands. "I feel nothing," he tells his wife.

I will myself to try harder, tell myself it doesn't matter whether or not I can sing. What matters is *that* I sing. While I struggle to join in, Záhilys rises from her seat to stand near Madelaine. He leans his body into hers, takes her hand in his. With his free hand, he touches his wife's face, her shoulders. Tenderly. Loosens her salt-and-pepper hair from its braid and combs his fingers through it till it falls down her back. Leads her into a slow underarm turn, first in one direction, then the other, their voices turning from the hymns they've been singing to a song I've never heard.

Ay Madre, Záhilys begins, *oye mi voz, oye mi voz.*

Oh Mother, hear my voice.

Misericordia, Poder Divino, Madelaine breaks in, his gravelly voice braiding a new refrain through hers.

Misericordia, Madre de Dios…
Misericordia para este ser…

My mind fixes on *misericordia*, this word that sounds like misery but means mercy as mysterious as everything else about this gathering. From the Latin root meaning "pity" and also "heart," it conjures that fine line between pain and glory, between holding on and letting go. It was the thing Catholics call Holy Spirit and Santeros call aché. The spirit my mother carried in her voice. I feel it surging inside me now, something like wings beating inside my chest.

"It's time to call your mother into the room," Záhilys says, motioning for me to stand. "Say her name."

I pause as I struggle to locate my mother's name among the jumble of the room.

"Mimi Meyers Huntman," I stutter, my throat still unaccustomed to making sound. And again, more loudly. "Mimi Meyers Huntman."

My voice gains strength with each repetition and the cadence of my mother's name forms a base beat for Záhilys's and Madelaine's chorus:

Misericordia, Madre de Dios…

Ay Madre, oye mi voz…

Mimi, I join in. Mimi. Then *Mother*. And then *Mamá*, both the Spanish and the child's name for her.

I close my eyes. When I open them, I feel a change in the room. A stillness has risen in the space between us. Not the kind I've seen in movies where an invisible wind blows in from nowhere to extinguish the medium's candle, but not entirely unlike that either. Madelaine, who is still singing, begins to stutter.

Záhilys nods. "He's going into trance," she tells me. "El Cimarrón is taking over."

I see the change in his body. His head bobs. His eyes widen. I get a sense that he is no longer looking at but through me. Madelaine, or rather this man who is now both Madelaine and El Cimarrón, takes my hands and lifts me from my seat. He turns me under his arm and dances me first in one direction, then the other.

Misericordia, he sings. His cheeks are wet with tears, and his voice is like the tearing of silk. The room fills with something that feels like church. An anointing, like oil rippling through the air.

Záhilys whispers, "The spirit is taking hold."

PART I
THE SIREN

She singeth merrily all day long,
She singeth each and every song.
MIMI MEYERS, JACKSONVILLE, ILLINOIS H.S. YEARBOOK, 1940

PORT OF ANGELS, 1974

I'm ten years old when my parents and I vacation in a small fishing village in Oaxaca, Mexico. My mother and I dig for seashells, pose in ankle-deep water while my father takes our picture. "Lift your chin a little," he tells us. "Turn your face to the left." This is his role in the family. He directs. Records. After my mother dies, he will spend months splicing together her greatest hits, a few images caught on Super 8 that over time begin to stand in for an entire life. I will watch as my mother poses again and again—on a honeymoon gondola; before one of her four children's birthday cakes; at the side of the house. From behind the camera my father instructs her to smile. She mouths for him to turn off the camera, then—when he doesn't—wills herself to follow along. My mother is beautiful—a sort of Ava Gardner meets Katherine Hepburn, with red lipstick and wavy brown hair, dressed always in a skirt and heels, a smile that both absorbs and infuses the air. Still, she moves tentatively, as if she might not be enough to fill these moments on film.

On the beach at Puerto Angel, she is playful. We laugh as sand tugs at our feet, invites us into deeper waters. None of us thinks to question why we are the only ones on the beach, that the waves that nip around us might not be mischievous but dangerous. By the time my father loses us in the viewfinder, my mother and I are far from shore, being pulled not just out but under.

Beneath those waves the world slows. Our legs and arms glimmer pale and strangely illuminated, as if they no longer belong to us. And then we burst to the surface where everything is churning—the waves darker, all sound coming as if from the other side of a tunnel. My mother's chest presses into my back. Her arms wrap around my waist. Both of us are coughing salt water in exchange for air. We don't die that day. Either way, though, she's not letting go.

[1]

THE REAL CHA-CHA-CHÁ

I WAS A SENIOR in high school when my parents first invited me to watch them dance. Their generation grew up with big bands and ballroom dancing, and in the early 80s they were still seeking out those places where their music could be found. On weekends they danced with the St. Louis Dance Club or at the Casa Loma Ballroom on the city's south side. Sometimes they drove to a KC Hall in Staunton, Illinois, where they waltzed and jitterbugged under a 260-pound crystal chandelier imported from Italy. My mother would be decked out in an evening dress she'd sewn for the occasion, her neck and arms strung with gold. My father in a suit and tie, his blue eyes twinkling over a silver mustache and beard. The orchestra always knew them and played "Mack the Knife" just for them. My father would snap his fingers, swing his body into shapes he invented on the fly. And while he was leading, he provided no recognizable steps to follow, which made it difficult for my mother.

For years she'd suggested they take dance classes and learn a syllabus of steps so they might both have something to hold onto. And so, when I was seventeen, my father signed them up for lessons at a Fred Astaire dance studio. My mother had spent the previous year fighting colon cancer, undergoing weeks of surgery and then chemotherapy. She was eager for a diversion and the studio offered group classes and private lessons, practice parties and competitions, showcases and festivals.

While my father struggled to memorize the foreign steps, my mother threw herself wholeheartedly into the endeavor. She bought a pair of strappy silver dance shoes and a wire brush to keep their suede bottoms clean. On Saturdays she carried the shoes inside a drawstring bag to the studio's theme parties, where she and my father danced with instructors they addressed not by their first names but by their honorifics: Miss Walker, Mr. McCullough. My parents would come home tipsy from punch they drank from plastic cups, with Polaroid evidence of their adventures in my mother's purse: my father dancing with an instructor a third his age, a bright handkerchief waving from his breast pocket; my mother in a crown, smiling almost girlishly as she posed before a backdrop of construction-paper jungle leaves.

I was mortified, both for them and for me, when they invited me to watch them perform at what their studio was calling a showcase. At seventeen I longed to rise above the version of myself I faced each day in the mirror, that girl with a long face erupting in pimples and a body that was all straight lines, not a curve in sight.

Everywhere I looked—from our house in the St. Louis suburbs, one of six brick homes that lined our cul-de-sac, each framed in boxwoods and magnolias, to the grids of farmland in Central Illinois where we spent weekends and summers—my life felt like a box someone else had arranged for me to inhabit. There were piano lessons and grades to master, colleges to apply for, a neighborhood just like Marvilla Lane waiting on the other side with a husband and children of my own.

My parents' ballroom dancing seemed as rigid and uninspired as everything else about our suburban life. And they were going to be performing a tango, a dance I equated with silent movies, irrelevant. As the evening approached, I complained to friends about the lameness of spending an evening at my parents' dance studio. Even so, I'd noticed how good this dancing seemed to be for my mother. I sometimes caught her practicing her steps in the living room—her arms raised as if to embrace an invisible partner, a loose curl falling over her forehead she was too intent to sweep away. A smile on her face that seemed to belong wholly to her.

It was just the three of us at home then. My two sisters and brother, who'd been teenagers when I was born, had long left St. Louis. My father was semi-retired, meaning that, after decades of running the Huntman family funeral home, ambulance service, and furniture store, he'd hung up his business suit to manage a few parcels of farmland in central Illinois. My mother divided her time between doctors' visits and sewing projects. Tutoring international students at Washington University. Singing in the church choir. And now dance.

On the night of their showcase, my parents dress from separate sides of their closet. My father puts on the black tuxedo he keeps for special occasions while my mother slips on a red and black ruffled dress that matches her image of the tango: a series of impressions culled from song lyrics and movie stills that spoke of leggy women who danced beneath streetlamps, their stilettos carving their presence into the night.

When it is time for the finishing touches, my mother calls me in to consult over choices in stockings and perfume. I help clip a silk rose to her hair. She leans forward to the mirror to apply a lipstick as red as any tango before turning to ask me, as she so often did, if it is good. Her brown hair curls in waves around her face; her smile is both uncertain and expectant. She is not perfect. The lipstick is already bleeding a little at the edges and a gold crown on an upper tooth interrupts her smile. Still, my mother is radiant.

As we pull out of our drive, Marvilla Lane disappears in the review mirror. It is the third week of December and our lawns and roofs are dusted in snow. In two weeks, my mother will begin a new round of chemotherapy. For now, she and my father talk only about their upcoming performance. Tonight, they'll be dancing their tango number not with each other but with their instructors. When they finish, the professionals will then dance with one another. Some of them are so good, my mother tells me, they're winning trophies all around the country, and her enthusiasm is so contagious that for a moment I forget that this outing is lame.

It's a ten-minute drive, just enough for the landscape to turn from tree-lined neighborhoods to apartment buildings and strip malls. My father parks in front of a vacuum and janitor supply store that sits on the first floor of a two-story office building and leads us up a flight of stairs to the second floor. Tucked between an insurance office and a bakery, the studio emits the smooth sounds of a foxtrot, which slip through glass doors etched with silhouettes of Ginger and Fred.

Inside, a few dozen students sit at tables sipping punch, the bravest among them foxtrotting in the ring of dance floor. Some are couples in their fifties and sixties who, like my parents, take lessons together. Others are widows—women in their seventies and eighties for whom this studio and the handsome instructors who partner with them are the center of their universe. But if the crowd is modest, still the room swells to the point of bursting. Brightly colored satin festoons doors and windows. Top hats and canes hang from walls. A mirror ball spins from the ceiling, with balloons and streamers radiating from it like the rays of a sun.

My father starts making the rounds, greeting everyone as enthusiastically as if he hasn't just seen them the week before. Both he and my mother seem overjoyed to introduce me to the people who make up their ballroom world. Among them is Mr. McCullough, a handsome man with a gold chain and a Magnum P. I. mustache who teaches my mother. She blushes when she introduces us, as if she has a crush.

When they excuse themselves to practice, I head to the refreshment table where the studio's famous spiked punch beckons from an actual punch bowl. The instructor who presides over it is glamorous in all the ways I yearn to be. Her blonde hair, crimped in waves, reaches her waist. Her eyes are powdered in blue and lined with kohl that draws them up like smoke. She doesn't seem to notice or care that I'm underage. I fill a plastic cup and seat myself at a corner table where I have a view of the room.

No one else in the studio is my age. At a nearby table a white-haired woman in chandelier earrings chats with her instructor. At another a group of ladies wait for their own teachers to invite them to dance. Circling the floor, the professionals carry themselves like royalty. Heads high. Spines erect. Some are dressed in prairie skirts and cowboy hats and I realize that, even though it's five days before Christmas, tonight's theme is country western. When one of them tips his hat in my direction I shake my head and move my chair closer to the wall.

The crowd is still circulating when the emcee announces my parents. As they take the floor with their instructors, my father is full of swagger, swaying and jitterbugging even before the music begins. His partner, a young redhaired woman, wears an off-the-shoulder ruffled dress whose hem, unlike my mother's, is cut short to show off her legs. Her eyes, like those of the instructor at the punch bowl, are powdered and lined with kohl.

My mother looks serious, either because she's nervous or because she's embodying the tone of the tango. She touches her hair, assures herself that the rose is still there, then rests her fingers on her instructor's shoulder.

There's a rustling in seats, and then the music, a classic tango I recognize from my mother's practice sessions, fills the room with violin and bandoneón. My parents' choreography is nothing fancy, just four or five basic figures they repeat on a loop. My mother holds her head high, directs her gaze over her partner's shoulder the way he's taught her, follows the syllabus of promenades and open fans precisely. *Slow, slow, quick, quick, slow,* I've heard her count each time she practices, her voice—almost a whisper—suggesting she knows these rhythms not as a set of instructions but as a mantra.

If my mother is the proud tango mistress, my father is Mack the Knife. He tips an imaginary hat. Turns every promenade into a jazz riff, dipping side to side like a drunken sailor. Each time he opens into a fan, he cocks a finger like he's shooting a pistol into the air. Still, my mother seems the crowd favorite. "Go, Mrs. Huntman!" someone shouts. I see the corners of her mouth twitch and I can't tell if she's smiling or counting.

"Olé!" the emcee shouts when the tempo changes from a tango to a paso doble. No longer the rhythm of romance under streetlamps, the paso doble is the dance of the bullfight. Its cadence, like the staccato march of hooves, invites the dancers to enter the bullring and inhabit its shapes—the matador. The bull. The cape, red and lurid, that distracts us from the awful inevitability of the match.

A trumpet sounds and my father clicks his heels, steps backward to invite his partner into the negative space he creates for her. She lifts her skirts like a cape and makes the pass. A man in the audience whistles. Someone else applauds. My mother swivels, carving figure eights into the floor with her heels. Presses her lips as she pivots into a final promenade. Again, the trumpet sounds, joining violin and accordion in a duel of brass and wind. A stampede of notes reaches a crescendo just as both my father and Mr. McCullough spin their partners out to face the crowd.

"Olé!" the emcee cheers.

Then, "All right, Mr. and Mrs. Huntman!" The room fills with applause. And while my father leads his instructor back to her seat, my mother and Mr. McCullough remain standing. There is no curtsy. My mother stands shoulder to shoulder with her partner. Their inner hands are clasped. Their outer arms open at a 45-degree angle, creating a V for Victory. Her smile fills the rest of us with the shape of all that possibility.

"*Bravo!*" someone shouts.

And again: "Bravo!!!"

My mother is still standing when the emcee starts moving the night into its next configuration. "We have a new crowning," he announces, gesturing toward the front of the room where two high-backed rattan chairs have been placed as thrones. Later, I will learn that the crown is awarded to the student who spends the most money on lessons. For now, it is just one more odd detail in a night of incongruities.

"Please welcome our new king and queen, Mr. Franz and Ms. Birdeneau!" the emcee trills. An instructor in a plaid shirt and cowboy boots leads the woman in the chandelier earrings toward the front of the room. The woman smiles as she receives her crown, and everyone applauds. I pour myself another cup of punch and seat myself with my parents, who are either too happy or too distracted to notice that I'm getting drunk.

When the emcee announces the professional portion of the showcase, a hush falls over the room. The rustling in and out of seats, the trips to the rest room and punch bowl, are replaced by an anticipation that has even me moving to the edge of my seat. The lights dim, then brighten. And when the professionals emerge, they too are changed. No longer in cowboy attire, the men are dressed in the cat suits then fashionable in the dance world, the women in Lycra and chiffon cut to show off every curve. I take in every detail: the shape and muscle of the women's legs accentuated by asymmetrical hems. Their bodices, cut from a flesh-colored fabric called Illusion that gives the appearance of being nude, strategically trimmed in hundreds of rhinestones. It isn't just their dresses that shimmer. Rhinestones spark from hair combs. Gold glitter dusts their eyes. Even their shoes—strappy and open-toed like my mother's— flash with still more sparkle.

The dancers begin with the foxtrot and waltz, smooth dances that, however beautiful, seem old fashioned and stiff. But when they break into the Latin rhythms—sambas and rumbas that send their bodies stretching and rolling like waves—something inside me shifts. The pageantry of glitter and twinkle lights, the exaggerated sensuality of teased hair and eyeliner, the mirror ball and streamers and rhinestones all adding up to something that is simultaneously over the top and just scratching at something even more fantastic.

These ballroom steps were only an approximation of the original Latin dances they'd been modeled after. And yet there was something undeniably real in the Afro-Cuban rhythms that lay beneath them. Even as I remained seated, a bass line grabbed me by my hips and feet, connecting me with a version of myself I'd always wanted to meet. A version opposite the straight lines and grids I'd been chafing against. A shape that was sultry and fluid, vast and alive.

Ah, so this is it, I thought without thinking.

For the next year and a half, my mother and I would share the same dance teacher. We picked out matching dance shoes we carried inside

matching drawstring bags to the studio's theme parties I both mocked
and adored. When it was time for me to start performing, my mother
sewed my first dance dress, cutting its skirts from blue chiffon she edged
in fishing line, which sent them rippling like water, and sequinning the
bodice in turquoise that shimmered like waves.

From that start in St. Louis, I'd go on to build a career as a Latin dancer
and choreographer. Most of my knowledge of those dances came to me
second-hand from the ballroom world, the original Afro-Cuban steps
streamlined and codified into European and then American syllabi.
Then, in 2004, when I was nearing 40, I traveled to Havana to study
with Lourdes Tamayo Fernández. I told her I'd come to learn the Cuban
roots of those dances so I could carry them back to the dance company
I trained in Chicago.

"Show me what you do," Lourdes asked at the first of many lessons
that would take place in the small square of her living room. Petite, in
her forties, she sat back in her chair, her face bright and expectant as I
danced what the ballroom world called a cha-cha and Cubans called
a cha-cha-chá. I pointed my feet and straightened my knees the way
years of Latin ballroom dance had trained me to. When I finished, she
applauded.

"That was beautiful," she said, laughing. "It wasn't the cha-cha-chá,
but it was beautiful."

Over cups of coffee and rum, Lourdes taught me the real cha-cha-
chá, a dance that traced its origins to the Afro-Cuban dances that connect us with the breath and stories of the gods. Dancing alongside me,
she demonstrated how to bend my knees and surrender to the earth.
Every step, every gesture, had a meaning. She explained how the Yoruba
of southwestern Nigeria tell of an age when Sky and Earth were one—
the world shaped like a gourd, its upper and lower halves fitted together
so snugly it was said that you could simply lift your palm and brush the
heavens.

It was through that scrim between worlds that the supreme god Olodumare had sent the intermediary gods known as the *oricha* spinning their way from Sky to Earth on spider webs to ready the Earth for human habitation. And it was through that veil that Lourdes now invited me to know the oricha.

There were hundreds of oricha and just as many ways to talk about them. Some were said to have been born directly from Olodumare. Others had been legendary kings and queens so great that when they died, they ascended to the realm of the gods. Still other oricha were anthropomorphic forces of nature. There were water oricha and sky oricha. Oricha who were as hot in temper as the lightning bolts they threw and the metals they forged, or as cool as the plants and waters they used to heal.

The oricha were our guides, Lourdes explained. It was by knowing them that we came to know ourselves and that we might come to know God. And so each of us was said to be born with a guardian oricha who would show us the way, and each of us would grow according to the characteristics of that oricha.

It was through our offerings that we came face to face with those divine exemplars. When we performed a ritual, whether it was through sacrifice or prayer or dance or song, we punctured the membrane between worlds, made our way back to the eternal time of the gods who gave us our shape.

Each oricha had a palette of color and sound, a symbology that allowed the dancer to inhabit their essence. For Eleggua, god of chance and guardian of the thresholds, it was a stutter step and cane. For the hunter-blacksmith Ogún, the machete and anvil he wielded to cut through obstacles. For the sea goddess Yemayá, it was her conch shell. And for her daughter, the river goddess Ochún, it was honey and sunflowers and copper and gold—bright, sensual things that pointed to the way she moved through the world.

Of all the oricha, it was Ochún who moved me. She was queen of the rivers, the ever-renewing source that bubbles just beneath the surface. The mighty shapeshifter who spins herself from weaver to oracle, from maiden to crone. She was a dancer. A musician. A sensuous beauty who adorned herself with beads and fans. She was a mother who helped others conceive. A wealthy businesswoman who held her riches in a calabash. The leader of the powerful women known as the *àjé*.

Through her steps I learned to work my skirt like a sail, lifting its white cotton outward and then back, my arms circling like oars. Both her dance and the *batá* drums that accompanied her echoed the swell and retreat of her river.

Something about the river goddess felt at home in my body, as if something or someone were beckoning me toward some deeper version of myself, asking only that I take her hand, close my eyes, and follow. First one step. Then the next.

Once I'd been introduced to the oricha, I discovered them on every corner of Havana. Their statues and symbols lined the shelves of the spiritual shops known as *botánicas*. They guarded the thresholds of businesses and homes. Their patterns rose in the cadence of musicians who played on street corners. Swirled across painted murals and canvases on display in alley shops.

In the afternoons, Lourdes and I walked to outdoor cafés where she introduced me to Havana's writers and artists—brightly dressed men and women who congregated around iron tables, drinking and smoking while they talked about art and religion in the same breath.

All art began with God, the ideal, they argued. Both Plato and Aquinas had known it. It was the spiritual substance of art, rather than the form, that mattered, for art was not meant to document but illuminate. To trick the mind, cause a double take. It was supposed to stir things up, incite you. Move you.

In the evenings, Lourdes and I danced at nightclubs where men and women shimmied with a freedom I'd never seen back home, their bodies as fluid as sea and air. But only on our last night together did I understand the depths of the dances I only thought I was coming to know. Arms linked, heads bowed in conversation that alternated between the topics of politics and men, we followed Havana's seawall to a nightclub in Vedado. Along the way we passed artists selling paintings and jewelry and couples holding hands; a musician playing trumpet and another playing French horn. Then, ducking into a doorway, we slipped down a staircase and into the smoke-filled basement of an underground cabaret.

Arriving just before the floorshow began, we grabbed one of the last remaining tables and settled into our seats. Around us men and women clinked their rum glasses. Lourdes squeezed my hand. The cleared space between tables was already set with the two-headed talking drums known as the batá. Carved from a single log, when filled with ritual medicines these instruments were believed to hold the oricha known as Aña, which was both the soul of the drums and of the drummer who played them. The voice of the drums was the voice of the gods, their call an invitation for the oricha to spin their way back to Earth. If they were successful, the oricha would accept the invitation, enter the room by mounting the bodies of the dancers who called them forth with their arms and feet.

The spectacle began with a cracking noise, followed by the flats of drummers' hands rising and falling in the patterns of pulse and silence that invite Eleggua into the space. The gatekeeper between worlds and messenger to the gods, Eleggua is first to receive every invitation. Dressed in red and black, the powerful trickster-warrior spun into the room. He staggered through the audience, stealing cigars and drinking from patrons' cups. He raised his club to remind us that it is he who is lord of *caminos* and opener of paths.

Next to enter were Ogún, the hunter-blacksmith, and the god of thunder, Changó. The two somersaulted through the space, taking turns to see who could lunge the farthest, jump the highest, twirl the longest. Ogún swung his machete to clear obstacles invisible to the untrained eye while Changó sent lightning bolts crashing off tables and chairs.

Then the cadence of the drums changed. There was a swelling of sound as the men made way for the mothers. First among them was

Oyá, queen of the cemetery and mistress of winds, whipping her fly whisk to stir the air between breeze and hurricane. Behind her came the sea goddess Yemayá, her blue and white skirts rippling as she moved between glassy waters and raging tidal wave. When she finished, it was Ochún's turn. Dressed from head to toe in yellow and gold, the river goddess entered, her undulating hips and steps tracing the curves of her current. I recognized her movements as those I'd been studying with Lourdes, could feel my own body wanting to move in my seat.

A pop of drums announced the invitation for the warriors and kings to rejoin the mothers. They were all here now—iron and thunder, wind and river and sea, all battling for floor and air in ever-increasing feats of strength. Each jump, each turn accelerated the momentum until the room became a vortex of motion and sound. The crackling of the batá, the rise and fall of dancers' feet drumming the rhythms of the oricha into the floor. The lifting of skirts and arms, machetes and clubs calling those gods from the realm of the spirits into the physical world, inviting them to climb dancers' bodies like trees, mount them like horses, until it was clear that the dancers had stopped performing the oricha and had *become* the oricha.

You could see it the moment the spirit took hold. Yemayá's eyes rolled back in her head. Eleggua stumbled, wide-eyed, through the crowd, demanding cigar and drink in a voice that was no longer the dancer's.

The crowd too changed. Only moments ago engrossed in drinks and conversation, they opened, as if on a hinge. An old man at a nearby table stood, his lips moving in prayer as he tossed a ten-peso bill in the direction of Eleggua. A woman across from him shouted, "¡Aché!"

I was among those changed. Everything I thought I knew about the body in space, about the line between performance and ritual, between skin and spirit, dissolved before me in a sea of cloth and sweat and prayer.

[2]

VENUS IN THE LIBRARY

⁓

WHEN LOURDES SAW ME off at the airport in Havana, I cried. I cried again when my plane touched ground in Miami, the applause of passengers—that distinctly Cuban custom of thanking the gods for a safe return—a reminder of all I was leaving behind. The thought of separating myself from Lourdes, from the worlds she'd opened up to me, was like ripping off a part of me I'd only begun to discover.

That was 2004. Nine years had passed since Lourdes and I had said our goodbyes. No longer the forty-year-old version of myself who was a dancer and a choreographer, I'd spent the last decade seeing my son through high school and off to college, closing my dance studio, and moving myself from Chicago to Ohio for graduate school.

Recently, I'd tried contacting Lourdes, but her phone was disconnected, and I wasn't able to track down her address. I wanted to get in touch with her because I was preparing to return to Cuba. The desire to go had become like a physical pull. I wanted to find a way back to what I'd witnessed on that first trip. There were wormholes in the universe, portals through which one could slip from one world to another, like in the books my mother had read to me as a child—collections of Greek and Roman myths; The *Chronicles of Narnia*—in which gods and children passed through secret wardrobes and doors.

A recurring dream came to me in the veil between night and day. Einstein and I are staring at one another, suspended underwater, separated by the thinnest of membranes, his nose just inches from mine. He tells me it has always been like this. Just this thin scrim between the two of us. Between us and everything. I can visit any time I want.

In the months after my mother died, the door between worlds swung easily on its hinge, the shape of her so palpable it seemed impossible that she wasn't really there. Her sewing machine in the corner of her bedroom was still threaded with its last bright spool. Her slips and stockings were still tucked in dresser drawers, as if at any moment she might step back into them.

It was more than the objects, though. I could *see* her—standing in the driveway each time I drove home from college to visit my father, her hand lifted to wave me through the front door. When I'd go to Schnucks market, I'd spy her pushing a grocery cart stacked with cuts of meat and vegetables for our dinner.

Part of me didn't accept that she was dead. She'd died in the night when my father was the only family member on watch. There was no funeral. I never saw a body. My mother had seen my father work as an undertaker, pumping bodies with formaldehyde to stave off the stench of death; caking cheeks with rouge to create the appearance of life; positioning hands and jaw to conjure the illusion of peace, as if the dead were not gone but merely resting. My mother wanted none of it. She'd asked to be cremated, and her ashes were released over a cornfield that my brother farmed in central Illinois.

Two months after her death, I was back at college in Chicago. It was the end of the first semester of my sophomore year, and I walked home from my last winter exam in the dim gray afternoon light. It was indescribably cold out. Snow crunched underfoot and a curtain of still more snow fell through the dusk, like ash. The stone walls of Alice Millar Chapel rose ahead, heavy and gray, from the landscape, its stained-glass windows shining impossibly bright against all that gray.

It would be years before I'd hear the Yoruba story about Sky and

Earth: how the world was once shaped like a gourd, its upper and lower halves fitted in an embrace. All I knew was that I'd aced my exam. I thought how proud my mother would have been. And, as I walked back to my apartment, I felt her with me, her appearance not a figment of a young woman's imagination but an actual, physical presence walking by my side, her footsteps falling in time with mine. I felt her hand, solid and substantial, fitting precisely inside my own.

I don't remember what we talked about as we walked the last half-mile. I might have told her how I'd put behind me my freshman year of drugs and sex, that clichéd rebellion against the confines of home. I was ready to make something of myself, become the daughter she'd hoped I'd be.

She might have talked about the last months of her cancer treatment, when she and my father had traveled to the Gerson Clinic in Mexico so she could receive a mix of holistic medicine and alternative cures—wheat grass and coffee enemas and oxygen therapy—which we hoped would heal her.

Whatever we talked about, for a moment that scrim between worlds parted and I felt my mother, the weight and breath of her occupying the space beside me, her eyes shining bright with hope. She and my father were still growing wheat grass in their windowsill, juicing calf livers and organic vegetables. She was going to beat the cancer.

But when I stepped onto my apartment stairs, I lost the feeling of her, my mother's hand loosening its grip before the rest of her faded into the cold.

Each turn of the calendar marked her loss: the first Christmas without her, the members of our family all looking at one another to see which one of us might step in and take her place. My first birthday without anyone thinking to send a cake, as she had, to my dorm. The marking of anniversaries: May 1, my mother's birthday; October 1, the anniversary of her death.

Certain challenges would announce themselves ahead of time: a college graduation, a wedding, the birth of my son. But these milestones weren't the hardest. I could see them coming and prepare for them, distract myself by staying busy. I could tell myself her absence made me stronger. I didn't need anyone. I was independent. I could push myself to get straight A's or raise a son by myself or start the best dance company anyone had ever seen. I could run a half marathon and whiten my teeth. Choreograph and direct and produce a show. Anything to fill all that absence I was pretending wasn't there.

And so, if the door between worlds had stood open, it was I who closed it, then constructed wall after wall between the self who moved forward to make something of herself and the mother she left behind. But this grief was subversive. While I stayed busy numbing myself, it searched for ways to break through.

Because her ashes had been scattered, there was no physical place where I could go to find my mother. No urn or gravestone that might mark or hold my grief. My mother was everywhere and nowhere, a mirage so solid in my wanting I could almost touch it.

She often inhabited my dreams. I walked corridors that took me to rooms I never knew existed. There I'd discover new pieces of her: lost rings stored in jewelry boxes. Dresses and coats hanging in forgotten closets. Each discovery offered a second chance to try her on, feel the drape and weight of her clothes. Slip a ring that had held her hand on my own.

In other dreams she returned, full-bodied, standing in the family kitchen cooking breakfast at the stove, looking over her shoulder at me as if to say she never left. In variations on this dream, I learned she'd never died. She'd simply left our family to live with another across town. In another she appeared covered in dirt, as if the earth might return her to me whole again.

By day I tried to write her back into existence. The semester I returned to college I took a poetry class. My first poems were filled with fleshy wombs and fetal blood, rambling longings about returning to that first cocoon that had given me my own shape. My college poetry professor—a rising literary star I wanted badly to impress—returned those first poems to me with a D- scrawled across them. I had been imprecise in the telling, melodramatic. He had thought I was describing the pain of a break-up. The spill of unedited grief on the page was deemed embarrassing.

Perhaps it was too soon to write about my mother, he suggested. I lacked the proper distance to create art from such a tender place.

Thirty years later, I am again looking for a way back to my mother. A forty-nine-year-old mother myself, a graduate student and retired dancer, I sit curled in a leather chair of the Ohio State University's library. It's winter again, and the view outside the floor-to-ceiling windows of the reading room flickers with students on their way to and from exams. On the table sits a stack of books about the mother—oversized books on art and psychology, myth and religion, with weathered bindings and pages as thin and translucent as onion skin.

It's 2013. This October will mark the thirtieth anniversary of my mother's death. In January, I'll turn fifty. These books, with their pebbly bindings and dog-eared pages remind me that it's time to feel like a woman. And yet I feel—as I so often do—like I am still that young girl yearning for her mother to hold her in place. It is no longer the fresh, sharp pain of the child severed from her mother, but an endless, deeper thing—a split stem searching for its root.

In shutting off the part of myself that grieved for my mother, I'd also shut off a willingness to be vulnerable and raw. I had not risked the kind of embarrassment my college poetry teacher had warned me of.

After three decades, I'd lost so much of my mother, the fullness of all she'd been flattened until she seemed as two-dimensional as the few photographs that held her image. I'd had a mother but what exactly had she looked like? She'd sung to me, but what exactly was the timbre of that voice? She'd touched me, but what was the precise temperature of that touch?

And yet, in spite of all I'd forgotten, and in spite of being, or perhaps precisely because I was, a grown woman—I longed for her. Deeply. Desperately. Shamefully. I missed my mother, but what was it that I missed? If I could barely remember her, if so much of her was lost, then what was I longing for?

My mother was there.

And then she wasn't.

I'd come to the library to search for images to complete the missing mother so that maybe I could see her: a 20,000-year-old Venus, her great hips and lap chiseled into limestone. A lioness-headed Sekhmet carved from granite. Athena and Aphrodite spiraling from marble. In each of them a clue. A shape, voluminous and lush.

What did it mean for me to render the mother? Reach my hand toward her, name her, pin her to the page. I'm trying to convince you, dear reader, that there is something in that image that is worth looking at—something in the life of a mother that might stand in for yours as well.

At the center of the reading room, an eight-foot replica of the Greek statue *Winged Victory* spreads her wings, her garments rippling as if in a strong breeze. Carved nearly 2,400 years ago in the likeness of Nike, Greek goddess of victory, she is one of the most celebrated statues in the world, famed for the way motion and stillness meet in one figure.

She is a woman caught between Heaven and Earth, her headless body straining to steady itself as she descends from the skies to alight upon the prow of a phantom ship. Her right hand, lost long ago along with her arms and face, is believed to have been cupped around her mouth to deliver the shout of victory before a triumphant fleet.

A century after her body was discovered, her missing hand, fingerless, was found under a large rock. The tip of her ring finger and thumb were later located in a storage drawer at a Vienna museum. The fragments eventually found their way to a glass case next to the podium on which the rest of her presides at the Louvre—a woman in pieces, asking us to fill in the gaps.

And here, in the middle of Ohio, the winged Nike stands replicated in plaster, her headless, armless body framed by bookcases, her phantom gaze toward the books piled before me, their pages filled with blueprints that might complete her form—goddesses carved in granite and marble. Madonna figures painted in oil and gold. Others that only alluded to her anatomy: ancient circles and triangles flickering across the walls of ancient caves.

Among them are a few pages about the Yoruba fertility goddess Òşun who ruled the banks of the Nigerian river that shares her name. The river's contours had been shaped by the footsteps she left in her wake, and the great shapeshifter had transformed herself with each of its bends, showing herself in one turn as a young woman admiring herself in her mirror, in another as a vulture flying messages to and from the gods.

The river goddess had crossed the Atlantic to watch over her Yoruban children when they were taken as slaves to Cuba. There her name had mixed with the new Spanish on their tongues, its spelling changing from Òşun to Ochún.

It was in the next pages that I read about a second mother, a small icon made of wood and vegetable paste who would become the patron saint of Cuba. On the eastern end of the island, she'd appeared before the African slave child, Juan Moreno, and the Indian brothers, Rodrígo and Juan de Joyos. All three young men were miners from the town of El Cobre, and they would come to be known in the telling and re-telling of the story as the three Juanes.

They were on their way to procure salt for the copper mines when they became lost in a storm. After a night filled with prayer, they spotted what they thought might be a bird. No, not a bird. A statue of the Madonna, just under a foot and a half tall and dressed in blue and gold, her copper skin identifying her as one of their own. Her dry robes amidst those turbulent waters announced that she was no ordinary figure. The words *I Am Your Lady of Charity* were etched into the wooden tablet beneath her feet.

They took the icon to shore and built a small hermitage where each night she disappeared from her altar, reappearing the next morning as if nothing had happened, her robes wet from her nightly swims—this second miracle an inversion of the first in which she'd emerged dry from stormy waters. The miners carried her to the mountain town of El Cobre where she continued to appear and disappear at will, sending a flash of lights across the sky to signal the hill where she wanted her sanctuary built.

Apolonia, an enslaved girl from the mines who was grieving the loss of her own mother, witnessed the lights and climbed after them in hopes of finding her mother waiting at the top.

In my time with Lourdes, I'd learned only of Ochún. And if Our Lady of Charity had been mentioned, or if I passed her image (which I certainly must have), I had not understood what it was.

Now, the miraculous icon opened a door I hadn't known I was looking for. Our Lady's miracles spoke to me, but even more compelling was the idea that for those Cubans who either practiced Santería or in other ways syncretized the figures of the African and Catholic religions of the island, Our Lady of Charity was nearly synonymous with Ochún. It was as if the crackling batá that announce the oricha had struck through the page, their rhythms inviting me to dance in the current that leads from river goddess to saint. Over centuries of devotion, their symbols had merged, Our Lady's copper skin and golden accouterments twinning with Ochún's love of the color yellow and sunflowers and brass and gold until the two mothers—one a Catholic virgin, the other an African fertility goddess—were revered as if woven from the same stream.

My country had no equivalent, no sweeping devotion to the mother, and certainly none as complex and mysterious as the one rising from the pages of the book. Here was a Madonna, virgin and holy, European in origin, an incarnation of the Catholic mother Mary, who was also an African deity of love and sensuality and rivers, an earthy goddess of fertility who could be summoned through dance and drums, the two of them together pointing to a single shape that was larger than the sum of their parts.

Holding the pages with their double portrait, I begin to tremble. This map of the mother was powerful and revered, a presence that changed form yet never truly disappeared.

On September 8th each year, Cuba's eastern highways and back roads fill with pilgrims making their way toward Our Lady's El Cobre sanctuary to celebrate her feast days. The Catholics among them carry rosaries; those who follow Santería wear the bright beads that mark the children of the Afro-Cuban saints. They come from Havana and Cienfuegos, from Santiago and Holguín, from Santa Clara and Miami. They come by plane and by bus. On foot and on knee, flocking in the thousands to petition the great mother for miracles of their own.

A certainty settles over me as I read about those pilgrims. I need to be among them, to climb the hill of Our Lady's sanctuary with the same reverence that brought her pilgrims on foot and on knee. I yearn to be swept up in that kind of faith and celebration. To witness a devotion to the mother that is larger than anything I've known.

I begin planning my own pilgrimage, a month-long quest that will start in Havana where Lourdes and I left off and end on the opposite side of the island in El Cobre in time to celebrate Our Lady of Charity's feast days. Over the next months, I immerse myself in study of the Yoruba and the oricha, Our Lady of Charity and Ochún. Seekers and scholars who have forged their own trips in search of the mother advise about the places I should visit and the people who might guide me.

The first fifteen days will be in Havana, where I hope to connect with Ochún through the dances and rituals that celebrate her and the religion of Santería that gives them their pattern. The second half of the trip will take me to the eastern part of the island where Our Lady's devotion is strongest. Between the capital city of Santiago and the nearby town of El Cobre that houses the miraculous icon, I'll meet with priestesses and anthropologists, historians and priests before attending the pilgrimages to Our Lady's sanctuary. Near there, in a small house covered in murals, a Spiritist named Madelaine will attempt to summon my mother's spirit.

The breadth and boldness of my plans take root inside me. The Taíno, the first peoples indigenous to Cuba, had known Our Lady as their great mother Atabey; the Lucumí, the descendants of the Yoruba kidnapped and enslaved to work the island's sugar plantations, called her Ochún. The Spanish knew her as the Virgin Mary, Stella Maris, Spanish protectress of the seas.

Still, she was more. She was the Aztec water deity Chalchiuhtlicue and the Persian Anahita; the Egyptian Anuket and the Greek Amphitrite. The Chinese Kwan Yin and the Slavic Kostroma. The Fon/Ewe knew her as Mami Wata. In Benin they called her Ezili.

Through books with their names, the snow falling softly outside the windows of the library, I can feel them, a watery chain of mothers tugging at my sleeve, mixing with a memory from long ago. My mother and I are digging for seashells in a Oaxacan fishing village and then the tide is pulling us out to sea. My mother's arms are holding me, her voice assuring me, *Shhh, I've got you. I will never let you go.*

This September 8th will mark the 401st anniversary of the day Our Lady first appeared before the three Juanes, and again before the enslaved girl Apolonia, announcing herself as their spiritual and most miraculous mother, Our Lady of Charity.

Could I become one of those pilgrims whose beliefs are so strong that they arrive before Our Lady on their hands and knees? Could I leave the polite confines of the library, climb after Apolonia and, like her, stand on the hill and call out for the mother?

Just this morning, I'd woken up on The Cloud, the name my partner Rick and I gave the Sleep Number bed we picked out the year before when we were still in that awkward phase between getting serious about each other and becoming a couple. The saleswoman who programmed our separate sides had avoided labels like boyfriend and girlfriend, husband and wife, referring to us instead as "sleep partners." Perhaps it was as good a title as any to describe the yet-to-be-decided nature of our relationship. We'd each been married before. Rick counted one divorce in his wake while I counted two. We had adult children from those marriages we wanted to protect. Which meant we were moving slowly this time, with equal parts caution and hope. I still kept my own apartment, a one-bedroom in Columbus's Victorian Village filled with books and art. But Rick and I were sleep partners three or four nights a week. I'd grown accustomed to our routines. With one eye I'd watch Rick shave for work each morning at his *en suite* bath mirror while I lazed under his sheets, Rick's rat terrier Skip at the foot of the bed. After he left, the dog and I would eventually get up to make breakfast before curling together in the corner leather chair where I wrote.

According to a friend who likes to characterize people by the animals they resemble, Rick was a bison. The kind of strong, no-nonsense man who listened more than he spoke. The kind of man who moved carefully through the world. It had taken him a year to confess he was in love with me. But he was also a man who loved deeply once he decided to. He showed it in the way he fathered his two children, now grown and making their way in the world. Or the way he devoted himself to Skip. And now me.

According to the same friend I was an egret—a former dancer, attracted to the showy and the shiny: the rhinestone-studded dance shoe, the feather-fringed jacket. The kind of woman who was most comfortable being admired from a distance. Throughout my adult life, I'd chosen my lovers as much for their inability to commit as their good looks and charm. Rick offered something different—a steady partner who might balance my flight. A bison.

Sometimes I'd take a break from my computer to wander Rick's house and touch his things, marvel at the exquisite strangeness of another human being and his habits. The way the artifacts, so different from my own, pointed to the man. In his closet seven pairs of khakis hung neatly above a pair of motorcycle boots. An acoustic guitar rested against a bookshelf filled with back issues of *Rolling Stone*, each of them read cover to cover. Stacked alongside them, whatever Lee Child or John Sanford detective series he was currently reading, a half dozen titles suggesting a variation on one solid theme: *Sudden Prey, Wicked Prey, Stolen Prey.* His drawers were filled with folded T-shirts—round-collared or V-necked, with or without pocket—another variation on theme. There was also the growing evidence of my presence in his life: the toothbrush I'd started keeping in his medicine cabinet; a head-and-shoulders portrait of me smiling from his nightstand. Before I leave for Cuba, I will leave loose photos around the house for him to find—the two of us taped to his bathroom mirror, inside a kitchen cabinet, above the basement washer and dryer—so he might keep me close during the month I will be away.

[3]

ELEGGUA: GATEKEEPER GOD OF CHANCE

EIGHT MONTHS AFTER THAT wintry day at the library, I board a plane from Columbus to Miami. A second from Miami to Havana, a charter operated by American Airlines that will travel the last ninety miles from the country I live in to the one that is calling me. That morning, neither Rick nor I spoke as we dressed to drive to the airport. I'd be back in a month. Still, I felt uneasy leaving this man whose predictable routines gave shape to my more dreamy ones. At the airport I cried. "We're in a good place," Rick assured me. And this is what I feared. I'd prayed for change during this trip. Prayed to learn about myself, to heal old wounds so I might come back more whole. But what if I came back so changed I no longer fit in Rick's arms? I worry that the changes in me might shift us from the good secure place where we've been. Would he recognize me? Would I recognize myself?

As my plane takes off, I watch the familiar Ohio landscape outside my window open onto a sea of ever-fragmenting geometry, squares of farms and subdivisions giving way to lake and river and ocean, the world I know growing smaller and smaller until everything that tethers me—the man I am starting to fall for, the one-bedroom apartment I share with three cats, my twenty-three-year-old son Alex in Chicago—recede with the terrain. Along with them, all the stories I tell myself about who I am—mother, girlfriend, dancer, artist, writer, teacher—grow smaller, too, becoming small enough to fit on the head of a pin until even the pin is gone and we escape into the clouds.

"Why have you come?" an unsmiling clerk asks when I hand him my passport in Havana. Perhaps it's the counter between us that lets me know I'm at a crossroad, or the uniform that highlights which one of us is in charge. I've been advised to keep my answers short with Cuban officials. No details, just vague answers about wanting to soak up the culture of the island.

"I'm here to learn about Cuban dance," I tell him. When he presses me for more, I add that I'm interested in Ochún, the West African deity of the rivers, and Our Lady of Charity, her Catholic counterpart.

As the non-smiling passport clerk continues not to smile, I worry I might not pass whatever test he's administering. I think of what I know about Eleggua: how the divine gatekeeper likes to mess with us to test our steadfastness. He is known to wait in the borderlands between worlds—at the threshold of house and marketplace, in the curve of the road, or the bend of the stream, granting or denying access to the other side. But he is also the meeting point—the speaker of every language, the bridge that joins things together that only appear to be separate, the choice point that changes our relation to the world. One choice leading to the next. A river branching, each tributary mapping the next course of our lives.

"Where will you be staying?" the passport clerk asks. I tell him I'm booked at one of the private homes turned bed-and-breakfast in Raul Castro's new experiment with free enterprise. The non-smiler records my answer in his notebook before buzzing me through the door and out to customs where attendants search my bags. Satisfied that the foreign object showing up on their screen is just a memory drive and not a weapon or cyber contraband, they wave me through a set of glass doors that open onto a horizon of blue sky and royal palms. A throng of Cubans are gathered on the other side, fanning themselves under Havana's August sun—already scorching at 10 a.m.—their faces scanning emerging passengers for loved ones.

"Rebecca?" an older man calls through the crowd. It's my driver, who tells me his name is José. He seems as relieved to find me as I am him. Even more relieved when he discovers my Spanish is fluent. I studied in school, and for most of my adult life I've lived and worked in Spanish-speaking neighborhoods and schools, which had me speaking more Spanish than English.

I follow him past the taxis that line the curb: 1980s Soviet Ladas and Moskviches tucked among American classics—a 1955 Ford Crown Victoria, a 1957 Bel Air. Among them is José's 1956 Buick. Once I'm settled inside, I find myself admiring the interior. I take in the worn leather upholstery, the manual locks and window cranks I remember from the cars my parents drove in the '60s and '70s of my childhood. Big boats of cars, with back seats wide enough for me to stretch out and lose myself in a Nancy Drew mystery or *Teen* magazine.

Other cars, majestic with age, pass us on the road, and the sight of them stirs a nostalgia in me. They remind me not just of the cars of my youth but of the 1950s Fords and Buicks my parents drove before I was born, cars I'd seen pictures of pasted in old photo albums. Seeing them is like seeing ghosts. Here under the Havana sun were the same cars miraculously running decades after they first drove off their Detroit assembly lines—Russian gearboxes and differentials replacing what were once American parts; tail pipes and hood ornaments recreated in back-alley shops from 1950s patterns and scraps of chrome. Brake fluid fabricated from soap and oil and shampoo.

Tucked among the deckle-edged photos pasted in a family album back home are four Polaroids labeled *Havana, 1951.* In the first one, my mother and father pose as they board one of the liners that shuttled North American passengers between Miami and Havana in the '50s. The next shows them seated on deck. My father is clowning around, his trousered legs splayed, his feet in the air. My mother looks neat and elegant beside him. She wears a black dress, and her neck is ringed with pearls. The final two show her alone. In one, she smiles before a banana tree; in the next, before a field of pineapples.

As José and I progress toward Havana, I can almost picture my parents driving in the lane opposite ours, leaving the city even as I draw near it. My mother would be dressed in the same cotton print dress she wears in the photo of her kneeling before the pineapple field. My father would have been behind the steering wheel, the sleeves of his white dress shirt rolled up, his jacket slung across the back of his seat as he points out the sights he thinks my mother should notice along the way. As they travel further, Havana's opulent hotels and casinos give way to the lush sugar and tobacco and fruit plantations of the countryside.

When he spots the pineapple field, my father cuts the ignition. He's a mortician, yes, but also a farmer. He's interested in the way these fruits do not spring shucked and cored and sliced from a can but grow close to the ground.

"Sit by that one," he tells my mother, pointing to a particularly robust plant. He lifts the camera, directs her to turn her body toward the pineapple, her face toward him.

Now, "Smile."

Over the course of their marriage my father will pose my mother before Mexican pyramids and Moroccan palaces. And when each of his four children are old enough to travel, he will photograph us too before landmarks we've either come to mark or to be marked by. Even on the beach in Puerto Angel, the day the waves carried my mother and me far from shore, my father had been photographing us, directing us to look at the camera as he snapped our picture.

For my father, it's important that we and the thing we've come to document exist within the same frame. The object in the background stands across time and space. Our presence in the foreground announces that we too are here—rooted, however briefly.

Decades after my father clicks the shutter, I will hold the photograph where my mother, then only twenty-seven, kneels among those pineapples, smoothing the folds of her cotton skirts until they fan from her waist, echoing the arc of leaves waving back to her.

Perhaps those plants stir something inside her. The way their slim stalks bow gracefully from their center. How the pineapple itself, only one per plant, grows from the same heart—an entire being radiating from one clear axis. She may have liked how this same geometry repeats itself as far as the eye can see, these neatly planted rows of fruit gesturing toward some distant point on the horizon.

As my mother poses, my brother Jon and sister Susan toddle golden-haired under the supervision of a babysitter back in Illinois. My sister Vicki, the barest breath of the woman she will be, is taking root in my mother's womb. My own birth is still more than twelve years in the future, but I see myself there among them, a small spirit hovering on the sidelines. Somewhere on that horizon is my mother's mother, and her mother's mother. Together we form a line of women and children, like those Russian nesting dolls, the Matryoshka, named after *mother*, each fitting inside the other. Womb inside womb inside womb.

"Calle Jesús María," I tell José when he asks for the address where I'll be staying. I smile as I speak the propitious-sounding name. Outside the car window, billboards punctuate the way. This one promises *un socialismo prospero y sostenible*. Another *¡Fin a la injustícia!* or *Aquí no se rinde nadie*. Che and Castro appear above or below the slogans, their fists raised under the white sun. Pastel buildings rise alongside them with equal conviction, their crumbling walls in various states of decay and repair. As the taxi enters Havana Vieja I watch as houses come into relief and recede, their balconies strung with laundry that flutters like flags. The sounds of hip hop and reggaeton drift up and down stairwells. Street vendors cry out their wares. My driver's voice adds to the cadence, calling out the window every few blocks to ask again for the street called Jesús María.

I close my eyes, focus on the feel of my spine against cracked upholstery, the weight of my purse and water bottle on my lap. Each of these solid points connects me to this moment before I rush toward the next.

Like the landscape, I too am a work in progress. With every atom of my physical being swapping out every seven years, my body has shed four sets of cells since I first grieved my mother's death, each new set wrapping around that loss like a cocoon. What of that young girl, I wonder, remains within its shape?

I try to hold her still behind my eyes: a girl who knew the sound and texture of her mother. She is digging for seashells in a port of angels before the tide carries them out to sea. She can almost feel the mother there beside her, can almost hear her laughter. But the mother won't stay still. Her image bleaches under the sun; its edges curl, then crumble. A dance of electrons. And then gone.

I hear the jangle of keys in locks. The woman who opens the door, Marta, tells me there's been a complication with the room where I've arranged to stay. The daughter of the family that was supposed to leave the night before is sick and they need to stay an extra day or two. Certainly I can understand how she can't throw the family out on the street?

We face each other on her doorstep. With short-cropped hair she dyes red and a manner that is both warm and stern, Marta gives the impression of a person who is savvy and kind, a no-nonsense woman who has found her way into the position of entrepreneur in this country that is just opening to the idea of enterprise. She pushes her thick glasses up the bridge of her nose, tells me she only wants what's best for me.

"You can come back for breakfast or advice any time you want," she assures me as she walks me down the block to a yellow colonial that belongs to her neighbor Miriam, where she's arranged for me to stay instead. Marta drags my suitcase behind her with one hand and holds my elbow with the other to help us maneuver past potholes and piles of rubble. Whenever a car horn sounds or a motorcycle rumbles by, she guides me onto the sidewalk.

There are hugs and kisses as Marta introduces me to Miriam. A white-haired woman with soft eyes and an even softer voice, my new host leads me through a house filled with heavy Spanish furniture. She waves toward the patio where I'll come for breakfast, and again toward the tree her pet parrot Cody calls home. At the rear of the house, we climb a narrow set of stairs to the roof. At the top, the concrete guesthouse—a one-room dwelling that will be my home there—perches under a bowl of blue sky. Miram shows me inside, pointing out a pair of beds with a set of floral curtains hung behind them to form a makeshift headboard. There's a corner refrigerator with space for bottled water and a shelf with pegs to hang my clothes. An air-conditioning unit rattles when Miriam turns the knobs and sends a cold rush into the musty room. In the adjoining bathroom, she shows me how to work the shower. And then Miriam hands me the key and lets herself out, leaving me alone for the first time since I left Ohio nearly 36 hours ago.

In the mirror above the sink, I catch a glimpse of myself. My face is stripped of makeup after two days of travel, my hair damp from the sea air. Everything that will define me for the next thirty days is still packed inside my backpack and suitcase. My camera and laptop are tucked among the five cotton sundresses I will wash and wear for the next four weeks, each of them short-hemmed to keep me cool under the 90-plus-degree heat. Stashed in there too are a handful of books about Ochún and Our Lady of Charity, as well as the journal I'd made for Cuba, its pages still mostly blank.

"This is a once-in-a-lifetime trip," Rick told me when he saw how little I was packing. "Why limit yourself?" But I'd *wanted* to limit myself— to these few possessions, to coming alone. I'd removed all my jewelry: the silver egret pendant Rick commissioned for our first Christmas together; the charm bracelet he gave me for our one-year anniversary. I'd wanted to come to Cuba without these ties to a life in Columbus, Ohio—to a history, to a partner or city or country—so that I might open myself to something new.

It wasn't just the jewelry. I'd spent the last two years trying to un-encumber, selling or giving away the contents of the house in Chicago where I'd built a dance career and raised my son. There was the garage full of tools and rakes. Then, scattered across the house, the trappings of decades of discarded hobbies and avocations: a pair of wall-climbing shoes; a closet full of half-finished art projects; boxes of '90s self-help books and spiritual guides. All so I might pare things down to the few all-important belongings that could fit inside a one-bedroom apartment 374 miles southeast of Chicago in Columbus, where I'd enrolled in graduate school.

I'd hoped that if I put the stuff behind me, I might also put behind me the experiences they represented—the last two decades I'd dedicated to raising a son alone; my fears about how he was to find his way through the world. My disappointments after two divorces and a retirement from dance. If I left behind the trappings, I might somehow leave behind the stories about who I'd been and make room to find a new one.

I'd been Becki Huntman, daughter of Bill and Mimi Huntman. Rebecca, wife to two men and mother to Alejandro. Ms. Huntman, the high school teacher, and Ms. Rebecca, the dancer–choreographer. Each of these roles had come with its own costume—the tailored dress I'd worn as a grieving daughter to my mother's memorial service, blood-red with ivory trim and a breast pocket that was just for show. The over-the-top satin wedding gown of the young bride. The pencil skirt of the school-teacher; the rhinestone-studded Lycra of the Latin dancer. Each uniform a new way to try myself on.

There was something both exhilarating and terrifying about each reinvention. To tether oneself to a story, gather oneself in the props that made up an identity, knowing that when one tired of that skin all one had to do was shed it for the next.

In the months after my mother's death, I saw a campus therapist who treated me through the lens of crisis intervention. Her job, as she saw it, was not to help me find long-term healing but to keep me from coming unglued so I could finish the semester. We talked about ways to compartmentalize my grief, to focus not on the mother who was forever gone but on the assignments that were due each day.

In the decades between then and now, I'd seen a string of therapists who ran the gamut in their approach: art therapists who had me paint my feelings, Jungian analysts who wanted to plumb the depths of my dreams.

The deep diggers among them seemed most interested in my father's story. My father had been largely absent during my childhood. He had also been wildly unfaithful to my mother, cheating on her again and again, and both these things naturally interested the therapists. It was no wonder my self-esteem suffered; no wonder that, until recently, I'd chosen unreliable men to date and marry. No wonder I'd sought my father's validation in jobs and trophies, always rushing toward the next prize.

But the absent mother was left largely unexplored. We never talked about the ways that, long before she died, my mother had been absent even to herself, vacating a career as a singer to marry my father and raise his children. Editing her tastes and preferences to match first his, then ours.

Nor did we talk about the ways that I, too, had turned my back on my mother. How I'd filled the void she'd left with schoolwork, then jobs, the full-time occupation of raising my son. How, in all my rush to avoid missing her I'd forgotten the precise tenor of her voice as she called me in the house each night for dinner, the scent of her perfume. Or how, all these years later, what I missed most was the missing.

With my most recent therapist we were finally talking about the mother. We talked about how I might fill the hole she'd left with self-love, with ways to listen to myself. Remember to forgive myself for not being perfect. To forgive my mother for her own imperfections.

All this was hard for me. Like my mother, I'd spent much of my life attending to the needs and wants of others. What would it look like to take care of my own?

On Valentine's Day I arrived in my therapist's office run-down with an undiagnosed sinus infection that left me cold and feverish. The day was rainy and gray. What I wanted, I told her, was to crawl back into bed. But I didn't want to disappoint Rick by backing out on the plans we'd made to celebrate that evening.

What would it look like, my therapist had asked, to tell Rick how I felt? Suggest we spend a quieter night together, make a plan that would feel comfortable to *me*.

This is what she and I had been working on. *My* comfort. After forty-nine years of being someone's daughter or mother, wife or girlfriend, wasn't it time to figure out what made me comfortable? To start mothering myself?

There was something about my inability to do this that seemed to make my therapist sadder for me than I was for myself. And so, she handed me the basket of shells that sat on the table between us during our weekly sessions. Sometimes, she told me, she gave one to a client who needed something to put in their pocket to remind them of who they were. Now she was giving them to me. Not just one, but the whole basket.

"Name each of them after a gift you want to give yourself," she told me. "The gift of not needing to be perfect. The gift of allowing yourself to have feelings. Of letting your wants be known. Of putting pleasing yourself above pleasing others."

"Carry the shells in your pocket," she said. "Let them speak to you."

"Let them remind you of those parts of yourself you need to remember."

Before I left for Cuba, I'd glued the shells to the cover of my journal. I'd spent weeks working on the book, binding the spine of a 6 x 8 sketchbook with gold bookbinding tape. Printing Our Lady's image from the internet and gluing it to the cover. Building up her skirts and crown through layers of paper and acrylic, colored pencil and beads, until she stared back at me in three dimensions.

On the inside I'd pasted an image of the river goddess Ochún—her palms lifted to reveal a fish in one hand, a heart in the other. The shells from my therapist were the final touch. Like the rest of the notebook, they were a part of me. My colors. My design. Its pages were a place to locate myself. The feel of those shells cool under my fingertips, like a rosary. Those twin images of Ochún and Our Lady a secret I'd spend the next month trying to decode.

Now at Miriam's, I open the cover and begin at the beginning. The date: August 14, 2013. My name: *Rebe Huntman, daughter of Mimi Meyers Huntman.*

[*4*]

THREADS OF IDENTITY

IN THE MORNING, I find Miriam dressed in a white work dress and sandals, her white hair tucked under a scarf that lends her the appearance of a domestic worker or nun. The expression on her face might be disapproval or disappointment or both. There is a quietness about her, a sadness that reminds me of abandoned dreams, secrets she doesn't dare speak out loud. The bed-and-breakfast belongs to her brother and his wife, but they are often away with their children in Viñales, leaving Miriam to tend to their ailing mother and a business that isn't hers.

"We're family," she explains. "And family looks out for one another."

Still, she makes sure I know she doesn't like any of it. The stairs are difficult to climb. She isn't much of a cook. And this never leaving the house except to go to the market is taking its toll.

It will take some days to settle into a rhythm. When I need help with practical things—where and how to find the *telepunto* to connect to the internet; how to use Cuban cell phone cards—I'll go to Marta. But it will be Miriam's that I call home. Not only because it is where I sleep and keep my things, but because she watches over me, making sure she buys ham and cheese—not always easy to come by in Cuba's uncertain economy—to add to my morning omelets; letting me know how proud she is that I've chosen to stay here in her home.

Where Marta's home is filled with books and advice, Miriam's is filled with images of the mother. A pair of figures flanks either side of the living room doors—the Virgin Mary carved in plaster on one side, on the other a wood carving of a feminine deity who might be Ochún. On the surface these two mothers appear as different as Marta and Miriam: the river goddess flaunting her exaggerated breasts and womb, the virgin hiding her own curves beneath modest robes. And yet here in Cuba, even in a Catholic home like Miriam's, the two are so often revered as one.

The Catholic Church was clear about the distinction. Our Lady of Charity was an incarnation of Mary, Mother of God. For the rest of Cuba, the lines often blurred. For the strictest of Catholics, she was Mary, but for others she was both Mary and Ochún. Still for others, her primary importance was not as a religious figure but as a symbol of national pride, a *mestiza* mother whose coppery skin and ties to the mines and slave rebellions of the town of El Cobre link her to the braided Indigenous and African and European heritage of the island.

For me, the ability to simultaneously hold the threads of their stories feels impossible. I'd been raised in a culture that looked to simplify rather than complicate, particularly when it came to women. A woman could be a virgin *or* she could be sensual. She could be a spirit *or* she could represent a nation. The ability to embrace more than one truth at once in order to make room for a layering of identity was something we had little practice in.

And so, as I try to grasp the complexity of the two mothers I've come to Cuba to study, I reach to simplify. In my journal I draw a Venn diagram. Inside one circle, I draw Our Lady of Charity, a physical object made of wood and paste and paint found floating in the waters four hundred years ago, who also embodied the Mother of God. Crudely drawn, her robed figure becomes a triangle crowned in a golden nimbus. At her breast she cradles the baby Jesus, who, in my rendering, is a stick figure.

Inside the second circle, I draw Ochún, the Yoruba river deity—a shapeshifter who could assume any form she wished: lover or warrior, vulture or crone, which made her difficult to capture as an image, and so I draw her as a circle. The round womb. The fertile calabash in which she stores both her riches and the promise of new life.

In the middle wedge where those two circles overlap, I write *water* and *devotion and motherhood*—three attributes where the two mothers converge before they begin again to circle out from one another.

If Our Lady was a virgin, the conception of her child immaculate, Ochún was voluptuous and fertile, a seductress who took but never kept her many husbands and lovers. If Our Lady was the mother of a singular god, Ochún's offspring were legion. They included the fish in her river, the trees in her grove, the children she either birthed herself or helped others to conceive.

And if Our Lady held her child at her breast, Ochún left hers for her own mother, the sea goddess Yemayá, to raise, so she could continue her wandering, her feet forming new tributaries with every step.

"How can the two be one?" I ask Miriam.

Miriam looks at me as if I've asked a most foolish question before she answers. "Before Our Lady became Our Lady, wasn't she a woman like you and me?"

Four years after my mother died, I asked the man I'd been dating for only a few months to marry me. It was the spring of 1987. I was twenty-three years old, a girl-woman who missed her mother, and who subconsciously thought she might fill the void left by her dying by stepping into those shapes she'd occupied as wife and mother.

The man I asked to marry me was both handsome and agreeable. Handsome in that he resembled a Mexican Tom Cruise, and agreeable in that he was young and anxious to leave the high-rise apartment he shared with his mother in Uptown, Chicago. Agreeable too in that when I proposed to him, in a rash moment after my sister told me about a scare with cervical cancer she was afraid might make her sterile and I became certain that at twenty-three I needed to get married and have a child of my own before it was too late, he did not say no. And by agreeable I also mean that, of all the women he might have chosen, he chose me.

My mother wanted me to apply myself in school, get good grades, make something of my life. I wanted to be pretty and popular—to feel like a grown woman, whatever that might mean. And so, if through my childhood we'd held each other close, in my teenage years we clashed. By the time my fifteenth birthday rolled around, we were so angry with each other she threatened to boycott any celebration. I created my own. On the night of my birthday, I snuck into my mother's closet and borrowed a black evening gown and a pair of green satin sandals, the ones she'd eyed for days at the mall before finally giving herself permission to buy. The ones she kept wrapped in tissue paper on the top shelf of her closet where they sat, waiting to be touched.

A friend and I snuck out to Houlihan's, where we spent the night smoking cigarettes and letting men twice our age buy us beers, a thing which to us felt both classy and grown up.

When I woke the next morning, I found my mother sitting in the armchair across from my bed, her dress and heels where I'd left them crumpled in a pile on the floor.

"Was it worth it?" she asked.

I never asked what exactly she meant by those words, but they've stuck with me all these years. Was it worth it to defy her? Leave the house on a day when the family should have been celebrating together? Forgo her homemade birthday cake and candles for a night with older men and beer?

Or did she mean something more subtle? Did she mean to ask if I'd had a good enough time to sully those exquisite clothes?

On a gray Thanksgiving weekend, Moisés and I exchanged vows at a banquet hall on the north side of Chicago. While I considered myself a feminist, I'd been unable to resist the lure of the wedding industry. I'd gone for it all—the engraved invitations and Jordan almonds wrapped in tulle. The puffy satin dress with giant bows that drooped from my shoulders. The enormous tower of a wedding cake with its ceremonial cutting. The throwing of the bouquet, a cascade of roses and freesia I'd fashioned after a photograph I'd seen in *Brides* magazine.

The feminist in me tried to mitigate my enthusiasm for these trappings by modifying them in ways that might indicate I did not fully buy into them. I had the dress, designed to be worn with a long train, cut above my ankle in a more modern style. In lieu of a traditional veil, I wore a puff of netting I pinned to the back of my head. My shoes, while beaded with pearls, had sensibly low—if not pointy—toes and heels. And rather than marry before a church altar, we married at a civil venue, exchanging egalitarian vows on a stage designed for musicians and emcees.

The result was disastrous in the way all things that lack the courage of their conviction tend to be. The dress looked ridiculously top-heavy with those enormous bows on my shoulders and no train to counterbalance their weight. The bob of netting perched precariously on top of my head only added to the sense of imbalance.

With one foot in the feminist camp and the other in wedding fairyland, I walked myself down the aisle. Perhaps my refusal to walk on my father's arm was just a slap at patriarchal norms. But when I look back, I think about how perfectly that solitary march captures how alone I felt. The one person I wanted more than anyone to be there with me was gone, her absence infusing every bit of the day—the miscalculations in wedding attire; the absence of anyone who might have told me that the makeup artist I'd hired to make sure I was the perfect bride had overdone it. Or that maybe I might be too young for this marrying business, and the groom possibly not as agreeable as he seemed. I walked myself, a girl-woman teetering on pointy shoes, her face caked with rouge, toward the twenty-one-year-old boy-man who waited for me at the altar-not-altar.

When the photos came back from the photographer, I complained to a coworker about how clownish I looked. She told me to wait it out.

"Years from now you'll long for the girl you were that day," she told me. "So young and thin. You won't care about the makeup."

And yes! I look at the photos now and think about how young I look, as ridiculous as a child playing dress up in her mother's clothes. And yet how beautiful! Beneath the makeup and naïveté, I see the kind of hope that belongs to the young. The belief that this is all one has to do. Put on the dress and the ring and wait for one's life to unfold.

The baby was, as the marriage had been, my proposal. The unfolding pregnancy narrative was intoxicating. There were books that told you *What to Expect When You're Expecting*. A nursery to stock with blankets and booties. There were mobiles to hang. Drawers to fill with onesies and baby bottles, talcum powder and teething rings.

While I spent the days of my pregnancy filling our spare bed-room-turned-nursery, the idea of the baby who would use each of these objects grew inside my head. Unknown yet bound for great things. Perfect and sweet smelling. And just as surely as the baby would be a perfect baby, I would be a perfect mother. I would take care of her the way my mother had taken care of me. Cut her peanut butter and jelly sandwiches on the diagonal. Arrange orange sections into flowers on her plate.

In June, I found myself in an operating room at Chicago's Illinois Masonic Hospital, surrounded by cold steel and bright lights. The midwife we'd contracted was nowhere to be found. The baby came, not by natural childbirth but by C-section. The whole situation was 180 degrees removed from the birthing room where I'd expected to do this. The anesthesiologist administered the epidural that would numb me from the ribcage down, allowing me to be both present and absent for the birth. With a screen placed between my collarbone and everything that was happening below it, I had only the nurses' voices to guide me. They would begin by cleaning my belly, they explained. I would feel a slight pressure. And that's all I felt. I lay on the metal table, experiencing every movement of doctors' and nurses' hands as a single sensation of slight but continuous pressure—the preparation as they cleaned my belly; the force of knife as it penetrated skin and muscle; the lifting of the baby into the cold air of the room; the cutting of the umbilical cord. There was no clear beginning, middle or end. No labor. No pushing toward a crescendo. No triumphant finale.

"Whose baby is that?" I asked a nurse when I heard a baby crying. I turned my head to locate the origin of the sound and found a tiny person with his eyes screwed up, his face purple with outrage at discovering his new life outside the womb. A stranger.

It wasn't until later, after I'd been wheeled to my room, hooked up to a morphine drip that helped manage the pain of being cut open, and the baby was brought to me that I saw how beautiful he was. Wrapped in a blue and white hospital blanket, his fingers worked under the tiny mittens that kept him from scratching himself. The smallest of bracelets was printed with his name: *Alejandro Moisés*.

A nurse showed me how to position him in my arms, how to place my nipple in his mouth so he could feed from the breast that had swollen, with no conscious instruction from me, with milk.

After the nurse returned him to the nursery, I slept. When I woke, I felt that severed umbilical cord like a phantom limb still connecting us. I followed it to the nursery where I found Alex joined in a line with other people's babies, all of them wrapped in identical hospital blankets, their heads crowned with pink or blue hats.

He was crying again, only this time I knew who he was. I told the nurse I needed to hold him. I'd never needed anything so much.

In a photo I keep on my dresser, my mother and I wade into an ocean that might be any ocean. I am two years old, my mother forty-two.

Our legs are rooted in water like a stem. Beyond us the deep blue of the sea meets the robin-egg blue of the sky. Only our torsos interrupt the palette. My mother holds one arm behind her back, extends the other toward my small hand, which I lift at the precise angle so our separate arms meet to form a single line. My mother's gaze over her shoulder connects with the line of her body that connects with the line of my own as she turns her attention entirely toward me.

With my free arm I wave into the shot as if to announce my presence. I stare into the camera. I am just trying myself out. And yet there in the middle, where our hands meet, we are not daughter. Not mother. But mother-daughter.

When I look at the photo it is always 1966, my mother and I still mother-daughter. And yet most times I can barely locate the shape of her. When I try to, it feels like looking at a photograph and thinking you remember a scene while everything outside the frame fades to white.

I need you to see my mother. It feels imperative that you know she existed: Mimi Meyers Huntman, daughter of Josephine Grubel, who was daughter to Lillian Horn, who was daughter to Leah Shaw. Mimi Huntman, who gave birth to Rebecca, who gave birth to Alejandro.

Alex was a year and a half old when our family of three became two. If I'd been paying more attention, I might have noticed that his father had been trying to leave for a while. And if I'd been honestly paying attention, I might have noticed that the life we'd made together hadn't been his idea at all. Twenty-one when we married, he'd hardly known what he wanted. Now at twenty-four he was living a life I'd chosen for us, a life he began to imagine he might simply slip away from and start anew.

A month before the actual leaving, he hopped a bus to San Antonio, Texas—a place he knew only from the brochures we'd looked at together as we dreamed of places we might someday live. He got a few hours away, the Midwestern landscape just beginning to turn to something new when he turned back. He was home before supper, full of kisses and promises to never leave again.

My father counted the women he took to his bed—over three hundred, according to stories that have somehow made their way to me. But the ways he punished my mother weren't limited to his infidelities. He drove too fast, faster when he sensed her fear. He bought scarves and chunky necklaces for her to cover the neck he found—for reasons I never understood—either unsightly or threatening. Mostly, my father punished my mother by not being present. He was charming at parties and at church and with the neighbors. At home he disappeared into the basement or the garage to work on a project, or to the farm to check on the crops.

In turn, my mother punished my father. She embarrassed him by raising her voice in public. She pushed him down stairs. Aimed the clothes iron at his face. Drove her car (family lore has it) through the wall of a motel cottage he was sharing with one of his mistresses. She punished him with the things she ate—gaining and losing forty pounds when she couldn't find any other way to communicate her hunger, her self-abnegation, her disappointment with both of them.

The day Alex's father left for good began like any other day. He and the baby waved from the doorway as I left for the high school where I taught. Two hours later I was standing in front of a U.S. History class, delivering a lecture about the Civil War, when a student I didn't know knocked on the door. He'd been intercepted outside the building by a man who'd asked him to deliver a letter.

As you read this, I'll be on my way out of your life, the note began. Who would write such a thing? I thought. I flipped it over to find the signature.

As I read and then re-read my husband's name, I felt my knees buckle. A part of me fell to the floor while another part kept moving, excused me from the classroom, made its way to the principal's office, then out into the rain. I'd ridden to work with a coworker and now I wasn't sure how to get home. I could call a taxi or take a bus, but to do either of those things seemed to require that part of me I'd left on the classroom floor. I stood looking out onto Ashland Avenue, the rain sloshing at the curb. All I knew was that I lived north. I began walking.

What I remember most about the months after Moisés left was how I lay each night on the floor of our Evanston apartment, listening to Mexican love ballads whose heartbreak matched my own. I wept. I fell apart. I needed a mother and she was nowhere to be found. I was alone and I was broken, emptied of the version of myself that was both a mother and a wife.

When I picked myself off that floor, I told myself I could do this parenting thing alone. Hadn't my mother in her own way been a single mother? While my father never formally abandoned us, wasn't he largely absent from our daily life, either physically gone or emotionally distant and critical? Hadn't my mother loved us enough for both of them?

Despite the hardship of her cancer as it progressed, my mother held on long enough to see my siblings make their own lives in Phoenix and Illinois. Long enough to see me off to college. In my last year of high school, she helped me fill out college applications, drove me around the country to visit campuses, quizzing me on lists of SAT vocabulary words we kept on the console between us.

I am so very proud of Becki, my mother wrote in her journal after she moved me into my freshmen dorm. *She is her own person—sets her own goals, plans efficiently and moves the obstacles around her.*

How strange, I thought when I later came across this entry, that in those months before she died, my mother saw me moving independently through the world when all I saw was how much I needed her.

There are those who might say that losing my mother at such a young age, compounded by my inability after all these years to stop grieving her loss, creates an emotional hole that keeps me from individuating. While I'd rebelled against my mother as a teen, I'd missed that thing daughters who keep their mothers into their adulthood get to both complain and brag about: that face-off when two grown women circle one another to decide how much they are alike and how they differ from one another. The push to decide: *I am,* or *I am not, my mother.*

I remember the exact moment I became a mother. It wasn't during pregnancy. The baby was still the *idea* of a baby. Nothing personal. Neither was it the moment I first saw him. But it happened. There was a moment, not soon after, when I realized: *This baby needs me. I am the one person who will never leave.*

The weight of this realization has never left me.

An eighteen-year contract is what I thought I'd committed to when I'd decided to have a baby. Eighteen years to raise a child and then they're off on their own. At least that's how it had been with me. Eighteen years and then college. Nineteen when my mother died. Gone with her was any template for how one might mother a child past the age of nineteen. My mother was not there to see me get married. Not there to tell me how to raise Alex. Not there to tell me that the task of the mother is never finished. The contract is never up.

When Alex was ten, I took him to see the pyramids of Mexico and Guatemala. There was something about those Aztec and Mayan ruins that held a key to his ancestry. A secret I wanted to know too. I imagined how we'd climb their summits and meditate before ancient gods. But Alex was a child who liked to climb more than he liked to sit. At Chichén Itzá's famed Castillo, I asked him to wait with a friend at the bottom while I climbed alone. I thought I might steal a few solitary moments for myself. But as I sat perched on a shelf of rock trying to still the noise of my thoughts, I felt the mental tug of Alex. *Would he be all right waiting without me?*

Nearly fifteen years later, I'd moved from Chicago to Columbus, stretching that umbilical cord far enough so that we both might make our own way in life but not so far that he wouldn't be able to find me when he needed me.

I've never let go of those hopes I'd had during pregnancy that my son would lead a perfect life, that he would be happy and successful without having to struggle. At twenty-three he's now the age I was when I walked myself down the aisle to marry his father. When he calls with uncertainties about how he should live his life, I feel their burden as if they were my own. I've always let him know he can tell me anything and that I would hold its weight with my own hands, try to help him figure a way through whatever troubles him. But it is one thing to rush in and rescue an infant who is crying in a nursery, another to try to smooth the way for a man who needs to find his own path.

As I'd sat on the top of that pyramid, caught between wanting to run down after Alex and trying to focus on the breath, on the clear center—whatever and wherever that was—I'd heard a voice cut through the chatter, soft but clear. It was a voice that came both from my own head and outside it.

This is how you'll have to learn to pray, the voice told me. Not in the still, idealized image of my fantasies where I could be a woman who sat, alone and unfettered, on a stone perch, but strumming through life, child in tow, and perpetually in motion.

In Cuba, I am again trying to find my center. I'd hoped for thirty days to put aside my own responsibilities as a mother so I could find the one who might mother me. Alex's and my usual lines of communication have been all but shut off. Internet connection is hard to find, phone calls difficult to orchestrate. Still, I find myself worrying about him. In the spaces between my thoughts and breath he is—as I imagine I was for my mother—always there. The world had changed so much since I grew up in it. Many of Alex's generation were having a hard time launching their lives. How much did Alex need me and how much did he need to set out on his own? Where was the sweet spot between holding on and letting go?

The first time I came to Cuba, I left my camera behind. I'd wanted to take the island in through my senses: to see and smell, touch, hear, speak its lexicon without the intermediary lens of the camera. I'd carried Cuba home inside me, every atom of muscle and bone still vibrating with its music and incantations.

This time I've packed a 35 mm Canon Rebel. Each day after breakfast I carry it to the streets and churches and museums I've come to explore. But now that I'm here I find my relationship with the camera awkward, not only because it's heavy to carry, but because the object identifies me instantly as separate from the landscape and people I'm here to know. The act of clicking the lens isolates me further.

With each frame, a decision to make. A vivisection. A body arrested as it moves through space is dislodged from the nuances of that space. A woman dressed in the white cloth of a Santería initiate is cleaved from the physicality of beads resting against her chest; a candle burning before an offering split from the scent of wax and smoke.

Even the air becomes a lie. A set of white sheets flap in the wind. The click of the shutter stills the sheets, erases the wind.

At the Casa de Africa cultural center I find a set of cast-iron bells, the dates in which they were forged written on placards: 1783, 1856, 1858. When I get home all anyone will see in the photo I take of them will be dates and bells, but as I stand before them I hear the clang of iron that once called enslaved men and women to church and to work—a reminder that the Afro-Cuban religion of Santería exists in the Americas only because of the Yoruba people who were forced across the Atlantic, bringing their gods along with them in song and prayer.

Upon arrival they were baptized and catechized before Catholic divinities and saints. A life of servitude, the Spanish argued, was a small price to pay for eternal life through Christ. And yet, even as the Yoruba kneeled—shackled and whipped—before those foreign deities, they searched for ways to keep their beloved oricha alive. They spotted them in the lush palms of the Cuban mountains where their warriors Ogún and Ochosi surely continued to hunt. They cradled them in the coconuts they quartered and threw to discern the will of the arch diviner, Orula. And in the very iconography of the oppressors, they found officially sanctioned symbols behind which their own oricha might live on. The blue and white robes of Our Lady of Regla provided a path to publicly adore the sea goddess Yemayá. The golden robes of Our Lady of Charity a way to worship the river goddess Ochún.

At the Museo de los Oricha I find a life-size sculpture of the river goddess standing over an actual stream. Her clothes are torn like the bark of a tree. Her arms open wide as if to embrace the world and everything in it. And at a sanctuary on Calle Manrique I kneel before her Catholic counterpart, a replica of Our Lady's actual effigy I'll see when I get to El Cobre. But where Ochún had appeared at the *museo* clothed in bark, Our Lady of Charity is dressed in finery and jewels. Her triangular robes fall from her shoulders in richly embroidered cloth. On her head she wears a sparkling crown.

What impresses me most, however, is not Our Lady's shape but the shape and scope of her devotion. The blocks leading to the sanctuary are lined with women who sit braiding sunflowers—one of the most ubiquitous symbols that link Our Lady with Ochún—into bouquets for sale. Inside the church a river of men and women dressed in yellow and white queue up to light a candle or leave a bouquet.

As I watch them kneel—faces ecstatic, mouths moving in

prayer—before Our Lady, I'm struck by the reverence even this replica of the miraculous icon commands. It's a reverence I find contagious as I work up the nerve to join them. I introduce myself. Shyly. Lay my own flowers at her feet. Tell her I've come to know her. Whisper the promise so many make before her image. That in a few weeks I will join the pilgrimage to her sanctuary on the other side of the island, in El Cobre.

For thousands of Cubans, the desire to make the pilgrimage to El Cobre is a given. They long to bend before the original effigy and pray that the miraculous icon will intercede on their behalf. Families take their children. Down the road those children take their own children. And for generation after generation, those who make the pilgrimage bring back carved *virgencitas* which are sold at the side of the road. Some are a few inches tall; others are so tall they have to be placed on the ground. On their backs are inscribed the words *Virgen de la Caridad de El Cobre* or *Nuestra Señora de la Caridad*.

Once purchased, these figurines serve as souvenirs of the pilgrimage, to be kept on dressers and altars as reminders of the promises made before Our Lady. Touchstones that bridge the pilgrims' homes and lives with that blessed sanctuary and the mysteries it holds.

Each time I pass in and out of Miriam's house, I stop in the dining room to admire the four virgencitas her brother has brought back from his own pilgrimages to El Cobre. I linger over them, stopping to wonder over the marvelous "stuff" of Catholicism, so different from the bare Congregational Church of my childhood. I remember a single crucifix, stripped of its flesh, Mary all but absent. We pulled her out at Christmas to round out the crèche scene but otherwise she remained silent, her role in the drama of God requiring she be receptacle rather than participant.

I'd grown up reciting the Lord's Prayer, my tongue tripping over its masculine sounds. *In the name of the Father, the Son, and the Holy Ghost.* The word "God" in all its iterations sounded both too male and too lofty to have anything to do with me, as hollow on my lips as a dry bone.

But I found the word "goddess" also problematic. Not just because of its deference to its root "God" but because in my mind it was a word made ridiculous by white New Age women, perhaps no different than myself, whose searching—my searching—embarrassed me. We seemed to have lost both context and claim to her, the word "goddess" floating in a bubble of distant imagery. If we think of a goddess at all, it might be in connection to the fat Neolithic artifacts unearthed in Germany and France. That is, as an ancient Venus with enormous breasts and hips, her secrets long ago buried with her people. Only the artifact remains, reminding us of our longing for something we barely dare to name.

Feminine. From the Latin *feminine* or *femina*; "woman, female," literally "she who suckles." Related to fetus, filial, fecund. Feminism.

The first time I had my hand slapped for using the word "feminine" was in response to a draft of a graduate school application. I'd used it twice to describe the work I'd been doing as a photography student at Chicago's School of the Art Institute. Freshly retired from dance, I'd spent two years searching for myself through the camera lens, throwing the dance costumes I no longer wore, but couldn't bear to part with, into the trunk of my car and hunting for new landscapes in which to bring them to life. I'd draped those skins that had held me over tree limbs and tombstones, sneaked them into dressing rooms where I photographed them hanging without me, still clinging to a shape I'd dared call feminine.

The professor who helped me edit my application materials told me I'd fucked up. Smart women couldn't afford to use such a word. I might as well write about kittens and butterflies. The world we lived in—a world still dominated by men, the literary world by editors and publishers who were still mostly male—didn't tolerate what she'd learned from hard experience they thought of as "women's shit."

It wasn't just male critics who had a problem with the word. The feminine was complicated. The images I'd grown up with often either missed their mark or barely scratched at the surface of their power. In the Sears catalog I pored over each Christmas as a child, the feminine presented itself as an assemblage of dollhouses and Easy Bake ovens. There was my mother's dresser top, arranged with gold-handled hairbrushes and bottles of Estée Lauder lipsticks and perfumes. The drawers beneath were filled with stockings and slips. Each of these items seemed to breathe with a secret life, a language that seemed alternately too shameful or threatening to speak of.

On the shelves of an upstairs closet my mother stored boxes of dress patterns, their paper glossy as onion skin and etched with dotted lines—a geometry of circles and squares to be cut and reconfigured as dress or blouse or skirt. I remember how she sat before her sewing machine, arching over fabric and needle as if before an altar, candy-colored pins protruding from between her teeth, others from the red pincushion she wore like a corsage at her wrist. A tape measure draped her neck.

My mother took pride in this sewing—the way pin and pattern anchored her in the objects she spun from her own handiwork: a kitchen apron trimmed in bric-à-brac, a gown for dancing cut from turquoise paisley silk. Each seam was sewn with knowledge that belonged first to her mother Josephine, and before her to Josephine's mother Lillian, and before her to Lillian's mother Leah Josephine—connecting my mother to a line of women who knew how to make and remake themselves with their own hands.

"She's a miracle," Miriam announces when she first speaks to me about Our Lady. We are sitting in her dining room, the four virgencitas her brother has brought from El Cobre watching over us from the sideboard. Her voice is barely a whisper as she tells me how the women of Cuba petitioned Our Lady for help in finding love and birthing children, and how Our Lady never let them down.

As Mary, Mother of God, she interceded selflessly on their behalf, holding them in her wide lap as they prayed for the safe passage of their lives and children.

And for those who saw her as Ochún, she oversaw those same acts of conception and delivery. She was Yeye, the Good Mother, the goddess of fertility whose rivers gave and sustained life. She who stood at the nexus of life and death, ensuring the continuance of humanity by linking the living with both the ancestors and the unborn. The mighty weaver who wove our destiny with her comb and with her loom. She whose name meant both *source* and *seep*.

This is the story my church had never spoken out loud. Its teachings suggested the shape of the feminine was small and shameful, but the shape of the feminine was expansive. It was a shape that privileged the conjunction *and* over *or*. A shape that was both African and European, cerebral and sensuous, spiritual and material. A shape so vast it multiplied in the generations who called her mother, its borders so fluid she appeared to them as both female and male, androgynous and trans.

The power of that shape was so obvious that for millennia it had been simply abbreviated as the triangle and circle. The ancients had carved the sacred geometry of vulva and womb onto bone and antler. Painted it across cave walls.

I don't limit my search to museums and churches. I look for her in the parasols of the women I pass on the street. In the men and women dressed in white who are rebirthing themselves as the children of their oricha, the ones draped in yellow beads as the sons and daughters of Ochún. I look for her in the smooth skin of a woman's dark cheek. In the dangle of a gold earring glinting above the rise of collarbone, and the tender concave flesh of the throat it protects. Again, in the flutter of a scarf. In a certain posture, the regalness with which some men and women remember to carry themselves. I look for her in the very names of the streets that turn from *Luz* to *Amargura*, and from *Jesús María* to *Gloria*

and *Lamparílla*. Again, in the homes I pass each day, their thresholds opening onto different tableaus—a yellow and gold statue of Our Lady of Charity tucked between white lace curtains, her copper face staring back at me through an open window. A portrait of the Madonna hung above a dining room table. A woman, her neck strung with Ochún's amber beads, calling out "my friend" to me from a doorway.

There, among these offerings, I spot a mother tending to the day-to-day activities of her life—fixing coffee for a neighbor, or sitting down to a family dinner of rice and pork. The sound of voices from the *telenovela* that flashes across the TV screen floats through open doors. The aroma of *framboyán* mixes with car exhaust and sea salt. The whispers of the oricha waft past, drawing my senses up toward balconies adorned with the artifacts of the living.

On Calle Cristo, a clothesline dips with a family's T-shirts and jeans. On Compostela, another with white sheets that blow in the Havana breeze. These sheets could be any sheets. My mother's flapping from our clothesline on Marvilla Lane alongside aprons and blouses she's pinned to the line. The heat of the day baking into the creases of a red and white checkered dress. The scent of Tide wafting from a neckline. I can almost feel the warmth of someone's skin, mine or hers.

EL SECRETO DE OCHÚN

T HERE'S A CADENCE TO Havana. A rhythm of sun and rain. A dance of pedestrian and car as taxis and bicitaxis weave among neighbors and shopkeepers on their way to and from someplace. Their dogs—a mix of terrier mutts that could be cousins to my partner Rick's dog, Skip— watch the world go by from shady stoops or join the traffic to and from. The pulse of salsa and reggaeton pours from open doors, where it meets the chorus of street vendors. "*Hay pan suave, tan suave,*" a man shouts from a bicycle piled high with soft buns in plastic bags. "*Reparo colchones,*" another cries. The scent of pineapple and sea salt tangs the air. All of it reminds me I am here not just to study the mother but to embody her.

Tomorrow I'll look for a dance teacher at the Callejón de Hamel, the Central Havana alley where each Sunday musicians and dancers perform the dances of the oricha. But tomorrow suddenly feels far away. I want to dip my toe in the water, feel my way back to the nightclub dances that hold those divine rhythms at their core: danzón and salsa, mambo and cha-cha-chá.

And so, on my fourth night in Havana, I head to a hotel off Trocadero I remember from my first trip: how from eight to eleven you could dine on its open-air patio while listening to a live quartet. Such an easy place to sit and pass a few hours on a summer night.

The Sevilla was the first luxury hotel in Havana. Its 1908 opening was one of the architectural triumphs of Cuba's new republic. Adorned with Alhambra-inspired columns and archways, the hotel welcomed the likes of Al Capone and Josephine Baker. By its rooftop pool, Cuban politicians and American businessmen met over mojitos and fine Cohiba cigars to negotiate the casinos and sugar mills that would turn Havana into the Paris of the Americas. Everything glinted with promise and prosperity. The white turrets of the presidential palace gleamed in the near distance. The men lifted their cocktail glasses, their toasts sparking yet more light. On the street below, Havana's elite paraded by on their way to shop or catch a show at the Gran Teatro.

I imagine my parents in 1951, walking among them, my father following the lines of women's seamed stockings and couture hats, my mother pretending not to notice. When they pass the Sevilla, they catch the notes of a quartet playing "Bésame Mucho" drifting through its lobby doors. My father closes his fingers around my mother's and leads her across the threshold, their heels clicking across tile as they rush toward the sound of palms striking bongos. A finger plucks an upright bass. A *shekere* shakes.

They sway a moment in the patio breeze while my father catches the beat and then they're off, the crowd scattered across the patio applauding as the couple from Illinois dance their way across the room. Even in this land of glitter and spectacle there's something about my parents that is worth looking at.

My father would have lost himself easily in the pulse of *güiro* and guitar. Gone are the duties he chafes against at home, all of them inherited from his family's businesses—the staffing and stocking of the furniture store; the midnight runs in the ambulance; the embalming and powdering of the dead. The endless stream of mourners waiting to be consoled.

For my mother, this letting go is more difficult. In her mind she is always gaining or losing ground. Either beautiful and charming enough to interest my father or not.

"I want to hold you close, see myself in your eyes," the singer croons, his voice erasing all thoughts of the women my father and mother both keep tally of at home. For a moment they are courting again, the thirty-three-year-old army captain returned from the war and the twenty-one-year-old soprano who compose love letters they send back and forth between their towns in Illinois.

"A world of flowers and beauty and love," my father writes as he imagines the life they'll build together. Not only is my mother enough; she is the whole world, the muse who will save him from himself. "Just to be near you is all I ask darling," my father writes. And, "Just left you this a.m. but am still Mimified."

"Kiss me, as if tonight were the last," the singer serenades. And then the ballad ends. The cadence quickens to a fast-tempoed cha-cha-chá. My father clicks his heels and launches into a jitterbug. His blue eyes twinkle. He is Mack the Knife, no longer here for my mother but to entertain the crowd.

It's almost eight o'clock when I arrive at the Sevilla, and the patio is just filling in. At one end, a pair of glamorous Cuban men press close to one another, their muscled arms peeking from pressed shirts. At the other, two French girls wear their youth like trophies, blowing smoke rings into the night air. The quartet is still setting up the instruments that will bring the Sevilla's patio to life: bongos and güiro, guitar and bass. The lead singer, a short, lively man dressed in plaid, makes his way around the room, stopping at each table to say hello.

I choose a seat near the French girls and line my journal and water bottle on the table before me, a set of props suggesting possible reasons for my presence. I might not be here for any other reason than to sit and write a few lines, or to catch a few notes of music over dinner before I head up to my room. Or I might be here hoping someone might ask me to dance. Who would know?

From the central wall of the patio, a life-size statue of Venus watches over us. One of many knock-offs of the marble Venus de Medici made in the style of the Venus Pudica or "Modest Venus," the figure evokes neither the Spanish Mary nor the African Ochún. Covering her breast with one hand and her pubis with the other, she is a different mother—a symbol of the pre-Castro Cuban republic that eschewed both its Spanish and African past. A mother rigid in her plaster, reminiscent more of Louis XIV, who owned five of these statues, than this exuberant island of the tropics. With her gaze cast to one side, she is shy, like me, slouching behind my journal, pretending not to want.

When the singer launches into the first song, a bolero made popular by Buena Vista Social Club, his deep voice takes me by surprise. It's such a potent sound to come from such a small man. And the music! That haunting mix of African, Spanish, Native and Arab rhythms that roots me in my breath and bones.

The band invites one of the French girls to join them on the dance floor. She shakes her head, mouthing that she doesn't know how to dance. But they keep after her until she stands. The singer hands her a güiro and motions for her to dance. She scrapes at the instrument, attempts a few steps. But she's awkward and stiff. Her ear doesn't catch the bass notes and she stumbles through the melody, searching for something to hold onto.

When the song ends, I watch with a mix of anticipation and terror as the musicians motion for the girl's friend to join them and I realize I could be next. I'm the daughter of both my parents, caught between letting go, like my father, and wanting, like my mother, to get things right. Eager to dance, to know myself as a body moving through space. Afraid I will be either too tall or too thin, too old or too young, too experienced or too inexperienced, to find anyone to dance with. No matter how many steps I've mastered, or how many trophies I've won, I will always feel like the girl at the sixth-grade dance. An object waiting to be picked or picked over. More than ever, as I approach fifty, the idea of exposing myself, a middle-aged body, seems all the more unbearable.

When the singer motions to me, I stand as if on autopilot. My hands receive the maracas he presses into my hands. My toes scratch for the beat. I don't look up from the floor. If my eyes don't meet the eyes of anyone in the crowd, I think, then they won't be able to see me either. It's the logic of a toddler.

The band is playing *El Cuarto de Tula*, a Cuban *son* whose rhythms I know by heart, and before I can think any further, I'm dancing. My focus shifts from my head to my hips. And even as it does, my heart breaks a little. Just a few years ago it would have been me on the microphone coaxing others onto the floor. I'd spent the last years of my dance career directing and choreographing, calling out shapes for others to populate. How easy it had been to coach from the sidelines. Harder but so much more fun to be the one dancing—to be the woman who knows the edges of her body, the movement of blood and breath as they course beneath her skin.

When the song comes to an end, I slink back to my seat. My knees barely make contact with my chair when I feel a tap on my shoulder. "You look like you can dance," one of the men I'd noticed from across the patio tells me. "Would you like to give it a try?"

As we take our place at the center of the patio, the man introduces himself as Angel. He's a professional dancer from Varadero, a man both natural in his movement and virtuous in his technique. For the next four and a half minutes I close my eyes and focus on the places where I'm solid. There, in my pelvis. There, where Angel's one hand cups my shoulder blade and the other cradles my fingers, the rest of us disappearing into sound.

"Wow! Those two can dance!" I hear the drummer shout as Angel leads me through a chain of increasingly complicated spins and turns. The patio bursts into applause. And then, just as quickly as it began, the set is over. I return to my seat, out of breath. My whole being vibrates. How wondrous, I think, to leave the girl hiding behind her journal and become the woman who dances four and a half minutes with Angel from Varadero. All you have to do is close your eyes, locate the pulse that lies just beneath the surface of things. That bass line that measures our steps in streams of fours or eights. To find it you have to wade through the top notes, the melodies, the digressive lines that take you this way and that. But it's there. An underlying rhythm. A larger version of the self just waiting for you to fill its contours.

It's mid-morning when I follow the *malecón* that leads from Miriam's to the Callejón de Hamel. Featured in paintings and postcards of Havana, it is this seawall that marks the line between land and sea. On one side, the waves of the Caribbean test themselves against concrete. On the other, the city stretches its limbs. The view along the way is bookended by sixteenth-century Spanish fortresses to the east, and to the west by swanky Vedado and Miramar. Sandwiched between them are the Central and Old Havana neighborhoods I explore each day.

The route is a study in pattern and permutation, a series of scenes that resolve and fade: Old couples walking hand in hand make way for young women in heels and painted lips, their suitors clamped at their waists; fishermen casting their rods into the sea give way to statues of martyrs and heroes, the ones facing inward toward the city paying tribute to Cuban protagonists, the statues facing outward to the sea celebrating foreign ones.

An artist whose work I'd admired during one of my walks had titled her version of the seawall *El Puente de Maravillas*. Her painting depicted a sea dotted with human faces and a sky populated with fish. Between those two planes she'd painted the great sea goddess Yemayá. When I gazed at the painting, the mermaid's black eyes met mine.

I'd lingered over the painting, found myself wanting to run my fingers over its texture, breathe in its scent. To be the mermaid in the painting, suspended between sea and sky, comfortable in her two textures of skin. It wasn't just the mermaid I envied but the artist too—a woman who was capable of seeing the world turned inside out, without the fear I so often felt that I would simply get it wrong. A suspicion that never leaves me no matter how much I see and learn. There was a secret to being a woman, a guidebook that lay just beyond my reach.

"She could do anything," my father boasted about my mother after she died—raise four children while finishing a master's degree, sew our clothes, host a dinner party for twelve. But while she lived, my mother struggled to live up to the impossible standards my father felt no shame espousing before her. A woman needed to be thin, but not too thin. An independent thinker who could discuss world politics, but from a liberal perspective, and certainly without interrupting. She had her own career. Was adventurous, but not too adventurous. She was a great housewife. A gourmet cook. A woman who would never embarrass you in public.

My sisters and I imbibed this message too, of course. And with our mother, we would roll our eyes, even as its manifesto seeped under our skin, mixing with our own breath until we understood it as our own. Its edicts directed us to rein ourselves in, arrange and rearrange our basic composition to become this third thing that was not us and not the world outside ourselves, but something else that sat always between us and the world. Our father's manifesto never failed to tell us how we measured up.

The worst threat to our well-being, according to both my parents, was to be mediocre. The word comes from the Latin *medius* meaning "middle" and *ocris* meaning "rugged mountain." Literally, to be caught halfway up the mountain. Which assumes there is a mountain to climb—some lower plane one must renounce in order to climb to higher ground.

For my parents, that lower ground was perhaps the small-town country roots they left behind them when they moved the family to St. Louis. Those same roots had given my grandparents their beginning. My father's father Johann Wilhelm worked his way up from immigrant day laborer to business owner-mortician-land owner. My father's mother Antonia left the dirt-floored cabin of her childhood to become his wife.

A half-century later, my parents sold the family funeral home and furniture store and invested their proceeds into the farmland that would fund their new life in the suburbs of St. Louis. They enrolled my siblings and me in private schools and music lessons. Made sure we stood tall and washed behind our ears. There was always another mountain to climb, and we must never be caught at rest.

My mother would dress each day in stockings and heels. She rolled her hair and painted her lips the same bright shade of red my father had asked her to wear since they first started dating, covered the neck he found unsightly with turtlenecks: long-sleeved ones in winter, sleeveless mock turtles in summer. I don't know what exactly it was about my mother's neck he found offensive. Maybe the proportions didn't live up to his sense of aesthetics, or perhaps the sight of the bare neck—its throat—frightened him. During his tenure as a mortician, he would have seen too many corpses not to understand how vulnerable our soft spots really are.

Sometimes I suspect it was the power of the voice that throat held. Before she met my father, my mother dreamed of becoming an opera singer, a radio announcer, maybe even a torch singer. As a teenager she'd sat in the back row of Jacksonville, Illinois' Majestic Theater watching Jeanette MacDonald and Nelson Eddy flash across the screen and imagined her own life might be that large. In a small recording studio, she recorded their songs "Rose Marie" and "Song of Love," yearning ballads about love and destiny, on a set of glass demo records. Her father and sister took turns accompanying her on piano.

At sixteen my mother entered the Illinois Wesleyan University's fifteenth-annual vocal contest. The youngest of 1400 contestants, she won its top prize—a four-year scholarship to study voice in Bloomington. By twenty-one she was on her way to that incandescent, silver-screen life she'd dreamt of. She rented an apartment with several other women in Chicago's Gold Coast, took voice lessons on weekends, and worked at a nearby furniture emporium to pay for them.

It was there in January 1946 that she would meet my dad. He was thirty-three years old then, an army captain returned from the second world war. A businessman making the annual pilgrimage to Chicago to stock up on inventory for the Huntman Furniture Store. He'd told his cousin Johnny he had a presentiment about the trip, an inexplicable but certain feeling that while he was in Chicago he was going to find a wife.

Unbeknownst to either of them, my parents' lives had been circling one another for more than a decade. The first time was when my father's mother Antonia was institutionalized in the Illinois State Hospital located in my mother's hometown. The second when my father attended university for a year at a college just blocks from where my mother lived on Edgehill Road.

The scene: My mother is seated behind the reception desk of Chicago's Farnsworth Television and Radio Corporation when my father spots her through the open door. There is something about her that makes him stop: the wavy brown hair. Those ruby-red lips. And there is something about my father that makes my mother take notice. He had a jaunty, irrepressible air about him—the gray fedora tipped over the brow, a twinkle in the eye that announced he just might be mischief.

Over the next five months, my parents will see each other eight times. Between visits they will send over a hundred letters. The first of them my father writes on January 20. *My dearest Mimi,* he begins. On March 12 he writes: *I want to get married.*

When they return from their honeymoon, my parents will move into the funeral home. It's an expedient business decision. My father will continue to work the family businesses he hates. When he seeks solace in other women's arms, my mother will rail against his infidelities. Her voice, that powerful, professionally trained instrument, will eventually get so loud with anger, with remonstration and recrimination, they'll have to leave the funeral home. First, they'll set up house in the country where there will be no one outside the family to hear their fights. Then they'll move all the way to St. Louis where there will be no one to remember their sound.

I'd wake in the middle of the night to my mother's voice shaking the house as she pressed my father about his latest affair, then the rumble of my father's voice commanding her to get a hold of herself.

"You're hysterical," he'd tell her and his voice, unlike my mother's, would be calm and cool. Sometimes I'd hear the crash of an object I couldn't identify—a framed photo? A hair brush?—being thrown across the room. Sometimes I'd hear a thud as my father ducked to avoid its blow.

"Simmer down," he'd tell her, "before you wake the neighborhood."

I'd pull my bedspread over my head to try to muffle their voices. Didn't they know I could hear them? Because my mother was louder than my father, I blamed her. Her anger seemed to rise from nowhere, or so I reasoned. I had no way of understanding the complexities of her feelings. How powerless my mother must have felt to have this voice, her greatest power, turned against her as her husband accused her of hysteria and her last-born child openly resented her for daring to rock the surface peace of the house.

I was a child hiding under the covers in a room both my parents and their generation had curated for me. The walls and carpet were rose-colored, the soft bedspread ruffled and pink. Beside the bed sat the dollhouse that my mother and I worked on together, sewing curtains for its windows and gluing parquet tiles to the floor of a miniature kitchen where a doll-sized mother cooked while the father read the newspaper.

The next morning my parents would face each other at the breakfast table, passing cream and sugar between them as if nothing had happened. And yet those nights when my mother's voice shook the house—while never acknowledged—took up residence inside me. What I took away from those nights was that to be lovable meant to keep my feelings to myself; to guard against the slightest hint of agitation or hysteria rising within me; to never raise my voice above a simmer.

"You're becoming hysterical," I hear my father say long after both he and my mother are dead, only he is talking not to my mother but to me, and it is no longer his voice issuing the warning but my own.

In my teens, I found a box hidden between leaves of sheet music my mother stored in a dining-room cabinet. Inside it were scraps of evidence she'd held onto—furniture receipts scrawled with women's phone numbers; personal ads that listed post office boxes for men whose names were thinly veiled versions of my father's.

My mother and I never talked about the box or the infidelities it represented. As close as we were, there was no way to break through the roles where she was my mother and I the daughter she wanted to protect. It is only now that I think about how much my mother must have been holding inside that box. How she grew up in an era that made it almost impossible for a woman to have, let alone give voice to, those desires that diverged from those of her husband and children.

Sometimes I caught my mother deep in thought as she went about her day, her red lips pursed, lipstick bleeding at the edges, tiny telltale feathers of distress. Did she think seriously of leaving my father? I've wondered. And if she did, what did she hope to make of a life that would be her own?

All these years later I want to decode the set of her lips. Ask my mother what it was she really wanted from her one and only life. There is no one to ask. She's gone.

The few clues are the ones I hold most dearly: the memory of her soprano voice filling the house with scales and arpeggios as she washed the dishes; another of my mother singing me in from the neighborhood. Ask anyone who grew up on Marvilla Lane and they will tell you how she leaned out our front door to call me in from a game of kickball or flashlight tag. "Beeeecki, it's time to come in for diiiinner," her vowels stretching the way she'd trained them to. Neither soft nor matter-of-fact, the call was operatic, booming, filling the night sky with the sound of itself.

Or those glass records she once recorded, brittle and warped after sitting for decades on a shelf in our hall closet—her voice rising from them, wobbly and distorted, a faint echo of its former power, but *there*.

I can almost see her, a twenty-one-year-old dreaming her future into being. A life whose only blueprints included sheet music and lyrics that speak of the divine design and glory of love.

And so, as I circle all the stories I know about my mother, I find myself landing again and again on that part of her life that began before she met my father and before I or my siblings were born. That brief window when my mother stood between being someone's daughter and being someone else's wife and mother. Those months just after the Second World War when she moved to Chicago to pursue a career in voice, stood at the threshold of her own life, and allowed herself to try herself on for her own pleasure.

It's almost noon when I arrive at the two-block alley known as the Callejón de Hamel. Originally famous for the musicians and artists who made it their home in the 20s, the alley has been re-envisioned by 65-year-old artist Salvador González as an outdoor art and performance venue dedicated to the gods. Every square inch of the alley's walls and ground are layered with donated paint and scrap metal, shell and stone. Mosaics gleam in concrete walkways. Brightly colored pinwheels bloom next to bathtubs that Salvador has repurposed as art objects. Plaster walls are painted with African gods who dance amongst lines of poetry and song. But the main draw of the venue are the professional dancers who perform the rhythms of the oricha each Sunday afternoon.

At the alley's entrance, a mannequin dressed in a plaid sports coat guards the threshold, a modern-day Eleggua overseeing the throng who've come to see the gods dance. The rumba *aficionados* and friends of dancers and musicians come on foot, while tourists arrive in taxis and bicitaxis.

I press my way toward the open-air stage where men and women have gathered, shoulder to shoulder, for the show to begin. There I find an upturned bathtub-turned art installation that offers a view over the crowd and climb on top. It's just past noon. I can feel the Havana sun searing my neck and shoulders. Still, I don't move from my spot. At any moment the dancers will take the stage. I want to see how they interpret the songs and dances of the oricha. Specifically, I want to see how they interpret Ochún. In the nine years since I studied the goddess's dances with Lourdes, I'd forgotten her steps. Now I'd lost Lourdes too. At the Callejón I hoped to find a new teacher: a dancer who might take over where Lourdes and I left off, lead me back to that theater where the scrim between our world and hers drops—that liminal space where the self-possessed seductress might teach me how to inhabit my own skin.

"Watch your purse," Marta had warned, alluding to *jinetero*s who hustled the crowds. But it wasn't just pickpockets she worried about. She'd spoken about *brujos* that inhabited the neighborhood, narrowing her eyes when she said the word, as if magic were something to run from instead of toward.

The dance group scheduled to perform today calls themselves *Los Ibellis de Merceditas Valdés,* a name that pays tribute both to the oricha twins known as the Ibeji and to the legendary Merceditas Valdés, a Santería practitioner who was among the first Cuban singers to record the songs of the oricha. They say that no one exceeded her interpretation of Ochún's dances. I've heard it described: how Valdés would enter with her neck strung with gold and her brass bangles chiming to the beat of the river. How when her torso undulated, it would seem more sea than flesh, and the flare of her upheld palms more like fins than hands.

The closest I'd come to such a thing was two decades ago when I went with my long-time dance partner to see Celia Cruz perform at Chicago's Aragon Ballroom. I didn't know then that the queen of salsa had been christened *de la Caridad*, promised to Our Lady of Charity since birth. Had grown up, like the great Merceditas Valdés, singing the songs of the oricha. Nor did I know how those West African rhythms had found their way into the very music Celia Cruz helped make famous: mambo and salsa, son, and cha-cha-chá.

It was the power of those rhythms that had brought me to the Chicago ballroom that evening, and I was far from alone. The dance hall thrummed with the excitement of those who'd come to hear the Cuban queen. She was sixty-seven, and still with another decade of performance in her when she took the microphone dressed in sequins and chiffon, her teased hair shooting from her head like the glorious nimbus of the Madonna.

Today's show begins much as it did the night Lourdes first took me to see the oricha. I hear the crackling of the batá as Eleggua jumps onto the stage. Everything about his performance is ordered and resonant with symbol—the way he dances backward and side to side, his hooked staff slung over his shoulder a reminder that it is he who holds the power to open and close our paths. Or the way he balances his weight on the left foot with the stutter-toe touch of his right to visually pun both the old man and the spinning top, for Eleggua is both as old as creation and as new as its latest spin.

Finishing in a flourish of acrobatic showmanship, the gatekeeper makes way for the hunter-blacksmith Ogún, who clears the stage of invisible brush with his machete. The thunder god Changó somersaults after him, his movements mimicking the strike of lightning and thunderbolt before he cedes the floor to Oyá. Like her masculine counterparts, the mistress of winds is a show of force. She sashays onto the stage, lashing her machete and fly whisk through the air.

Now it is Yemayá's turn. The sea goddess raises her blue and white skirts as if ready for combat, facing off against each of the male oricha before turning to the audience. With each of us, her message is clear. She is queen. She takes her time to announce herself, lifting and lowering her skirts—slowly at first, sending them rippling as if in a delicate breeze. Then faster. Round and round she spins, her skirts gaining greater and greater speed until the dancer wearing them disappears inside a blur of blue and white.

I close my eyes and anticipate the rhythms that might accompany the river goddess when she joins the others. Slow and sensuous, the way honey might sound. The movements of her body strong like her current yet rippling with surprise. If I could pay enough attention, if I could memorize each movement of waist and torso, hand and foot, take note of every touch of gold, I might know her. Might know that part of myself that was the Ochún-ness of Ochún. But Ochún does not appear. And when Eleggua returns to close the performance, I realize I will not see her today.

As the dancers leave the stage, I step off the bathtub. My head is swirling, my body trembling with dehydration and disappointment. I drink from the water bottle I keep in my purse and move toward the shaded catacombs that lead to the Callejon's coffee shop and art gallery.

Down a set of stone steps, I enter the cool recess where the artist Salvador keeps his studio. Its walls are hung with portraits of the oricha, each of them identifiable by their colors and attributes. I spot a rooster painted in red and black that signals the trickster-gatekeeper, Eleggua. For Ogún, a green and black mask peers from forest foliage. But I am looking for Ochún.

"¡Aché!" I hear the voice before I see the body it belongs to. A bubbly man dressed in an African print tunic and pants introduces himself as Salvador's assistant, El Señor Licenciado Elías. "Here to serve you," he announces. His reddish-brown curls bob as he bows.

"Are there any paintings of Ochún?" I ask, hoping that if I can't see her dance, I might at least glimpse her image.

Elías leads me to a rack of paintings and flips through brightly colored canvases, selecting the ones flecked with Ochún's yellow and gold and setting them one by one on an easel for me to study. I'm surprised to see how varied each of the artist's interpretations of the river goddess are. I'd been struck already by the correspondences and differences between her and Our Lady of Charity. Now, as I gaze at the portraits, I see that she herself contains multitudes. The river of her splits into a thousand tributaries, each offering up a different version of the goddess. There is Ochún Yeye Moró, the flirtatious one who loves to dance, and Ochún Ololodí, the deaf mermaid who doesn't dance but owns the sixteen *caracoles* that divine the will of the gods. There is Ochún Niwe, who lives in the jungle. And there is Ochún Ibú Akuaro, who lives between river and sea and whose domain encompasses both fresh- and saltwater, just as her own identity can switch and change.

Ochún appears again and again—as Ochún Sekese, the serious one, and as Ochún Aña, the one who plays the drums. As Ochún Funké, the wise one. And as Ibú Kolé, the vulture who delivers messages to and from the gods and is the leader of the powerful women known as the *àjé*.

"Àjé"—such an interesting and layered word. If you look it up in an English dictionary, the translation you are likely to get is "witch." But you'd have to unravel it from all the prejudices implied even now by that term in wider American culture—the idea that a woman's magic is a dark or evil thing. A thing to hide away in shame. A power to be feared more than revered.

As I'm coming to understand the word in my time here, I find that the truth about the àjé cannot be reduced to any single word. For the Yoruba of West Africa and their descendants in the diaspora, the àjé are women who are known for their authority over life and death: their power to conceive and nurture, to bring into the world that which did not previously exist. To be a mother.

This idea that there are women with such immense power is not a belief but a knowing. The towns of southwestern Nigeria and Cuba are filled with stories of women who keep their power inside a calabash and use it to turn themselves into birds. They are the elderly women and female ancestors, goddesses, and healers known as *iyami* (my mother) and *iya agba* (old and wise one). Members of that group who are known collectively as *awon iya wa* or "our mothers".

Some wear egret or parrot feathers in their hair, for it is their bird power that enables the mothers to accomplish whatever they wish. But mostly their powers are not visible from the outside. Every family knows there might be a member of the àjé in their midst. She might be your sister, your aunt, or your grandmother. She might be your mother—an ordinary woman in lipstick and a turtleneck who can shake the house with her voice. And so every woman must be respected, for the àjé are fearsome in their powers.

Elías and I are working our way through Ochún's paintings, each portrait offering another way to know the river goddess, when the artist joins us. A handsome man with salt and pepper hair and a white dress shirt he rolls at the sleeves, Salvador approaches just as his assistant pulls a new canvas from the pile. It's different than the others. Stiller, less adorned. Unlike the other paintings, the symbols that so often define Ochún are absent: her five brass bracelets; her half-moon and oars and bells; her sunflowers and buttercups; her honey and machete and crown. In their place, set against a palette of ocher and black, three eyes and a mouth float among the play between the light and dark of the river.

This painting is the first image I've seen that scratches beyond a surface personality or form. Not the doll-like replica of Our Lady I'd seen dressed in robes and jewels at the church, and not the proud statue of Ochún clothed in bark at the Museo de los Oricha. Neither circle nor triangle. Not bird or crone. Only this half-delineated figure that hints at the secrets of the natural world. Something truly wondrous hidden within the dark and the deep. Not the pathway to but the thing itself. The source.

"This one is special," Salvador tells me, his voice low as if he were sharing a great mystery. "I wanted to paint the moment when the initiate first goes to the river and asks Ochún to reveal her secrets."

I imagine the stillness to be found at the river's depths. The initiate must come to this place, separated from the rest of the world's sound and light, to know the goddess. There she will strip herself of her dress and jewelry and descend, like the Sumerian goddess Inanna, naked and alone into that strange underworld. Around her the enormous pressure, the darkness, the silence, of this realm—this place where the unknown is knowable, and the riches and treasures of the world abound.

I remember swimming as a girl with my mother at the farm. Our pond, tucked like a secret pocket between fields of soybean and corn, hides us from the road and all the places it might lead. We sun ourselves on the dock, wash our hair with Nexxus shampoo that smells like coconut.

We won't know for some years that she has cancer, and it won't be until years after that—until after she's dead—that anyone will think to question the harsh agricultural chemicals that seep from the fields and into the water where we swim.

On that day, we are mermaids. Sea urchins. Nymphs. These waters are a respite from anything that has or will ever touch us. A place to dissolve. I float on my back and focus on the places where I am no longer solid. My torso becomes an anemone waving from the bottom of the sea. My arm an octopus tentacle rolling through green water, my wrist and elbow as fluid as seaweed swept along the surface of the sea. My mother swims beside me, and the built-in skirt of her one-piece balloons around her like a jellyfish. The sun above projects sunspots onto the insides of my eyelids that morph into shapes I don't yet know how to interpret: a bouquet of sunflowers. A golden crown. I hear the ripple of water like the jangling of brass and gold as Ochún's bangled wrists invite me to dance with her.

"Do you know of a teacher who can teach me Ochún's dances?" I ask Elías and Salvador, suddenly remembering why I've come. Elías' face brightens. "We have just the person for you," he answers. He points to a rooftop loft that sits above the art gallery. "One of the best percussionists in town is changing clothes on this very roof."

Salvador remains in the studio as I follow Elías up a ladder. At the top we find the dancers and musicians changing from the finery of the oricha into the tank tops and flip flops of their ordinary lives. Elías wants me to meet their director, Daniel. A man who might be cast as Javier Bardem in the movie of his life, the drummer greets me dressed in jeans and a sleeveless cotton shirt that shows off the tanned muscles of his arms. A pair of sunglasses is perched on top of a ball cap. A cigarette dangles from his lips. There is nothing casual in the casualness of his appearance. The jeans and shirt look not only pressed but starched. The ball cap is spotless.

Later, I will learn that Daniel is a Santería priest and a devotee of the smooth-talking thunder god, Changó. One of the oricha Ochún took as her husband, Changó is said to have fathered her children, the Ibeji—those Yoruban twins who remind us to look for where we are yoked to something more than our own self.

I smile when I think how coyly Ochún has appeared before me today—not in the dances I'd come to see but here in the flesh-and-blood embodiment of her husband, Changó. What secrets, I wonder, might this personification of the thunder god help me unlock?

They say that while everyone else merely exists, Changó lives. He is the connoisseur, the visionary, the artist. The ruler of fertility and king of the drums. The lover of life and of women. The black cat who always lands on his feet. All this is written in Daniel's body, in the almost feline cast of his amber eyes and the certainty with which he responds to my request. For the next week I'm to report to a pink house on Calle Concordia where he teaches. He will provide two hours of private percussion instruction followed by two hours of dance with one of the women performers. The charge: $20 per day. We begin tomorrow at noon.

[6]

PLANTED

⌒

IN THE MORNING, I retrace my steps to the house where I am to report for lessons. I could take a taxi, but walking feels more honest. I like the way the city measures itself beneath my feet—the reassurance of my shadow dancing against the malecón; the feel of time and space ticking with each step.

At the statue of Antonio Maceo, I turn inland toward Central Havana's web of narrow streets and alleys. Right at the Ditú Pollo stand onto San Lázaro. Left onto Aramburu. Past the Callejón de Hamel and onto Calle Concordia where I duck through the open door of the pink house where Daniel teaches.

A woman introduces herself as Daniel's *comadre* and greets me with a burst of kisses and rapid Spanish. Dressed from head to toe in white, she explains she has just made *santo*, meaning she is a child, newly reborn in the religion of Santería as the daughter of her spiritual mother, the sea goddess Yemayá. For the next year, Miriela will follow the rules of the newly initiated—among them to dress always in white, and to eat her meals on a mat away from others, using a bowl and utensils only she will use.

Every inch of Miriela's house showcases her devotion. The stone head that represents Eleggua stands watch from the doorway, his cowrie shell eyes surveying all who enter. A porcelain statue of Our Lady of Charity is tucked in a corner near the TV. On the main wall a shelf carved in the shape of a conch holds the *fundamentos* of Miriela's guardian oricha Yemayá. At the arrangement's center stands the blue and white *sopera*, or soup tureen, that holds her sacred stones. These *otanes* are considered to be the most fundamental, tangible representation of the oricha. They are in fact believed to be the very remains the gods left when they departed the primordial community of Ile-Ife by descending into the earth. For those who know how to listen, the stones they left in their place can be found among ordinary stones—ocean rocks that vibrate with the breath and spirit of Yemayá; meteorites for the thunder king Changó; river pebbles for Ochún. Their voices can be confirmed through divination; the ones that pass the test are consecrated by a priest before being placed inside a sopera like the one on Miriela's shelf.

Miriela introduces me to the drummer who's here to help Daniel with our percussion lesson. A family friend who toggles between his roles as drumming assistant and beloved uncle, Jorge Luís is seated on her couch. His gray hair tufts from beneath a ball cap. Seated next to him is Miriela's son, a thirteen-year-old whose sunglasses and cane mark him, as they had my mother's father, as blind. Jordan is, like his mother, all hugs and kisses. He shows me the beaded *elekes* around his neck that tie him to his spiritual parents, a red and white strand for Changó and a yellow one for Ochún. He talks me through the teaching drums Daniel keeps stacked in a corner of the room: congas and *cajones,* and the double-headed batá I will be learning to play. All of the instruments are painted red or white, the colors of Changó, king of the drum.

At ten minutes after noon, Daniel strides through the doorway and takes immediate possession of the room. He directs us all to our places and passes out our instruments. When anointed with secret herbs and medicines, the batá are said to become inhabited by the oricha known in Nigeria as Àyàn and in Cuba as Aña, the spirit that inspires and is the soul of both the drum and the drummer who plays it.

"*Suave,*" Daniel tells me as he positions and repositions my hands on the mid-sized batá that drives the rhythms of Ochún. Suave, meaning both smooth and soft. My job is to maintain a steady rhythm, like a metronome. And to do so gently, without trying too hard.

The job is more difficult than it seems. One must locate the sweet spot of both hand and drum to produce the right sound. Over the next days it will become obvious I have more talent for movement than drumming and the lessons will turn almost entirely to dance. But on this first day Daniel works with me until my palms turn red and raw.

I'm relieved when my dance teacher arrives. Once we finish with the drums, Daniel will introduce her as his niece Zunilda, the dancer who performs the dances of Ochún with his troupe, the one whose absence at the Callejón had left me disappointed. But even before the introduction, I know she is my teacher. Everything about her appearance announces her as the personification of the river goddess—her yellow mini-dress with holes cut like portholes at the sides to emphasize her petite waist; the green headband and flower that crown her wavy hair; the long curved yellow and green artificial nails that on her do not seem gaudy but inevitable. When she smiles, the gold cap of a front tooth flashes. When she speaks, her words tumble from her mouth like stones made from honey and smoke.

Over the next six days Zunilda will teach me the steps that make up Ochún's repertoire. We begin with the zigzagging foot patterns that mimic the advance and retreat of her river, as well as the circular movements of hip and torso that call to mind the fullness of her waters. We lift and lower our ruffled practice skirts in imitation of the rise and fall of her waves.

I watch as Zunilda demonstrates each step, taking note of her undulating hips, her soft laugh, those fantastic green and gold fingernails tracing invisible currents in the air. When I try to imitate her, I'm all elbows and knees. From time to time, I do something that pleases her and she flashes her beautiful gold tooth. But mostly I fail.

"Try again," she tells me. I must keep my movements soft and fluid. Feet together. Knees bent. I focus on coordinating legs and torso, wrists and skirt, until my face and body drip with sweat. Then again.

There is nothing private about our private lessons. While Zunilda and I dance across the tiled floor of Miriela's kitchen, neighbors and family filter in and out of adjoining rooms. They smoke. They watch television. They visit. From time to time, Miriela jumps off the couch to stir a pot on the stove or fuss with laundry on the line.

All the while, we keep working. Daniel and Jorge Luís on drums. Zunilda instructing. Now Zunilda on drums or napping in a chair while Daniel instructs, his hands guiding my hips and shoulders, my feet. Now Zunilda again beside me while Daniel directs from the chair, his voice ushering me toward those coordinated waves of torso and pelvis that belong to Ochún.

The intensity of the rehearsal is familiar. In the years I trained as a ballroom dancer, I practiced for hours every day. When I trained my dance company, I trained them just as hard. There were shows to produce. Applause and awards to be won. Beneath each achievement the same nagging questions: Were we good enough? Had we done enough to earn our place on this earth?

Here, on Miriela's kitchen floor, the goal is not to make my mark but to sync my breath and pulse with the rhythms of the oricha. Step into their skin, inhabit their character. My entire body has become an instrument I must tune to their language. There is something in me that knows about Ochún, I just have to remember it. Her line of curves, the unquenchable voices of her daughters taking flight, the memory that we are each born of water.

It is Ochún's sensuality, her willingness to be present and attentive to her own body, that most characterizes the river goddess and her devotees. They are beautiful not because they measure up to someone else's ideas of beauty, but because they measure up to their own. Because they remember—as Ochún does—to revel in their own way of moving through the world, to fulfill the promise of who and what only they can be.

Daniel opens my journal to a blank page and draws the new lexicon I must master. He begins with a crown, taking time to decorate each of its five points. Next to it he writes the Yoruban word *ade.*

"When the *akpwon* calls ade," he tells me, "she is cueing the dancer to make a fuss over Ochún's crown.

"*Abèbè* means she is drawing attention to her fan.

"*Acho,* her clothes.

"When she calls out *oyin,* she is referring to the honey she spools from her jar. *Okokan* or *okan,* her heart."

"Follow me," Zunilda says as we try on my new vocabulary. She leads me through the steps where Ochún relishes in the movement of her hips and skirts, takes pleasure in combing her own hair. We synchronize each of our movements with the batá drums that accompany us, for Ochún is more than just an image or a story. She is a rhythm. A cadence. A template that can be accessed through sound and breath. And so, to summon Ochún you must know the drumbeats she likes best. You must move as she does. Your steps trace the flow of her current, your skirts lift like sails, your hands like oars. With each step you leave rivers in your wake.

And to summon Ochún you must also know the objects that are sacred to her—her fan made from peacock feathers, her five-pointed crown. You are a river queen preening before her sacred mirror; a sensuous beauty draping her neck and wrists with amber and gold.

I remember my mother's vanity topped with lipsticks and jewelry boxes, hair brushes and perfumes. Did she know these objects as mere instruments of vanity and decoration—as part and parcel, along with kittens and butterflies, of what the professor who once helped me with my grad school application had called "women's shit"? Or did she know them, as Ochún did, not as separate from but intrinsic to the power of her other attributes—Ochún's coquettishness a way not only to moderate her roles as warrior and leader of the àjé, but a way to give them added weight. A heft and texture woven as much from grace as from strength.

Outside Miriela's door, two men busy themselves under the hood of a 1957 Chevy. Children play soccer. Fruit vendors roll their carts up and down the street. An occasional passerby stops to peer through the doorway at the river goddess and her North American protégé, white-skirted and barefoot, while we serve invisible plates of fruit to imaginary suitors; while we dance the dance of the fan. With each of our movements, the dancer turns herself into an object—not for the pleasure of others but for herself. And here Ochún again upsets our pre-conceived notions, for her vanity is neither gratuitous, nor selfish. Her ability to focus inwardly not a call to narcissism but a reminder to cherish the self—to travel inward to those parts of ourselves that are both strong and sweet. It's a form of self-love that might serve as an antidote in a world that can foster so much contempt and self-hate.

"Hay que sacar miel," Zunilda tells me when she demonstrates the step where Ochún pours honey from an imaginary pot, lavishing its sweetness first on herself before offering it to the world.

It wasn't until she was dying that my mother remembered her body was not a bargaining chip but the vessel without which she could no longer move through the world. At the Gerson Clinic outside Tijuana, she learned to replace chemical-laden cleansers with glycerin. Abandon hair dye in favor of revealing hair that had been white for over a decade. Exchange processed foods for wheatgrass and organic juices. For the first time in her married life, the food she ate was not a tool to alternately punish or reward either herself or my father, but a gift to nourish her own precious self.

Shortly after I left for college, my mother and father closed up their house in St. Louis and re-located to Arizona's Sun City West where they could have access to the organic vegetables that hadn't yet made their way to the Midwest, leaving behind anything that didn't fit into their new one-bedroom condo. Then, a week before she died, my mother asked my father to take her home to St. Louis so she could touch her life one last time: the sheet music she kept folded in the drawers of a dining-room chest; the closet with her evening dresses hung ready for dancing; the green satin heels with the delicate straps that crisscrossed her ankles, the ones so special she could never bring herself to wear them. She wanted to feel herself solid again in the weight of a perfume bottle, breathe the scent of a woman who was still alive in the folds of a blouse or skirt.

"Suave," Daniel repeats when he wants me to soften my hips, shorten the distance between steps, stop trying to cover ground and focus on what's right in front of me.

"Plant your feet," he reminds me that within that softness lies a strength I needed to master. The confidence to get off my toes, bend my knees and surrender to the ground beneath me, trust that it will hold me.

I close my eyes and imagine myself planted in the earth, my toes plunging deep into its soil, my arms lifted toward the heavens. A stone rising from where the river goddess once descended to the center of the earth, leaving this part of herself still ringing with the aché that marks her spot.

"You have to believe you're Ochún," Zunilda tells me.

This is the difficult part. The steps are easy. I'm a dancer, practiced in mimicking movement. What Zunilda wants is not for me to mimic the river goddess but to embody her. I think about Miriela who has dedicated her life to Yemayá, been crowned in the *kariocha* ceremony that aligns the head of the initiate with her guardian oricha. What would it feel like to dance these steps not as a student but as a believer? Turn my body into a vessel through which Ochún might truly move? Leave behind the woman locked inside her stereotypes and become the river whose character changes at every bend, whose particular mix of restlessness and grace reveals the beauty of Heaven and Earth.

She is both the shallow pool and the raging current; the seductress who lures her lovers to her with honey and the vulture who picks over the bones of the dead. A mother who is both nurturing and ferocious—sweet in her ability to coax a child into the world and strong in her power to lead her through it. How to commit to such a vast shape?

"*Está bien*," Daniel announces when our four hours of instruction come to a close. My feet and hands ache. My skirt and top are soaked with sweat, and my head dizzy with instructions on where and how to place my arms and hips.

Daniel opens a jar of hemp cream to soothe my palms, which are still tender from my efforts to locate the sweet spot of the batá. I watch as he massages my left palm, then my right. Slowly. This man I've just met, Daniel Rodríguez, artistic director of *Grupo Ibellis de Merceditas Valdés*. This child of Changó, father of lightning and thunder. His tenderness reminds me of a dance coach in Chicago who used to buckle his prized student's shoes for her. This touch of the master's hands on his apprentice that is both paternal and sensual and, dare I say, even maternal. I close my eyes and relax into the feeling of being cared for. A feeling that is echoed when Daniel leads me to the bathroom so I can bathe my feet, grimy after dancing on the tile floor. Again, as he fills a bucket with warm water and calls to Miriela to bring the washcloth.

WAKING THE ANCESTORS

Tʜᴇ ᴛᴇʀᴍ Aꜰʀᴏ-Cᴜʙᴀɴ ᴅᴇᴠᴏᴛᴇᴇs employ to express the multiple guises of the divine is not faces or avatars but *caminos*—literally roads or paths. They are the surfaces that define a journey. The route or course of a life. Caminos have a source and a goal, a point of origin and a point of destination. Connecting those points is a story.

"The ancestors are watching over us," Miriam tells me when she catches me eyeing the altar she keeps on a dining-room sideboard. Framed wedding photos of grandparents and great-grandparents are flanked by prayer cards and candles, as well as the statuettes of Our Lady her brother brings back from his pilgrimages to El Cobre.

Neither Catholic nor African in origin, the *boveda* is a Spiritist tradition. A form of mediumship founded by the French philosopher-scientist Allan Kardec in the nineteenth century, in Latin America his ideas took on local Catholic and African overtones. The crucifix and prayer cards on Miriam's table all nod toward Catholicism. The photographs she keeps of the deceased echo those African religions that hold at their core the idea that family is not just made up of those who are living, but of an entire group of living and dead who share a common ancestor—all of them eternally linked in a daily exchange between worlds.

There is nothing symbolic about this arrangement. The Yoruba don't say "I'm going to speak to the spirit of my mother" but rather "I'm going to speak with my mother"—a throwback to the days when the Yoruba buried their dead beneath the floorboards of their home so the dead could continue to take part in the day-to-day happenings of the household. Here in Cuba, it is the boveda that serves as a tangible place where family can ask for guidance and know their ancestors are listening, prepared to intercede on their behalf.

Both the living and the dead know their roles. The duty of the dead is to protect the offspring they've left behind, guiding them through dreams and whispering in their ear, like an inner voice.

The duty of the living is to remember the ancestors by tending the boveda. Setting out their photographs and belongings, their favorite foods and drinks. A goblet of water placed at their center is the medium that allows for communication between the living and the dead. The candles are a way to illuminate their path.

In the world I came from, we didn't speak of making contact with our ancestors. The dead were dead. We wrote their names on family trees for school projects, displayed their portraits in the hallway that connected my parents' bedroom to mine. There the family hung framed like a sepia-toned map—German immigrants who'd traveled oceans, then rivers across the Atlantic and up the Mississippi River, from New Orleans, toward the Midwestern lands where they made their lives as farmers and teamsters, teachers and railroad car operators.

I was pregnant with Alex when I first took an interest in their stories. It felt important that I tether myself and my unborn child to something larger than my own narrative. Give him a sense of where we'd come from and where we might be headed. While his father was only one generation removed from his Mexican roots, my familiarity with my heritage could be reduced to a pair of *lederhosen* my parents brought back from Germany when I was ten and the German ravioli my father's mother had invented and my mother cooked each year for my father's birthday. My last name Huntman, one letter removed from the original German *Huntmann*.

In the months before Alex was born, I plotted family names on charts and trees. Some I could link to those photographs that lined my parents' hallway, others were just a name accompanied by the date of their birth or death.

The men's stories were the most complete. Their lives had been recorded in military records and census reports. They'd been heads of households and soldiers, farmers and railway men. The women's stories were harder to locate, their lives documented simply as housewives and mothers. Their names made them even harder to track, breaking off with each marriage as Horn became Grubel, and Grubel became Meyers, and Meyers became Huntman. A line of women, each preparing the way for the next generation before fading into oblivescence.

They were all gone now. My mother Mimi and her mother Josephine. My father's mother Antonia. My great-grandmothers Lillian and Anna, Wilhelmina and Margaretha. Only those moments bright enough to be caught on film or memory survived: a photograph of my father's grandmother Margaretha, tucked like a doll at the side of her husband Gerhardt and holding their first-born child on her lap. My mother's mother Josephine, beautiful in her 1920s lace dress and button-up shoes and peeking flirtatiously through the branches of a maple tree, this still-young version of the grandmother I knew as a formidable old woman with hairy chin moles. My father's mother Antonia posing stiffly in her feathered hats.

The rest of their stories floated outside the edges of those picture frames. Some stories were too awful to be spoken, such as how Margaretha lost six of the twelve children she carried in her womb. Other stories were repeated so often they came to stand for the woman herself. The ones about Josephine stressed her penchant for writing poetry and refusal to wear a corset, qualities that marked her as a rebel. That reputation had only solidified when she left home to teach at the Illinois School for the Blind and fell in love with the blind, handsome music teacher who became my grandfather. About her as a girl all I knew is that as a child she'd shot peas across the table at her brother Roy.

Sometimes it was the awful thing in the story that came to eclipse the woman. With my grandmother Antonia, it was her mental illness that did this, so that my sense of her became not the woman herself but the tales of her madness. There were colorful stories, like the one about how she woke my parents after their honeymoon by standing at the foot of their bed with a breakfast tray just for my father. Others we dared not speak out loud, like her two stints at the state mental hospital. Or her suicide, three years before I was born.

I had to imagine the rest of those women's lives, try to zoom in and dilate the image to take in those days that held their day-to-day stories. My great-grandmother Lillian at the sewing machine mending her husband's railroad operator overalls. My grandmother Antonia adding her own German twist to an Italian neighbor's recipe for ravioli to make a dish that would become a family treasure.

For the next week I return each day to the house on Concordia to work with Zunilda. Always Daniel and Jorge Luís are with us—accompanying us on drums; directing from the sidelines. With each day our comfort with one another grows as we develop a rhythm that moves between dance and storytelling. Daniel and Jorge Luís lean back in their chairs, filling the room with cigarette smoke as they recount the *patakis* of the oricha. Zunilda chimes in from the chair next to mine as she rummages through her bag for mascara or adjusts her skirts.

For each story there are competing versions and timelines, and not only because these stories have traveled over great distance and time from their origins in southwestern Nigeria, their shape changing with each telling, but because the oricha are by nature complex and ever-changing. Their stories change because *they* change.

What you got with Ochún depended on what part of her river you stepped into. She could be sweet and nurturing—her current transparent like glass—or she could be foul and static, murky and deep, ferocious and unpredictable. Her waters birthed and destroyed; they brought fortune or affliction. Their flow was the flow of life.

It was after the creation of the land, Daniel tells me, after the chameleon and the chicken tested and scattered the earth, that Olodumare sent the seventeen major oricha to infuse it with their quintessential powers: the iron of Ogún; the healing herbs of Osanyin. The science of Orunmila and the creativity of Obatalá. The thunder of Changó and the cooling waters of Ochún.

Ochún was the only woman among them. And when the male oricha met to discuss their business, they did not invite her. They didn't know that Olodumare had given her all the aché, the invisible power that makes things come to pass. That without her magic the plants they sowed would not produce fruit, or that their own semen would dry up. That disease would not be cured. And that when rain fell, the chickens would just pick it up and eat it.

And so, when each of these misfortunes came to pass, the male oricha consulted only with one another to find their remedies. And when epidemics festered and death and sickness prevailed and rain refused to fall, still they did not confide their troubles in Ochún but headed for the heavens to ask Olodumare what they should do.

"How many of you are here?" the supreme god asked them.

"Sixteen," they answered.

"And when you were leaving Heaven, how many were you?"

"We were seventeen."

"The one you left behind is the solution to your problems." Olodumare instructed them to apologize and make sacrifices to Ochún. When they arrived before her, the river goddess told them that she would help them, but first she wanted to be initiated in all the rituals they performed for men and by which they kept women behind. And she wanted every woman like her to know them too. So the male oricha called Ochún to them and showed her everything.

And so it is. Ochún is the awakening: the source whose waters sustain and heal. The quintessential creatrix and the leader of the àjé; the owner of the sixteen cowrie dilogún that divines the fortunes of humans and gods; the wearer of gold and brass whose crown and jewels are not mere adornment but symbols of her vast strength and worth. The queen of the markets who keeps her wealth and power inside her calabash.

To envision such a world, picture a gourd. Perhaps you're imagining something hollow and dry that has sat too long on the holiday table. Picture it again. It is a pumpkin, freshly cut. Now lift the top and find the two halves of the world. Plunge your hands inside. Feel your way over flesh and seed. Do not pull away. It is here in this wild, hidden place that you will find the womb of the world.

It is Ochún who sits with us at the side of her river before we are born, parting our destinies with her beaded comb. And it is her lips that first speak our names out loud, tossing them like flowers into the current that carries us toward our futures. First Lillian, then Josephine. Mimi, then Rebecca. A line of mothers both sweet and strong in their power to hold generations.

[8]

ORACLE

⌒

It's impossible to describe how hot Cuba gets in the summer, or how much those scorching temperatures can take out of you. The plans you make before you leave your room for the day evaporate the moment you step into the heat. The plans were only a suggestion anyway. Almost nothing in Cuba unfolds the way you think it will. You must make room for surprise: a morning sun that turns to afternoon showers, or a pile of rubble blocking your path. The buildings of Havana aren't just quaint but in serious decay, making the streets, while virtually clean of violent crime, often difficult to navigate.

I pick my way around cracks and puddles, the debris left by colonial walls that crumble into the streets faster than city workers armed with brooms and buckets and the occasional small front loader can move out of the way. The city is a perpetual work in progress, its potholes and sewer lines opening their veins, exposing whatever might lie underneath.

Within moments of leaving the house, the space beneath my fingernails fills with a gray gunk the Spanish call *mugre*—a mix of sweat and dirt that seems to hold the entire contents of the air, ripe with papaya and ginger lily and exhaust fume.

There is something else to the city. Something lush and electric. You feel it drifting on a wave of music. There again on an unexpected breeze. Perhaps you catch a glimpse of something out of the corner of your eye—the remains of a sacrifice tossed into the street. A candle burning in a window. A mirage that shimmers in the sun. If you reach your hand in any direction, you might feel the gods impregnating what you'd thought of as empty air, the hunter Ogún at their lead, carving through negative space with his machete as the oricha spin their way to Earth.

You have a feeling you've been here before at the beginning of the world. A memory from childhood when you still danced with invisible friends. Before the adults around you told you they weren't real.

On our third day of lessons, I ask Zunilda about the braided strand of yellow beads she wears around her neck. We're enjoying a break from Ochún's repertoire, giving our bodies a chance to cool before the next round when they catch my eye. I've seen them marking the necks of girls and women as daughters of Ochún, been told that receiving these elekes was one of the first steps of initiation into the religion of Santería. The beads were a way to yoke one's spirit to the oricha who watched over you. Each time I see them I've wondered how one went about earning a set of one's own.

There is nothing rational about the way I want those yellow beads. Their color, brash and bright, does not flatter me. Nor is it their quality, an inexpensive dime-store bead, that makes me want them so badly. I want the beads the way I once wanted a letter jacket or a class ring. The way I'd wanted a wedding dress more than I'd wanted to be married, or the way I'd wanted those rhinestone-studded costumes that defined me as a dancer almost more than I'd wanted to dance. In my eyes the beads of Ochún flash like a badge, a pass of admittance into a club of women willing to mark themselves as daughters of the river.

My mother had strung her wrists and neck with copper and gold, her fingers with diamonds. Even as she lay dying in the hospital, it was her rings, and not the woman wearing them, I kept my eyes on. After she died, I continued to fixate on them, my longing for them seemingly a way I might hold onto those last moments when they'd still held her. I lobbied my father to give them to me, then after his death I gave them up as my sisters asserted their rights to them. They reminded me that she was their mother, too. I was the youngest; my brother and sisters were eleven, fourteen, and sixteen when I was born. My siblings had come first, had known for longer than I how those rings flashed from our mother's fingers as she taught us to bake cookies and combed our hair. Perhaps my sisters felt as I did—that those rings might still hold something of our mother's spirit, her aché still embedded within those facets and grooves of metal and stone.

When I ask Zunilda how I can get a necklace like hers, she tells me that Daniel made it for her, that he'd prayed over the beads and given the necklace to her in an initiation ceremony.

"There has to be a ceremony to consecrate the beads," Daniel explains. "Otherwise, they're just beads."

The beads Zunilda wears had been *lavados*—meaning washed, christened, consecrated in Ochún's favorite plants and herbs: buttercup and coralillo, hierba niña, romerillo, and yellow elder. And they were lavados also in the blood, the *sangre*, of her sacrificial dove.

The casualness with which the word sangre tumbles off Daniel's tongue startles me. Until now, I'd been focusing on the parts of Santería that were easy for me to absorb—the music and dance; the glorious pantheon of gods, their various caminos offering a thousand ways to live in the world. The idea that I might have a guardian oricha, someone who might be watching over me, showing me the way.

On our first day together, Zunilda had asked if I loved Ochún. I hadn't known how to answer. The word "love" implied a certain level of intimacy with the goddess, and I was just getting to know her. But the Spanish word *querer* meant both to love and to want. And that I *wanted* to love Ochún I was certain.

Now the mention of blood threatened to eclipse that wanting. Its shadow was a reminder that there was more to being planted in this religion than just pretty beads. The price of admission challenged me to shake the prejudices of the literature I'd consumed over the years—every TV crime drama I'd ever watched where the bad guy was a practitioner of Vodú or Santería; Eleggua depicted not as trickster but devil; Santería priests not as healers but as crazed and vengeful monsters. Their rituals, plucked from the contexts that gave them their meaning, portrayed as savage and strange.

Daniel gestures toward the red and white beads of Changó that mark his own neck and wrist, the blue and white of Yemayá that mark Miriela's. Each set of colors represented a language that connected the wearer with the god they adored. All of them had been steeped in the aché of the oricha's favorite plants and herbs, and in the sangre of their sacred animals.

"A badge of protection," Daniel tells me as he touches his own beads. "A way to say: God of mine, protect me; don't leave me alone."

I turn the words over in my head, trying on the word Goddess in place of God. *Goddess of mine*, and *don't leave me alone*.

Then *badge of protection*.

"Is there someone who can make Ochún's eleke for me?" I rush to ask before I lose my courage. Daniel nods. He will talk with his *obá*, he tells me, a Santería priest who is trained in casting the sixteen cowrie shells of Ochún's oracle. Daniel will ask if Yolersi can come to the pink house before the week is up to read my caracoles. Ask the gods if I'm ready for beads.

I leave Daniel eager for something tangible that might connect me with Ochún and Our Lady: a prayer card, a picture, perhaps a figurine. In Old Havana I sift through galleries and souvenir shops, each of them offering the same goods I've seen for sale elsewhere—inexpensive paintings of street scenes; T-shirts and postcards stamped with Che Guevara and the Cuban flag. The only images of Ochún and Our Lady are the mass-produced statues I see lining the shelves of botánicas, their features rendered crudely and gaudily painted. Still, there is something about their ubiquitousness that reminds me of why I've come to Cuba. A tactile reminder that it is the mother who dominates the imagination of an island that has made her their patron saint.

In a gallery on Calle Obrapía, I find a plaster statue of Our Lady of Charity. Just under a foot tall, she is delicately crafted and painted in rich blues and golds, as if the artist who made her understood the responsibility of representing such an image and took their time. The owner of the shop, an artist named Generoso, tells me she was made long ago. How long ago, he doesn't say and I don't ask. It doesn't matter, I love her. The price is twelve CUCs, the equivalent of twelve dollars, and I only have ten, but Generoso promises he will hold onto her until I come back; he will wrap her carefully so she won't be damaged during my travels.

I leave the shop with Our Lady's delicate image in my head and wanting more. In a gallery on Obispo, I find a silver pendant engraved with Our Lady of Charity's image, her triangular figure holding her child in one hand and rosary in the other. At her feet, the three Juanes lift their hands in prayer as they look to the great mother.

I too am under Our Lady's sway. No matter how grand my lessons with Daniel and Zunilda, or how enthralled I am with Havana, it is the pilgrimage to Our Lady's El Cobre sanctuary that has monopolized my thoughts ever since I'd first read about her at the Ohio State library.

In my journal I keep a running countdown to her pilgrimage.

Two-hundred-and-forty days from when I'd first read how the ground swelled with the multitudes who arrived before the great mother on their hands and knees.

Twenty-six from the day I'd first left for Cuba.

Now there were eighteen.

I'd been shy to talk with Daniel or Zunilda about that next leg of my trip, worried that my anticipation for Our Lady's pilgrimage might detract from our focus on Ochún. But Zunilda had smiled when I'd told her. She seemed both pleased and impressed that I wasn't just another tourist taking dance lessons for the sake of cultural curiosity but perhaps a true pilgrim. She'd pulled a small stone flecked with copper from the lining of her bra and held out her cupped hand so I could admire the souvenir that had come all the way from El Cobre.

"The ground there is littered with copper," Jorge Luís had chimed in, happy to add to the conversation. Remnants from the copper mines that gave the town its name and Our Lady's narrative its spine. It was miners who first encountered the copper-skinned effigy. The three Juanes had been looking for salt for the mines when they were lost in the storm that brought them to their spiritual mother.

And it was the daughter of miners—the young girl named Apolonia—who, following a burst of lights across the sky she hoped would lead her to her own mother, had found Our Lady waiting at the top of a hill.

For the last four centuries Our Lady's devotees had followed Apolonia's footsteps, carrying offerings of candles and sunflowers as they climbed the hill of Our Lady's sanctuary. Descending that same hill clutching slivers of copper and virgencitas they brought home with them as touchstones of their faith.

I hand my money to the woman behind the counter, and then, because there is no cord to fasten the pendant, I circle down the street to find someone who might sell me one. At an outdoor market I find a jeweler with a spool of black silk. As he cuts and ties the string that will secure Our Lady's image around my neck, I hear Miriam's voice in my head.

"Our Lady brings love and children to the women who pray to her."

I think about what these things must mean to Miriam who has never married or had children. Do I imagine it is their absence that lies at the root of her sadness? Or am I making assumptions about what a woman might want?

I think again about the copper Zunilda tucks in her bra and how she'd told me she keeps it with her wherever she goes. What was it, I wondered, that Zunilda asks for when she cradles that amulet?

"Carry it with you always," Zunilda had told me about the piece I'd find in El Cobre. "She will bring you luck."

Now, as the artisan places Our Lady's image around my neck, adjusting the knots in the cord until it rests against my throat, I ponder my own questions and desires. There is something enticing in the idea of yoking myself to a story larger than my own. Something that stirs in my chest at the prospect of joining the tens of thousands of pilgrims who celebrate Our Lady that might carry me to my own mother. And there is something about those bright beads of Ochún that causes the same feeling, like they might take me there too.

I touch the pendant at my throat and feel my way over its raised image, tracing the lines that connect Our Lady's crown with the right and left hem of her robes. At her feet the three Juanes extend the bottom line of the triangle. In her hands she holds her rosary and child.

But it isn't just Our Lady's shape that I notice. The entire scene is held within a circle that might be Ochún's calabash, or the sopera that holds her five sacred stones. The womb that holds the whole world, its two halves still holding one another.

I was three years old when my father had our house on Marvilla Lane built from the apple orchards that made up the part of West County, St. Louis that would become the suburb of Frontenac. Our house was the first of six to carve a cul-de-sac from the land—a circle of homes, red brick and trimmed in white, each fronted by a neatly mowed expanse of green lawn.

Outside the perimeter of that manicured circle stretched what felt to a young girl like endless fields of milkweed and thistle. It was a habitat of bumblebees and wild rabbits, its rhythm a chorus of tree frogs and song-birds. And it was at the intersection of those two worlds—there, on the boundary where our property dropped off into prairie—that I'd find my mother kneeling over her garden. There, on the fringes of the world my father and his architect had built that my mother seemed most herself. And there, on the edges, where the magic happened.

Between our house and the house behind ours grew a thicket of trees and brush. I wandered through it, imagining I was discovering lost and uncharted worlds. When I found two boards nailed together to form a cross, I believed I'd found the actual site of Christ's crucifixion. I was too in awe of my discovery to tell anyone. I knew adults could be wary of things that appeared clearly before the young.

My discovery seeded itself among the other mysteries of the neighborhood. A half-mile from our cul-de-sac my friends and I found a pond cut from a limestone quarry. We followed the creek that fed it, searched the stones beneath our feet for fossilized tooth marks, footprints, entire strange-bodied vertebrates trapped inside ancient sediment: cephalopods, brachiopods, trilobites, mollusks, echinoderms, corals, and bryozoans rising from their five-hundred-million-year-old Paleozoic shells into our fingers and pockets, joining the turtles and crawdads we carried home.

We knew what a thing meant without understanding it fully: how the sunbaked rock we cradled in our palms held stories greater even than our imaginations. How it mapped the journeys of creatures that crawled the earth before us; and before that, when there were no creatures at all.

At night the air grew heavy, not just with the heat of summer but with its very substance. In the backyard, behind a playhouse my father built from boards that had once made up the box that carried my grandfather's prized piano, my best friend Susie and I huddled together telling stories. We'd squint and watch the dance of fireflies, squint again and see particles dancing in the air.

"Can you see them?" Susie asked me.

"Yea, I see them."

"You see the molecules?"

"No," I answered, even more in awe of my ability to see things others needed a microscope to see. "I see atoms."

The night before the oracle-priest Yolersi divines my shells, it rains. The unrelenting downpour beats against Miriam's roof and walls, breaking down the border between outside and in. Within minutes the torrents push their way through the wall behind my bed, soaking my pillows and mattress and filling the room with a dank, sour smell. I find Miriam downstairs, mopping up water that's flooding the floors faster than she can keep up. She's never seen such rain, she tells me as she moves her bucket from room to room. Not even when Hurricane Sandy struck the island nearly a year ago.

For the next hour Miriam tries to save my room before she gives up and moves me to a room on the first floor that is dry but unfamiliar. I fall asleep to the sound of rain and dream I'm underwater. My mother is there, the two of us separated by the thinnest of membranes. We stare at one another like twin images in a mirror, her nose just inches from mine. So close I can almost reach out and touch her.

I wake with the sound of water still in my head. At the foot of my bed a cockroach the flood has turned onto its back waves its spindly legs in a last effort to right itself.

Zunilda and I are dancing when Yolersi slips across the threshold. Dressed in shorts and sandals, I hardly recognize him as the great oracle I've been awaiting to divine my shells. However casual his attire, he wears it well. His skin is smooth and dark, his clothes crisply pressed like Daniel's. He and Miriela drink tea at a table in the living room while Zunilda and I work and rework Ochún's repertoire. Occasionally Yolersi will glance in our direction, and each time he does I feel myself hoping to impress him, like a child showing off for a parent.

When Zunilda and I finish our lesson, Daniel and Yolersi lead me to a back bedroom that doubles as an impromptu ceremonial space. Yolersi unrolls a reed mat and invites me to sit at one end. From his pocket he removes a pouch. Inside it are the cowrie shells the Lucumí believe hold the voice of the gods. He calls for Miriela to bring a blue composition notebook so she can record their instructions.

Yolersi shakes the cowrie shells and watches the way they drop to the mat. Teeth up. Teeth down. He translates each fall into the *letras* that trace their origin to the beginning of time—this mat, this space drawn in the midst of this very house a stand-in for another threshold, a meeting place between worlds at the ancient Nigerian city of Ile-Ife.

Here lie the crossroads of creation where Orula—the mythic founder of the oracle who knows each of our destinies because he was present at the creation of the world—and Eleggua, the force of randomness and whim that defies certainty and turns fate aside, guard the scrim line between worlds.

On the earthly side, the priest opens his mat, shakes the sixteen cowries that intuit the will of the gods between his closed hands. The sequence of their fall becomes the answer to the question asked.

What seems like chance is the breath of Olodumare. The answer that falls—teeth up, teeth down—falls from his mouth. Each signature, each outcome of those casts, corresponds with one of the 256 figures called *odu* that form the poems of Ifá.

The oracle priest knows them by heart so perfectly they recite themselves through him. Their oration translates the wisdom of the ancestors: stories of how the gods and ancestors overcame obstacles at the beginning of the world. How they fought off death and disease, infirmity and loss, and how we might do the same.

For each of us, it is the withdrawal of Sky from Earth that is the all-important line in the sand. The demarcation between before: a time of cosmic eternity and perfection, ruled by the proximity of the sky-world, Orun.

And after: a state of worldly temporality and imperfection, dominated by the earthly realm of Aye, now separated from the distant sky.

The oracle bridges the gap by translating the fall of shells that hold the language and will of the gods. Its answer points to the particular crossroads you are standing at: whether you are in a state of balance or imbalance; what prayers and offerings you need to offer to regain harmony; whether you are ready to move ahead as an initiate in the religion.

Yolersi holds his closed fists out to me and tells me to blow on them.

"What do you want?" he asks. I feel the weight of the question, the idea of being pinned down to an answer more frightening than anything else I might encounter in this room. The array of possible responses dances in the air before me, daring me to catch one before they fall like caracoles to the mat.

I look to Daniel for help but he only raises his eyebrows back at me, letting me know the question is mine alone to answer.

What did I want?

It had something to do with the comings and goings of the house. The way life didn't stop just because we were talking with the gods but kept spinning: the sounds of Jordan and Jorge Luís's laughter drifting from the living room; the cadence of Miriela's voice and hands as she washed dishes or pinned laundry to the line.

And it had something to do with the materiality of things: statues that stood in for Catholic and African saints. Batá drums that called the sacred rhythms of the oricha. Water goblets that allowed one to communicate with the dead. Zunilda's beautiful golden beads that tied her to Ochún. Each of these objects held an invitation for the spirits to join the living, incarnate through the medium of image and drink, song and dance, body and prayer—Yolersi's shells not just caracoles but a way to channel the very voices of the gods. How many initiates had sat, like me, waiting for their deepest questions to be answered by the sequence of their fall?

I study the hands stretched before me—Yolersi's hands—and see not one man's hands but a line of hands. It is a line that stretches from this pink house on Concordia all the way to Nigeria where kings and priests first received the oracle from the gods. Using kola nuts or cowrie shells, for generations they practiced each cast and fall, memorizing each letra, distilling its translation and interpretation. So that even when the descendants of those first priests were shackled and chained and forced onto the ships that would take them to the Americas, they brought their wisdom with them. In their hands they clasped the muscle memory of casting nuts and shells. In their heads they stowed the knowledge of secret offerings and herbs. On their tongues they ferried the songs and prayers of the gods.

Ochún was there among those men and women as they traversed rivers and oceans. She watched over them as they crossed the great Niger River and its tributaries west through Nigeria and Benin to the Gulf of Guinea and out into the Atlantic where, centuries later, her rhythms and stories would find their way to these very rooms where I'm learning to plant myself. Each afternoon Daniel and Jorge Luís's palms find their way to the sweet spot of their drums. Zunilda's wrists trace the currents of Ochún's waters. My own hands lift and lower my skirts as I dance my way back to a mother who once held her daughter in a port of angels. Yolersi stretches his fists before me. His hands are the bridge to all the hands that have paved the way for this reading.

When I remember that long-ago day in Oaxaca, Mexico, when my mother and I were nearly pulled out to sea, it's not just my mother's hands I think of when I recall those churning waters nor how tightly she held onto me. Also central to the story is that someone came to save us. This part of what happened spins itself from some place imperceptible to the logical mind. The woman who heard our shouts for help wasn't around when we first dipped our toes in those waters. Nor was she there when they pulled us out to sea. But she was present that day nonetheless. I like to think that some sweet voice whispered in her ear, suggesting that a walk by the ocean might be just what she needed. Some invisible arm pulled her onto the beach just in time to hear our shouts. She let out a cry of alarm.

And the divers who answered her call? What web of circumstances enabled those particular men—their arms and legs, muscled from diving for black coral, a perfect match for those roiling waters—to be within earshot of her call? What I take from this story: Someone was watching out for us, and because of that my mother and I were destined not to die but to live.

The Yoruba tell that we are born with a specific path. It is our duty to travel it. And it is the oracle's duty to show us the way. The last night I saw my mother, I'd stood in the threshold of her hospital room not looking at her hands but her rings—those atoms of carbon and gold that still connected her to the tasks of the living: to the wooden spoon and red-enameled colander she used to cook. To the strappy heels she kept wrapped in tissue paper on her closet shelf. To a note she left only a few months before on my pillow, the words *Because I love you always, Mother* engraved in blue ink. What remained of her body was skeletal, hovering between worlds; the rest of her was already floating somewhere I could no longer touch.

Now I stood in another doorway, one that seemed to be open and which, in return for my entry, asked only that I too be willing to open. Let go. Surrender. Move past the borders of what I could see, hear, and touch. Find that portal back to the original world of union when Sky and Earth still held one another, and Olodumare's breath coursed through each and every thing, reminding us we were still one.

What did I want?

Could I tell Yolersi that what I wanted was to be part of the club? To have a cool necklace like Zunilda's? That I wanted to join without the cost of commitment? That I wanted just to dip my toe in its shallowest waters? Without any animal sacrifices or other rituals I didn't yet understand?

Could I tell him that those unfamiliar rituals were exactly what I wanted? That in fact I hungered for them? That I wanted to drown in their deepest waters? That I wanted to be overcome? To step over the line and make contact with a world beyond the finite one I kept bumping into. Abandon caution and common sense and reach out and seize a memory of wholeness.

Again, Yolersi shakes the cowrie shells, watches as they fall—teeth up, teeth down—to the mat. Calls out the verdict of the gods. I am to receive the five sacred stones and the beaded necklace of Ochún. But first I need to receive the four *guerreros* who will guard and protect me.

The first of the warriors, Yolersi explains, is Eleggua, the gatekeeper who will open my roads to good things and close the doors to all the forces that might do me harm. The next is Ogún, the blacksmith who will clear my path of obstacles and give me the tools to build a better life. The hunter Ochosi will help me hunt for the good things in life and keep me from losing my way in the wilderness. And the guardian Osun—not to be confused with Ochún—is the protector of health and stability who will watch over my head and wellbeing.

Yolersi doesn't say the word and I'm too new to the religion, too dazed by the novelty of what is happening to think it out loud, but what Yolersi is calling for are the first initiations into the religion of Santería. The objects that hold Ochún and the warriors' spirits will be washed, along with the beads, in herbs and blood. My receiving them is the equivalent of a baptism—a ritual to align my life with the gods they represent.

Yolersi and Daniel confer with Miriela about how they can pull all this off before I leave for El Cobre. The ceremony will have to take place tomorrow, and there is much to purchase and prepare. There are the fundamentos of the oricha: the cement head that will be consecrated with the herbs and prayers that are sacred to Eleggua, and the iron cauldron of Ogún. Ochosi's bow and arrow. The five river stones of Ochún. There are the herbs and animals that will be offered to each of them. And yes, there will be beads! A strand of red and black beads for Eleggua; another of yellow and gold for Ochún; a third made of peony seeds Yolersi says will help me be more decisive.

"You have a hard time making a decision?" he asks, although he already knows the answer. Even now, I feel thin-skinned and uncertain. As porous as a ghost, the world pouring in and out of me as I think about moving forward with the plans being discussed. I understand so little about what it means to receive these gods. I can feel all my fears about getting caught up in things I don't understand bumping up against the part of me that wants to jump in with both feet.

I think of Rick back in Ohio. What would he think of what I'm about to do? Rick, who was the bison to my egret—a man who could zero in on a decision while I had to circle each and every possibility.

On our third date, Rick and I had our fortune read at the state fair. The man running the booth entered our birth dates and handwriting samples into a computer that spit out its prognosis for our future: Our relationship would either be the best or the worst ever. Mostly, one year in, the relationship steers toward the best. Still, there is much to negotiate. After years of being on our own, we are finding our way into what it means to be in partnership. The intersection between Rick's analytical brain and my more intuitive ways are where we most often collide. We disagree about the plausibility of astrology and the right way to rake the yard or paint a room—he prefers to tackle tasks in quadrants while I like to start where the mood strikes. Finding ways to listen and understand one another amidst such differences had become both our steepest learning curve and, when we were able to do so, our greatest strength.

Now I stood at the threshold where my own mind toggled between longing and logic. On the one side, a lifetime of indoctrination from a culture that privileged reason over intuition, the linear over the mythical.

On the other, an invitation to step into a world where time measured itself not in the before and after, but in circles—the gods and ancestors always only a breath away.

For the final roll, Yolersi tells me I should think of a question, one question only, that has a yes or no response and let him know when I have it ready in my head.

As I search the air for questions I might ask, one rises clearly from the field.

Am I ready?

I nod to Yolersi to let him know I have my question and close my eyes. He places what is either a stone or a shell in each of my hands and asks me to choose between them.

Am I ready? I turn my question in my head. Am I ready to receive the warriors and Ochún? Am I ready to continue down this rabbit hole and move closer toward their secrets?

Yolersi opens my hand and calls out the answer.

My response, a large, shy grin, takes me by surprise. I haven't realized how much I needed it to be a yes.

CITY OF GODS

IT IS DURING THE ceremony known as *asiento* that the oricha determined to be one's guardian is seated inside one's head. The ritual seals a fundamental bond of consciousness between human and spirit. From that moment forward the devotee no longer needs to listen for the call of the oricha because the voice is her very self.

For days Daniel has been inviting me to a *cajón*, a term I know only in its relation to the box drums he keeps stacked in the corner of Miriela's dining room. Now we are rushing to get there on time. Yolersi is still folding his mat as Daniel pulls his drums out onto the curb where Jorge Luís and Misael, a drummer I recognize from the performance at the Callejón, are waiting in a peso taxi.

It is Jorge Luís who explains what we're on our way to do. A woman named Cristina who lives in the town of Regla is getting ready to celebrate the anniversary of making santo, becoming a daughter of Yemayá. Tomorrow there will be a birthday party, but the festivities begin today with the purification ceremony known as the cajón, which is named after the drums that will be used to call the oricha into the room.

I sit in the backseat with the drummers. Daniel's red drums nestle between us like the taxi's fifth passenger as we wind our way to the ferry that will take us across the harbor to Regla.

As we shove off to sea, I imagine the ship that brought my parents to Cuba sixty years ago as it set anchor in these same waters. It would have squeezed through the Spanish fortresses that line the jaws of the harbor—El Morro and La Cabaña on the northern stretch, Castillo de la Punta to the south—the three garrisons holding my parents gently in their teeth before releasing them into the bay. I can almost hear my parents gasp as they catch their first glimpse of the island. Before them, Havana would have spread her shores, a dazzling paradise framed by blue seas and royal palms. To the west on the periphery of their vision lie the swanky hotels and nightclubs of Vedado where movie stars and mobsters come to play. To the east, the town of Regla.

When I'd asked Marta and Miriam about Regla, they'd spoken in quiet tones. Its residents were said either to be great priests or dangerous thieves, depending on who was reporting.

"A town of witches," Marta had cautioned.

"A center of great mysteries," Daniel now promises.

It's in the town of Regla that Santería priests and *babalawos* have made their homes since the 1880s. Here where the streets are said to thrum with the rhythms of batá drums and incantations. Here that the àjé are said to live.

And it is here among them where the Black Madonna, Our Lady of Regla, rules over harbor and town. Like Our Lady of Charity, Our Lady of Regla is a mother who is too expansive to confine herself to one religion. She is an incarnation both of Mary, Stella Maris, Catholic star of the seas, and the Yoruban queen of the seas, Ochún's mother, Yemayá. And it is her church in Regla, like Our Lady's in El Cobre, that is the focal point of her devotion.

Daniel tells me how the inhabitants of Regla say she swims the length and breadth of her bay at night. The fishermen have seen her—a mermaid with mother-of-pearl scales and silvery hair. Her eyes, they say, are round and white, her dark irises fringed in lashes. They describe how the stars light her skin as she swims. By morning, she has resumed her place in the sanctuary and can be found there standing erect and still—her forehead still wet with perspiration from the exertion of her nocturnal swims, her robes still dripping from the sea.

I like to think she and my mother might have spotted one another across the harbor. That my mother might have heard the voice of that great sea goddess inviting her to join her in her nightly swims. Know herself as a woman clothed in stars and sea: a woman with the power to come and go as she pleased, revel in the fullness of herself as she dips between worlds.

However afraid my mother must have been as she faced her own death, she never talked about it. Not when she received her diagnosis, and not when she underwent weeks of surgeries and chemotherapy. She allowed herself only the luxury of complaining about the Jell-O the hospital served with every meal and the vanity of trying to hold onto the woman she'd been before the cancer. The day of her first surgery, she made me promise I would bring her lipstick to the recovery room. She didn't want anyone to see her looking "undone." In the waiting room I twisted the metal tube between my fingers, relieved to have a job. When the doctors came out to give us an update, I twisted the tube again as I listened to them recite the list of organs they'd excised from my mother's body— uterus, ovaries, fallopian tubes, half her colon, several feet of intestine, a portion of her stomach.

In the recovery room I found my mother looking small and defeated in a hospital gown that was suddenly too large for her. When I showed her the lipstick, she looked at me as if she couldn't remember a time when such a thing could have felt important.

For the next seven weeks, my mother lived at the hospital, recovering from one surgery, preparing for the next. In between came the needles—the ones the nurses inserted for IVs and the ones they stuck her with to draw blood. With each needle came the struggle to find a point of entry, my mother's delicate veins broken after so many pokes. And with each needle, my mother turned away a moment to brace herself before turning back to again offer the white underside of her arm.

When we dock in Regla, the drummers and I thread our way through dirt streets and alleyways, stopping occasionally to ask for directions. Above us clouds turn black with the rains that threaten to break at any moment. Residents duck for cover, leaving the narrow streets empty, the only sign of life an occasional bicycle parked outside a house. Even the sanctuary feels dark and deserted as we pass by. The ivory statue of Our Lady of Regla outside its doors takes on a gray hue that reflects the gloom of the day.

We find the house we're looking for just as the first rain hits. We are, as Daniel feared, late. Cristina is waiting for us in the doorway, already dressed in the colors of her saint: a blue and white skirt and tank top, white footless tights and headscarf. A pair of bright yellow sandals are the only interruption in the sea goddess's template of blue and white.

Like Daniel's comadre Miriela, Cristina has undergone the asiento ceremony in which she has aligned her head and spirit with Yemayá. But whereas Miriela is still completing her first year of making santo, Cristina is years in. The rituals that will take place today and tomorrow mark the anniversary date when she first became an *oloricha* of the sea goddess. These celebrations are a way to strengthen the bond she sealed during the asiento ceremony, demonstrate her devotion, and invite Yemayá to come dance with her.

Cristina leads us through a narrow strip of kitchen that takes us to the main room of the house. A square no more than 10 x 20 feet, the room serves as living and dining room as well as shrine. Its shelves and glass-doored cabinet are filled with soperas and statues dedicated to the saints, and every piece of furniture except for a table set in the middle of the room has been cleared for the ceremony about to take place.

Cristina is a hurricane of activity, directing family members to bring us bottled water and soda and cups, setting the table with plates of chicken and rice and avocado. We are honored guests, Daniel explains. No matter that we're late. The drummers who play the consecrated drums that bring down the oricha must be fed.

When we finish our meal, the crew and guests click into place. Cristina calls for two men to remove the table. She sweeps the floors and smooths her skirts. The drummers move to the chairs Cristina has set for them against a wall. Family and neighbors migrate from the kitchen to the main room. There they hug the walls, leaving the center of the room clear. I search for a place as far as possible from the activity, settling on a spot near Cristina's teenaged children at the back of the room. Her daughter, dressed in a miniskirt and an off-the-shoulder tee with the letters "Diva" spelled out in rhinestones, moves between checking a pink smartphone and admiring her reflection in the glass doors of the cabinet that houses the saints. The girl's brother, his hair cut into a Mohawk he's dyed red and black, sits on the stairs behind us busying himself with an MP3 player.

From the front of the room, a stout gray-haired woman who Daniel tells me is the santera in charge instructs us to cleanse our faces and hands with herbs and perfume water. She leads us in a call and response of the Padre Nuestro, then cedes the room to the drummers: Daniel and Misael on the cajones, Jorge Luís on *clave* and *agogo*. The instruments sound out the invitation for the oricha to join us.

The men close their eyes as they feel their way into the rhythms that call Eleggua to enter the room and open the threshold between worlds. Jorge Luís lights a cigar, blowing smoke to tease the deity into the room.

Cristina kicks off her shoes and begins to dance. There is nothing performative about the way she moves. Unlike the structured steps I've learned with Lourdes and Zunilda, Cristina's first steps are slow and tentative—not the result of studying an official lexicon but rather an extension of her own sensibility as she feels her way into the pulse and cadence of the goddess.

The drummers lead the way. Over the next hours they will transform. Gone will be the men I traveled across the harbor with on the ferry, the ones who joked and argued as they dragged their drums behind them. What I'll see in their place is something moving through them: another throat informing the tongues that alternate between Lucumí and Spanish chants. Their voices sing out at a greater volume than is required in such a small space. Their hands strike their instruments in intensifying waves.

Cristina too is changed. This woman who moments ago served us lunch, who directed the moving of furniture and the sweeping of floors, the woman who was in charge of *everything*, now submits to something only she can see—a latent image of the goddess impressed at the time of initiation that reveals itself fully to her now.

I can tell the instant the spirit catches her. Cristina throws her head back and laughs, and when she looks out at us again her eyes are wide and bright, as if she were suddenly able to take in more of the world. I remember this look from the dancers I saw nine years earlier with Lourdes. Their eyes had swelled as if to accommodate the inner vision of the spirits that rose to mount their limbs, climbing them like trees until they came to rest in their heads. I could still recall how every affectation of those dancers' worldly selves had dropped away as they made way for the oricha now moving through them.

It's not just Cristina's eyes that are changed. She stumbles through the room as if drunk, her limbs loose, as if they no longer require the support of mortal bones. And when she dances, she dances as Yemayá, lifting her skirts as if they were sails or oars.

The crowd claps their encouragement, and people mark time with their feet as they follow Cristina across the threshold. Jorge Luís relights his cigar, puffing up a line of smoke like incense into a room already hazy from other cigar and cigarette smoke. Cristina reels along the wall, coaxing men and women into the center of the room to dance with her. They are dancing now, as their ancestors once did in Ile-Ife, in the beginning of time. Even Cristina's children put down their electronics to join.

I watch the circle of dancers before me, wondering what it was that allowed them to drop the veil of skin and gesture, invite the gods to dance with and through them. I am both surprised and disappointed at how shy I feel. Since I'd arrived nearly two weeks ago, I'd been hoping I might witness a Santería ceremony. Now that I'm here I feel painfully self-conscious. Terrified I might be called upon to leave my safe place at the back of the room and join in.

There's a break in the drumming—a signal that it is time for Yemayá to rest after her long journey from Orun. The santera offers Cristina a drink of water to help clear her throat. Together, they walk around the room, the old woman's arm draped around Cristina's shoulder like a boxing coach.

When she's ready for the next round, Cristina breaks away to circle the room on her own. She touches the faces of her children, hugs one of the men. When she gets to me, she grazes my forehead, almost lovingly, her fingers moving like those of a priest as she marks me with the sign of the cross. Her eyes widen as if to take in more of me. I feel something shift inside me, something blooming at the root of my spine. Its voice, if it had one, tells me not to be afraid.

Hour after hour the drummers fill the room with the call of their voices and hands. Hour after hour Cristina answers with the drumming of her feet and the circling of her skirts. The crowd ebbs and flows with her tide, waving more smoke into an already cramped space. I vacillate between feeling caught up in the happenings and feeling them wash over me. The drummers' hands rise and fall as Cristina's feet rhythmically hit the ground; her blue and white skirts whip the air. Voices. Drums. Feet. Hands. The borders of my own body begin to feel as if they are taking on unreliable dimensions. A mole on my forearm I've never noticed before seems to grow before my eyes. I watch it pulsate. I can't breathe. Choking on something that may or may not be smoke, I push past the blur of dancing limbs, through the kitchen door, and into the alley to clear my head.

Outside, the rain falls in solid sheets, and the slender overhang of the roof provides only a little protection from the monsoon that soaks the hem of my skirt and feet. I lean against the wall of the house and feel the concrete damp against my back. I am not the only one who has come outside for air. Around me, hands and faces move in and out of focus and cigarette smoke mixes with rain. Cristina's daughter shivers next to me in her miniskirt and Diva top. The writer in me feels like I should talk to her. If I weren't so dizzy, I might ask her how it feels to see her mother mounted by her oricha.

The closest I'd come to such a thing was when I'd watched my mother practice her dance steps. That smile that crept over her face as she discovered something within her: a grace and restlessness she could call her own. Again, after she got sick. Not right away. Her first attempts at healing were surgical and chemical, but after. Once she and my father stumbled upon the holistic health movement. Signed up for macrobiotics classes. Traveled to the Gerson Center in Mexico for treatments they couldn't get at home: laetrile and coffee enemas and oxygen therapy; a diet of organic fruits and vegetables; liquid meals concocted from calf livers and wheatgrass. Such things were unheard of in the St. Louis suburbs of the early 80s. My mother was a renegade, an adventuress tossing aside the conventional wisdom of her oncologist with his steel tools and chemical drips and heading south to the healing power of plants and herbs. Whether initially spurred by fear or faith or both, she became a true believer. While I was at college, she wrote long missives about the importance of nurturing my own body.

Please, Becki—do some looking around at whatever interests you in the health area, my mother wrote. *We are all being poisoned by our environment—the chlorine and fluoride in the water … food additives that have passed the Food and Drug Act and yet are toxic in small degrees in your body.*

You <u>must</u> be in charge of your own body. You must read and learn how to take care of beautiful Becki.

As I stand under the dripping ledge of the roof, my legs feel weak. My ears are ringing. And when I look back at my arm, the mole, seemingly larger than it was a few minutes before, swims under my gaze. Suddenly I feel far from home. Homesick—and not just for Rick and his steady touch and my apartment in Ohio. I am homesick for my small room at Miriam's. I miss the familiarity of having a place that lets me know who I am: my two beds, the one I sleep in and the other where I stash my journal and books. I miss my suitcase with my sundresses rolled up inside it. My window with my toothbrush and shampoo lined along the ledge. And then I remember how I lost those four walls to last night's flood. How the water beat against the house, rushing through every crack in its armor.

I feel so far from you, my mother confided in her letters. *I can't wait to see you, Becki,* she wrote before our last real visit: *It's been awful missing you; I can tell you now.*

All at once I realize I can't breathe. Rain and smoke close in on me, saturating every particle of oxygen. I'm going to pass out if I don't lie down. Right now. But where? There is nowhere to lie down. I haven't seen a bed or even a couch. The only chairs are occupied by the drummers. The sky is black. The rain is coming harder and faster. It's a long way back through town to the ferry, even if I remembered my way.

Inside the house the dancers are still dancing, the drummers still drum-
ming. The shape and sound of them reach me as if from very far away.
I need to make my way to them before I pass out, I think, let Daniel or
Jorge Luís know that I'm not feeling well.

I expect the drummers to be angry when I interrupt them, but Jorge
Luís takes one look at me and gives me his chair. Daniel leans over me.
"You're cold and pallid," he tells me, touching my face. The santera
douses my head and neck with perfume water, prays over a glass of water
she instructs me to throw on myself, brings me fresh water to drink. As
if from the other side of a tunnel, I hear the slap of Cristina's feet on the
floor. "Ah, ah!" she cries in a voice that rides the line between ecstasy and
pain. And then my dizziness lifts and I feel myself returning to the room.

Cristina too is coming back to herself, barely able to stand from
exhaustion as she regains her awareness. After hours of demonstrating
her devotion to Yemayá—calling the sea goddess to dance with her,
recommitting before family and friends to the bond she first sealed with
the divinity during the asiento ceremony—Cristina has reached some
sort of climax. The old woman walks her in circles, talking her down.
"Not everything can be accomplished in one day," I hear her say and I'm
not sure if she's talking to Cristina or to me. After nearly four hours the
drummers launch into their closing rhythms, the ones that sound their
final praises for the oricha before petitioning Eleggua to usher the spirits
back to the invisible world. And then all is quiet. The men pack up their
drums. The old woman returns to the front of the room. She leads us
in a final blessing, calling out for the good to follow each of us, then
herds what's left of the crowd into the kitchen where she ladles soup and
orange soda into plastic cups for us, signaling our re-entry back into the
world of ordinary things.

The rain is just letting up as we retrace our steps back to the ferry, the mood among us jovial as Daniel and Jorge Luís replay everything that has happened.

"Did you see Rebecca?" Jorge Luís asks Daniel, reliving the details as if proudly recounting a war story. "She was cold and white!"

"And dizzy," Daniel joins in.

"There was a lot of spirituality in that place," Daniel turns to me, his voice growing solemn. "And you were able to feel it. That opening between worlds. Not everyone can.

"When you come to the house tomorrow, dress in white," he adds. "You will be a child reborn into a new religion."

Yes, I think, a child. How much I had to learn about this religion that was just revealing itself to me! During Yolersi's divination, the oricha had said I should receive Santería's four warriors so they could guide and protect me. That, having opened that first door of initiation, I should also receive Ochún. The gods had not said whether she was my guardian oricha. That information would come down the line should I choose to pursue the path Miriela and Cristina had. Undergo the asiento ceremony in which one invites her guardian oricha to seat herself in one's head. *Hacerse santo.*

For now, I was just dipping my hand in the river. Yolersi and Daniel had described tomorrow's initiation as an opening. A series of rituals in which I would ask the warriors and Ochún to watch over me. As a sign of their protection, I would receive their fundamental ritual objects. Miriela had compiled a shopping list of all we would need. Among them were the warriors' stones and tools and the beaded eleke of Ochún. More than ever, it is those golden beads that call to me—a way to yoke my spirit to the river goddess, open the first channels of communication between us.

"Tomorrow is a big day," Daniel reminds me, and for the first time in hours I think about the birds on Miriela's list.

"They're going to be killed, aren't they?" I ask Daniel, although I already know the answer.

"Don't look," he says.

[10]

DULCE Y FUERTE

I'M NOT LOOKING WHEN Daniel buys the birds. He slips behind one of the butcher shops at the market and emerges twenty minutes later with two cloth sacks dangling from his wrists. I've seen Miriela's list and so I know that what he holds in those sacks are two chickens and two doves. Not the ones the butcher sells out front but the ones he keeps in back, the ones that have been consecrated and blessed, prepared especially for Santería initiations.

Except for an occasional squawk, the birds are silent as we move between market stalls and botánicas, Miriela ticking off each remaining item on our list—bottles of rum and palm oil; the sacred stones that hold the oricha's spirits and the *herramientas* that accompany them—a five-pointed golden crown that announces Ochún as queen of her river. A set of brass oars to carry her between the spirit and material world. A brass bell I'll ring when I want to speak with her.

For the warriors there is a cement head set with cowrie shells for eyes that will hold the secret herbs of Eleggua; Ogún's metal cauldron and anvil; the hunter Ochosi's bow and arrow; a metal rooster to stand in for the guardian Osun. Each of these items are to be bathed in the blood of the birds Daniel carries in the sacks at his sides.

Daniel assures me the sacrifices are more like a rabbi's kosher blessings than those crazed portrayals I've seen on TV. Their slaughter is clean and quick, with every bit of flesh shared among the humans and their gods, and those parts we could not consume left outside for the street dogs to finish off.

Still, the dread of what's to come hangs over the morning. My only experience with dead animals has been confined to what can be bought from the Meat section at the supermarket: cuts of beef or chicken neatly wrapped and bearing little resemblance to the living animal from which they came. I remember watching my mother tear through plastic and Styrofoam, then skin and fat, to expose the naked bird that lay beneath. Holding under the kitchen faucet the severed root where the animal's head was once fastened to its flesh, her hands turning it under the flow of cool water. As a child I'd recoiled in horror at the sight and dreaded the day I too might have to touch such a thing.

Even now I find myself wanting to evade the thought of their bodies: raw, naked, wholly vulnerable. It goes deeper than just concern for the animals Daniel carries at his side. It is the idea that, underneath all our efforts to disguise it, we were all dying even as we live.

With Daniel I was learning to embrace that the conjunction joining life and death was not *or* but *and*. We were mortal and alive. Human and spirit. Both alone and enveloped by the spirits who guided us. The items we were purchasing weren't just objects but portals through which we might make contact with the nonmaterial world. The blood they would be bathed in a way to feed the oricha, give back to the invisible world something of what it gave us, thank them for guiding and protecting us. Invite them to keep working their magic in our lives.

At a botánica near the Callejón de Hamel, Miriela fusses over strands of beaded elekes for me to choose from—Eleggua's in red and black, Ochún's in yellow and gold—while Daniel picks over the *ildes*—beaded bracelets worn by the initiate at the wrist. He chooses a smaller one woven from yellow and gold beads for me to wear every day, and a more extravagant one, with bits of real coral interspersed among yellow beads and a cowrie shell as a clasp he tells me I can wear until we get back to Miriela's.

"Your bracelet is old," he tells me, pointing to the frayed threads that dangle from its clasp, casting shadows on the ground beneath us as we make our way to the pink house, the strings of the sacks that hang from Daniel's own wrists casting a twin shadow alongside them. I feel the cowrie shell press against my pulse point, its mouth opening, unabashedly female, like a vulva. Those bright yellow beads a reminder that I am not alone.

We return to find Yolersi already waiting for us. A second priest, Aristedes, is at his side. Over the next hour and a half, we work to turn Miriela's house into a space fit to be a meeting place between humans and gods. We unpack the market items, and they're arranged in a precise way across the house, which is now serving as a stand-in for the sacred spaces of the Yoruba towns where these rituals originated. The front door represents the gate where Eleggua and Ogún stand watch between worlds. The back bedroom, the inner sanctum where divinations and initiations take place. The bathroom becomes the riverbed where Ochún's waters bring renewal and health. The living room stands in for the town center of communal worship and celebration while the kitchen is the grove where sacred plants and herbs are cultivated for medicine and magic.

We throw ourselves into our work. Daniel and Jordan are in the back room with Yolersi and Aristedes preparing herbs; Jorge Luís and Miriela at the stove; I am at the kitchen table shredding coconut into piles. When we finish, Yolersi gathers us into a corner of the kitchen for the *coco al muerto*, a ceremony to honor the ancestors that precedes all Santería initiations.

We stand in a circle. A candle on the floor casts its amber glow on the offerings we've set before them. Plastic cups have been filled with coffee and rum, tea and soda, and quartered coconut coated with palm oil and placed on plates. The coconuts, like the traditional kola nuts and cowrie shells, are a way to divine the will of the gods. The ratio of pieces falling face up with those that fall face down yields their answers.

"First the dead, and then the saints," Daniel whispers, explaining that we need to ask the blessing of the *egún*, the departed ancestors of those who've gathered in this circle, before we can continue with today's initiation.

"They're our intermediaries and unless they give their permission, the oricha won't talk with us," Daniel explains. He draws a cross on my forehead with *cascarilla*, a white chalk made from ground eggshell he says will protect me as we call forth the dead.

Yolersi lifts a staff covered with colored strips of cloth and bells and taps it on the ground. This tapping is a way to mark the meeting point between Heaven and Earth, its sound a way to call forth the dead, once literally and now symbolically buried under the floor.

Daniel stays close to me so he can explain each step of the ceremony. He tells me how, together, the dead and the living form a symbiotic chain. The unborn are dependent on the living and the divinities to give them life, while the ancestors and divinities are dependent on the living so they might exist in the world—not just through the offerings we leave that give them nourishment and form, but because without us to remember them, they would simply disappear.

"You're a child today," Daniel reminds me when it's time to turn my back so the egún don't try to slip under my skin. I am vulnerable and must be protected.

I look down at the dress I chose this morning for the day. It's a floor-length cotton sundress, white with a pink and gold print around the bodice and hem, the closest I'd brought with me to pure white. What did it mean to be a child—a daughter—here among the dead?

I listen as the others take turns reciting the names of their ancestors—not only blood relations, but mythological and spiritual kinships: a lineage of godfathers and godmothers that link them to this religion of ancestral kings and queens. A spiritual pedigree that carries them back to the beginning of time when the oricha first settled at the center of the world, in the city of Ile-Ife. The litany of kinship pours easily from their mouths as they recite each name by heart.

Daniel nudges me when it's my turn. I open my mouth to speak but nothing comes. I search for the names of my own dead among the Spanish and African names taking shape in the room. But they feel as distant as those ancestral trees where I'd once tried to root them, more like a research project than something I might touch with my voice. I close my eyes and try to conjure them—a grandmother named Antonia. Another named Josephine. Their images swim past me not in whole pictures but in fragments: a name inscribed inside a family Bible. A corset. A plumed hat. My mind and jaws grasp after them, but even my parents are difficult to catch.

When I finally speak, I do so slowly, deliberating over each syllable, as if I'm speaking their names for the first time. Not *Mom* and *Dad* but *Mimi Meyers Huntman* and *John William Huntman*.

Josephine Grubel and *Frederick Meyers*, I add my grandparents, relishing the fullness of each name. *Antonia Schreiter* and *Johann Huntman*. A softening as I realize how much my body wants to pay tribute to them. Nothing I can remember in all my life has felt more holy. Something like wings beats the air. A warm breath pillows the room. The uttering of these names is not just a remembrance but a physical act, an invitation for the beloved to raise themselves from those two-dimensional Bibles and family trees and join us—join *me*—in this room.

There is a hierarchy to the religion of Santería, a series of initiations that take one closer to its heart. The receiving of the warriors and the elekes are only the first. As a novice, there are parts of today's initiation that must remain a mystery to me. And so I wait with Miriela in the living room while the men move to a back bedroom to work their secrets. We drink coffee. Make small talk. But mostly we sit in silence, watching the television screen morph from *Despicable Me* into soccer games, the announcer's voice filling the room with animated shouts of *¡Gooooooooooool!*

"This is how it is to be an initiate," Miriela tells me. "To wait and see." From the back room I hear the men singing in a mix of Spanish and Lucumí, the sound of hands slapping the walls and floors of the room to hold their rhythms in place. From the kitchen the squawks of the birds fill me with a growing sense of dread for what is yet to come.

As if reading my thoughts, Miriela tells me, "Better not to think about the sacrifices until you have to."

Most of my mother's dying happened behind the closed doors and curtains of hospital rooms. After her first round of surgery, my best friend Jill and I arrived at the hospital as nurses prepared the nasal gastric tube to clear my mother's stomach of the food she couldn't clear on her own. We were juniors in high school. My mother's cancer was still a thing we believed we would all survive.

We watched from the other side of the curtain as they threaded the tube down her nose to her esophagus and into her stomach. We watched as the tube filled with what looked like green slime but was somehow coming from inside my mother. Jill squeezed my hand. If she hadn't, I might not have believed I was really there. And then I turned away.

Two years later my mother would find herself back at St. Luke's, only this time there would be no tubes; she had stopped eating altogether. It would be the last time I would see her. Still, I couldn't look.

I know that that final night, after I left the room, my father sat at the edge of her bed holding her hand in his. But I wasn't there to see when the nurses tapped his shoulder to let him know it was time to let go, that the cold hand he held would not be warm again, no matter how long he held it. Nor was I there to see them prepare her body to be transported from the hospital to the funeral home. Or present when the undertaker bathed her body before sending her to be cremated. It is only now that I wonder—as he worked his hands from one end of her body to the other, washing each site along the way—if the movements of his hands were merely perfunctory, those of a technician. Or if they were tender, the hands of a priest aware of the holiness of those last rites.

After what might be an hour or two or four, Daniel returns to claim me for the part of the initiation called the *rogación de cabeza*—the cleansing of the head that strengthens the spiritual bond between one's heavenly head and its earthly counterpart—translated literally as "head prayer."

Motioning for me to sit in a chair he's set in the middle of the dining room, Daniel kneels before two bowls he places at my feet. He dips his fingers into the first bowl and begins washing the tops of my feet and knees; when he finishes, he moves to my palms and elbows, the front and back of my throat. The movements of his hands are slow and gentle as he works his way from foot to head. I close my eyes and welcome the pleasure of his touch on my temples and scalp, their circular pressure reminding me of my mother's as she washed my young head in the kitchen sink. That surge of gentleness as she worked her way toward the fontanel, the last site of the infant's skull to close. That most tender spot sometimes referenced as the gateway to the gods.

"This is your *ori*," Daniel tells me when he reaches the top of my head. "Your inner head. The god within your head who rules your thinking process.

"It is our ori that kneels before Olodumare before we are born and chooses our destiny," Daniel continues. "And it is our ori that comes into the world to fulfill it.

"Your ori is the path of your life. The seat of your soul. The part of God who, like the Holy Spirit, lives inside you, literally guiding you through your head."

I think about what I know about the oricha. How they not only have, or follow, paths but are themselves paths—a moving, flowing current to be tapped into or "made" by the devotee's commitment. Was it possible that before I was born I'd knelt before God and chosen the precise circumstances of my life? To be born the youngest daughter to John William Huntman and Mimi Mabelle Meyers? To be nurtured, challenged, and bound to my mother only to lose her just as I was finding my way in the world? To travel all the way to Cuba—to this living room where I sit before Daniel, preparing to cross into a world so far from the one I was raised in—so I might find my way back to her?

Two months before my mother died, I'd stayed with her in Mexico at the Gerson Center, sleeping each night in the twin bed next to hers. But even then, I hadn't taken in what was happening. I didn't register the sadness with which my mother's doctor looked at her. Instead, I went shopping in Tijuana, accepted the doctor's invitation to have dinner with him, sat with his friends pretending I was living a different story than the one that was unspooling right before my eyes.

"I'm writing a book," I'd boasted to my mother's doctor and his friends. I wasn't a writer. I hadn't taken my first poetry class. Had never written a short story, let alone a book. And yet the novel I now spoke of seemed not only conceivable but inevitable. A book so masterfully written it might save both me and the world from the circumstances in which a daughter could lose her mother. This scene with the doctor seemed as likely as any other to make its way into its pages.

How naïve I was to think I knew my story! To think I was the one controlling the shots of my life, as if I were in charge of the narrative that was writing itself without me. In a few months my mother will be dying in the oncology wing of St. Luke's, her shape more bone than flesh, her hair a mad halo of white as she glides between the living and the dying, looking wildly at the air, as if she sees things the rest of us are unable to see. I'll be a sophomore in college, a woman just beginning her own life with so much she still needs from her mother. And my mother, at fifty-nine, will be too young for this dying.

"You are so loving," she will tell me just hours before she dies. And yet even then it will be impossible to imagine into the space where she is no longer there.

"To the next Márquez," her doctor tells me, raising his glass.

"To us," I answer, my voice joining a chorus of clinking glasses. I'm too young to know that what I'll remember most about this night is not the story the doctor and his friends and I are telling but what is happening back at the Gerson Center without me. How my mother sits at the edge of her bed, dressed in the pink embroidered dress I've bought for her in Tijuana, looking out at the empty bed next to hers that is mine. Her fingers—long and slender like my own—cradle her pen as she writes the note she'll leave on my bed for me, her handwriting breaking at times into uncertainty before finding its way again. The loops of her m's curlicue at the top, like birds taking flight. The blue ink bleeds into the page like water.

I won't know about my mother's letter until I stumble home drunk from tequila and kissing. And yet it is the letter, and not the doctor and his friends, that I want all these years later to pin to this page. I need you to see what I was too busy to notice. How my mother places the finishing touches on the note she'll leave—a heart and arrow encircling her message—before positioning it on my pillow so that her words will be the first thing I see when I get back. Twelve words inscribed in a heart: *Be my valentine in August Becki. Because I love you always, Mother.*

It was that word *always* that had gotten me into so much trouble. My belief in it that prevented me from looking at what was really happening. It was all there in front of us. We knew how ill my mother was. And yet, even in the face of her impending death, our family clung to a conviction that she couldn't die, a certitude that seesawed between childishness and arrogance.

Never did it occur to us to drop to our knees and ask whatever gods looked over us for our mother's salvation. We were too educated, too cultured, too polite, for such a thing. The closest we came was the year my mother was diagnosed with cancer and a Japanese friend showed my sister and me how to fold paper into origami cranes. If we made enough of them, she told us, we could string them together, hang them in my mother's hospital room where they could oversee her recovery. If we made a thousand, legend had it, we could surely save her.

We invited friends to join us. And while the hospital surgeons worked to clear the malignancy from my mother's body, we sat at her kitchen table—where years before she'd taught me how to fold paper into dolls—and folded birds.

It was slow work, this folding. For each crane, twenty folds. To reach a thousand, a total of twenty thousand folds. By the time we reached a hundred birds, my mother was almost ready to come home from the hospital. So we stopped our folding, hung what we'd finished above her bed, and hoped for the best.

My eyes are closed and my body is beginning to soften when Daniel finishes circling my temples with the sacramental water that will cleanse my spiritual head. He reaches for the second bowl at our feet, fills his hands with the coconut I shredded hours ago, and revisits each of the sites he's just washed—feet, then knees, palms, elbows, neck, temples. Again, he works his way toward my fontanel, placing a ball of coconut at each site and covering it with cotton before continuing onto the next. From time to time, he pauses to ask the blessing of the spirits. And then he retraces his movements, removing clumps of cotton and coconut he passes for me to hold between my hands. When only the coconut on my skull remains, he ties a white scarf around my head.

"Let the coconut do its work," Daniel tells me, referring to the wait for the bond between my human head and my heavenly head to take hold.

"*Pedir*," he tells me. "Ask for what you want."

I feel my mind grow white and cold as it struggles to find purchase within such vast possibility, either because I don't know what I want or because what I want feels like too much. I want my mother. I want to know Ochún. I want someone to open the secret door and let me into the mysteries of life and death. I want all these things but I don't want them to be frightening. And how could they be anything else?

In the end, we didn't succeed in moving the obstacle that began with the obstruction of my mother's colon. Not with the trips to the Gerson Center in Mexico nor with the pounds of calf livers and wheatgrass my father pressed into juices. Nor with the hundred origami cranes my sister and friends and I folded and hung over my mother's bed.

In the end none of it mattered.

I blamed everyone and everything—the chemotherapy that had compromised my mother's immune system and the hospital that had fed her Jell-O and fried chicken after all she'd sacrificed to make herself well. The American Medical Association's emphasis on excision rather than prevention and wholeness. The economic system that privileged profits over health.

No one was immune to my anger. I blamed my father for taking my mother for granted for so many years, for cheating on her with so many women. I blamed myself—for fighting her when I was a teenager; for not visiting enough at the end; for not folding more cranes.

Silently, burning beneath those other furies, I blamed my mother. After promising to be there, she'd given up. Allowed the system to beat her. Proven not to be invincible, but utterly, disappointingly, human.

Daniel tells me to fill the now-empty bowl with the coconut I've been praying over, then covers it with a cloth napkin and places it on the floor.

"We'll light a candle to Eleggua here," he says, handing me a white taper like the ones I've seen people light before church altars. He holds his cigarette lighter to its base until wax drips hot onto the floor, forming a foundation in which he roots the candle.

As the wax pools and congeals, I hear my mother's voice in my head. Not so much a voice as a gasp. She and my father prided themselves on an immaculate life: yard and nails manicured, clothes pressed, floors polished—each of these things a testament to the power of gleaming surfaces to keep disorder and vulnerability at bay. This sacrilegious dripping of wax onto the floor feels as far removed from my upbringing as anything else that might happen today.

The day my mother first told me about the tumor her gynecologist had found in her colon, she'd excused me from school to take me to lunch, a thing she did from time to time so we could share an hour in the middle of an afternoon. We'd sat across from each other surrounded by the civility of white cloth napkins, the polite pairing of salad and dinner fork nestled side by side.

Two years earlier such an outing would have felt impossible. I had raged against my mother. But we had found a way through that anger. And though we still sometimes clashed—around attire and appearance, curfews and rules—we had begun leaning back toward one another.

On this day I was bursting with conversation that seemed to matter—news about school friends and boyfriends, plans for the weekend, plans for college—when my mother interrupted me.

"I have cancer," she'd whispered, and the sound of those three words was like cloth ripping in two.

Daniel leads me to the back room where the men have been working. The air wafts across its threshold thick with the scent of herbs and prayer. Inside, the fundamentos of the oricha are lined along the floor in shallow clay bowls: Eleggua's cement head and Ogún's cauldron; the metal rooster of Osun; the five stones of Ochún someone has placed inside a soup tureen.

Squatting before them, Aristedes casts sections of quartered coconut onto the floor to ask the gods if we have their permission to continue.

"*Alafia,*" Aristedes calls out when all four segments land belly up, a sign that the spirits have said yes but asked for a second throw for confirmation.

"*Ejife,*" when they fall two segments up, two down: a definite yes.

I stand between the men as we again offer coconut and prayers to the dead. Yolersi and Aristedes lead the way, and Daniel signals when it is my turn to recite the names of my own. I speak more boldly this time, savoring the feel of my parents' names as they river off my tongue: *Mimi Meyers Huntman. John William Huntman.* Again, I feel their presence fill the room, not just the idea of them but an actual weight in the air.

From the hallway I hear the scrabble of birds scratching against cloth as someone pulls the first of them from its sack. I try not to make a face when the men carry it toward me. I am to give thanks to the bird for giving its life to nourish my own, Daniel tells me as they form a circle around me, touching the live bird to my head and then my shoulders.

"Don't look," Daniel had told me when I first asked about the sacrifices. Now he grabs the camera I've left on a table and begins documenting each moment. I hear the shutter click as Daniel captures the birds' wings beating in the air above me. Another click as my hands open to receive their blessings.

The flutter of wings is a tactile reminder of the life that still throbs inside the animal and the thin scrim that separates this moment from what's to come. I feel my father standing beside me, telling me this is how it was for him as an undertaker and ambulance driver. He reminds me how many times he had stood at the door between life and death—pulling bodies, still pulsing with their last breath, from crashed cars; washing and preparing those bodies for their caskets; and again, as he sat at the edge of my mother's hospital bed, holding her hand long after she'd passed.

Now I can't help wonder what might have happened if my sister and I had approached the task of folding those birds with more urgency. Sacrificed whatever breaks we took for food and sleep and school and kept folding until we reached a thousand. Completed the job as if someone's life depended on it.

I didn't cry in front of my mother. Not the day she told me she had cancer or any other. We went on, talking over dress designs she'd sew me for high school proms and dance competitions and freshman formals. Preparing for AP tests and SAT Exams. Pretending that, each time I left her—for dates, for dance classes, for school and then college—we could trust that she'd be there when I returned. It wasn't just me. My father busied himself growing wheatgrass in the windowsill and cracking apricots to extract laetrile at the kitchen table. Never did he name the illness his efforts were meant to cure. Nor did my siblings and I ever speak out loud our fears about what might become of our mother if those efforts didn't succeed.

We were practiced in this kind of dance. We'd absorbed my father's exhortations to never, under any circumstances, get hysterical. We knew to stay silent about our grandmother Antonia's suicide. Silent about my father's affairs. Now the family again tiptoed around the thing we dared not name, pretending that the holistic treatments my mother was depending on were foolproof. Ignoring that they'd been designed to work with patients whose immune systems had not been compromised, as hers had, by the harsh chemotherapy the hospitals were using in the early '80s.

It's only now that I wonder how much that pretending cost us. By willing my mother to live forever, we denied her the complexity of her last months—that she was both a living and a dying creature, caught in the ancestral web that moves inexorably between birth and life and death.

How might I have reacted if I hadn't been a child—seventeen, eighteen, nineteen years old and scared of death—but rather someone whose courage to face what was happening might have offered some comfort. Someone who might have dared pierce the shroud of politeness we'd hung over my mother's dying, pushed fearlessly toward those places in both of us that felt fragile, vulnerable, undeniably human, and reached for my mother's hand. Confronted head-on the terror of death—that mysterious void from which we come and to which we return—and asked her, asked both of us: *Are you scared?*

When Aristedes reaches for his knife, my reflex is to again avert my eyes. But I fight to keep looking. This ceremony is on my behalf; I have a responsibility for what is happening. And so I watch. I watch as Aristedes holds the chicken upside down by its feet, and I watch as he winds its neck around his fingers. Three twists and a snap. I watch as blood pours red down the blade of the knife. Again, as Aristedes' index finger directs its flow onto the fundamentos of the warriors—the cement head of Eleggua first, then Ogún and Ochosi's cauldron and the metal rooster of Osun—and the aché within this sacrificial blood gives life to these bits of stone and metal we plucked just hours before from the markets.

Yolersi presses my hands into the pulsing sides of the bird. He wants me not just to look but to touch. Inhabit this moment when the bird beneath my hands hovers between life and death. Witness the precise moment its aché seeps from its body to infuse the objects before us. There is no way to distance myself. The bird in my hand does not come packaged in plastic and Styrofoam from the grocery store. I've heard its song, felt its legs scuffing the air above my head.

Yolersi places my right hand under a wing. With his free hand, he demonstrates how to pull its feathers and scatter them into the clay bowls that hold the fundamentos of the oricha, then instructs me to continue without him.

"I don't want to," I tell him. But Yolersi doesn't back down. I pull half-heartedly, both revolted by the task and disappointed at my inability to rise to it. The feathers stay fastened at their root, refusing to budge under my half efforts.

Who was my squeamishness serving? I wonder. This pretending that I hadn't asked to be here, hadn't wanted to cross this threshold so I might earn the eleke of Ochún. Who was I to think I could cross without paying the price of pressing my hands to this still-warm body?

"*Fuerte*," Yolersi tells me as he places my fingers between his, moving our hands in unison as we yank a handful of feathers in one burst, then tells me to try again on my own.

I remember what the sculptor Generoso told me about his Ochún. She was sweet and nurturing. A mother. But she was also a warrior. A shapeshifter who could change herself into a vulture when she needed to. A badass mother who rode naked on a white horse and brandished a machete.

I pull again at the feathers, both sickened and in awe of the reality of the bird in my hands. Struck that the action of participating feels somehow more compassionate than turning away.

I manage to rip out a few feathers before Yolersi takes mercy on me and takes over. I watch as he tears out handful after handful, letting them settle over the warriors' bowls. When he finishes, he shows me how to collect the bits that have scattered into the blood on the floor, moving my bare hands in circles across the floor as together we mop up feathers and blood.

"Pedir," he tells me. "Pray for the things you want in your life."

Two birds are sacrificed for the warriors, another two for Ochún. Each time, the knife, the blood. Each time, my hands move in circles across the floor as I mop up feathers and blood. And each time, I ask the gods to show me the way.

When we sacrifice Ochún's birds, Yolersi hands me her brass bell and tells me to ring it as I pray. Its sound clangs clear and deep, and its vibrations reach like fingers inside me. I pray for Rick and for Alex. I pray for my writing and my health. But mostly I pray that Ochún show herself to me. That she remake me in her image, both *dulce y fuerte*. Both sweet and strong.

When Yolersi tells me I can stop ringing, the silence feels more suffused than any sound. Daniel unwraps my headscarf so he can remove the remaining coconut and adds it to the bowl we left before the candle, which is still burning on the dining-room floor. How many hours had passed since we first lit that flame?

"We're almost finished," Daniel announces.

I am almost reborn.

For my final purification Yolersi hands me a pair of buckets, one filled with clear water, the other with an infusion of herbs and water made sacred by the chants and prayers the men have spoken over them.

I carry them into the bathroom and close the door. Before me stands the shower, its feeble stream a stand-in for Ochún's river. When I step back into the house, I will be reborn. But born into what?

I lift the bucket made holy with herbs and prayer over my head and let it wash over me. As the sacred *omiero* swirls into the drain at my feet, I replay those images from moments before when I'd kneeled to mop up blood. At some point the grotesqueness of the scene had given way to some sort of beauty, as if those scarlet droplets were not bits of blood but Easter egg dye dropped into vinegar, or wine into holy water.

I wash my body—working my fingers across my scalp, as Daniel and before him my mother had. Wasn't it she who had first taught me to revel in the sensation of my own skin. To feel my way over my own borders, those places where flesh met water, met soap, met air.

Hadn't it been through her body that I'd first learned about the wonders of my own? I remember how cocooned I'd felt each time I crawled into her arms and lap as a child. Enveloped in the sensation of blood beating under skin and bone, both hers and mine. Aware each time I studied her—as she dressed to go dancing with my father, as she worked at her stove or sewing machine, as she sang in the choir—of the creativity that resides inside each of us: the ability to spin thread and needle into cloth. Arms and legs into motion. Voice into song and prayer.

Wasn't this what the spirits hungered for when they came to receive the breath and blood of our offerings? This body the thing they missed most. The thing we couldn't hold onto no matter how much we caressed it. The thing I would lose no matter how many times I circled it with fingertip and cloth.

When I step out of the shower, I will slip my white dress back over my head and make my way to the dining room. There, I'll find Yolersi waiting to share the wisdom he's received from Eleggua and Ochún. He will tell me how to care for the five stones that hold Ochún's spirit, that I am to find a golden soup tureen where I'll keep her stones covered in water. And he'll tell me I am to visit El Cobre. "Find a piece of copper while you're there and place it alongside Ochún's sacred stones," he says, putting a final point on Jorge Luís and Zunilda's advice.

When we finish, Miriela and Jorge Luís will serve up plates of pork and rice with avocado and plantain. Jorge Luís will be proud of his cooking. "A true chef!" he'll announce. The ceremony is over. It's time to eat and laugh. Daniel will scoop from the bowl the coconut that hours before crowned my head, wrap it in white butcher paper, and hand it to me.

"On your way home, find a church and leave it there," he will tell me. "Any church will do." But I know I will take it to the sanctuary that houses Our Lady's replica and slip it between offerings of sunflowers. I will kneel before her image and thank both her and, through her, Ochún—for guiding me today. For protecting me. For illuminating my path.

As I leave the church, the skies will open, sending torrents of rain into the streets, covering everything with the sheen of new life. Street vendors will pass, their carts loaded with chocolates and fruit, and the scent of papaya and banana will mix into an air already ripe with salt and mist. Veins of rubble will course with rainwater. Saturating everything will be the smell of blood I carry, despite my shower, on my fingers and clothes.

At Miriam's, I'll load the photos Daniel took onto my laptop and replay the day through the lens of his eye—my palms lifting to receive the blessing of a white dove Yolersi holds over them. Those same hands washing the floor in circles of feathers and blood, then ringing Ochún's brass bell as I pray for the river goddess to make herself known to me. To teach me to be both sweet and strong.

When I hear Miriam's footsteps, I will close my laptop. These images feel too fresh, too intimate, to share. It's not just the smell of blood that's followed me home. I will feel transformed. And while I don't know if I would use Daniel's word "reborn" to describe my metamorphosis, it will seem impossible that my day is not written on my face.

Tomorrow I will kneel before Miriela and Jorge Luís, Daniel and Jordan as they crown me with my beads. The red and black strand of Eleggua will come first, then the yellow and gold of Ochún. The strand of peony seeds last. I will follow Daniel's instructions as he walks me through this last piece of my initiation, throwing each necklace onto the floor three times, picking it up and kissing it after each throw. And then, with the beads held between their pinky fingers, my new godfamily will place each strand over my head, yoking my story with theirs.

The day after, I will fly to the eastern side of the island to follow the lines of another story—a miraculous virgin who'd appeared before three miners lost at sea, and again before the young Apolonia who climbed, grief stricken, up a hill in search of her own lost mother.

For now, as I stand under Miriela's shower, all I know is the feel of my hands moving over skin. Each movement asserts that I am here. Here in this shower, where the stream of water flowing over me is a stand-in for Ochún's river, the herbs and prayers spoken over these buckets a baptism into a religion that is not separate but braided into life. A religion that hums and sings through blood and bead and metal and stone. You could call it forth by dripping hot wax onto the floor. You could hold its pulse in your hands and feel it beating in time with your own.

What would my mother have thought about my traveling to Cuba to reconnect with her through rituals so far removed from the life we knew together? My answer depends on which part of the stream I step into. My mother was many things. Like all mothers, more complicated than their children like to think or give them credit for. There was the mother who named herself *Me-Me*, the one whose voice rang out, filling church and neighborhood with the sound of herself. The mother who delighted in the artifacts of womanhood, who filled her dresser with stockings and perfume, and dressed herself in Moroccan caftans and evening dresses to go dancing with my father. There was the mother who relished the motion of her arms and legs as she swam at the farm. The earthy, magic, dare I say witchy mother who reached toward the power of plants and herbs to heal herself, and who taught me to protect my own body. *And* there was the mother who lived and died according to the rules she was given—that to be a woman was to be gracious and polite, to keep a tidy house and raise even tidier children. There was the mother who kept a box she might use one day to divorce my father and set out to define her own life. And there was the mother who stayed. This is the mother I find myself not only wanting to recover but to set free, give her a do-over, let her live again, this time in the mythic realm. Allow herself to be wild and messy, larger than life. Perhaps it is this, more than anything, that drew me to Cuba. To find a larger story that might hold us both.

PORT OF ANGELS REVISITED

AFTERWARD, THE STORY THAT would be told was not the one about the mother who held her daughter in the waves, but about the various men who swam out to save them. How, after my father realized what was happening—that his wife and child had been pulled out to sea, and that he was the only one on the beach who might save us—he threw his camera onto the sand and jumped in after us.

He couldn't make it, and two local men would vie to become the heroes of the story, claiming to have pulled my mother and me from the waters. A crowd had gathered by then, and the two men stood on the beach, puffing their chests and telling their tale. Meanwhile, the man we believe did save us—a coral diver who swam against the tide to the rescue—slipped quietly away.

Whoever it was, they had to save my father too. By the time they brought him to shore, he'd been knocked unconscious. He was sixty-two years old then, a slighter, gray-haired version of the army captain who'd swept my mother off her feet. It wasn't clear if he'd live. And so, it was the father of the story, not the mother and child, who had to be carried up the hill to the hotel where we were staying, my mother and me following on foot. And it was for the father that I was sent back down the hill to fetch some bottled water.

The part I haven't told until now is the part where one of the men who claimed to be but in fact was not our savior followed after me. I was ten years old, skinny and flat-chested, all arms and legs in a one-piece swimsuit that was starred and striped like an American flag. He was curly haired and dressed in bell-bottoms. Since the hotel had no bottled water for the father who might be dying, we walked down the hill to the town where I hoped to find some. And while I worried about whether or not I would find water and whether or not I would make it back up the hill to deliver it in time, the curly-haired, bell-bottomed man tried out a handful of English phrases he knew.

"Kiss, kiss! Love, love!" he told me. At one point he reached for the place on my body that in a few years would grow into breasts. At one point he tried to steer me off the path.

Somehow, I kept us moving toward the store that sold bottled water and back up the hill where we delivered it to my father. Somehow, my father survived. The town doctor was called to monitor his improvement. The water I brought helped. The next day we celebrated with the family of the man we believe saved us. We drank wine and ate lobsters pulled fresh from the sea while we told and retold the miracle of how we'd been saved by one man and how another man had come so close to death.

When the town newspaper published the story, they told of the local hero who saved the three Americans pulled out to sea. When my father spoke of it, he too dwelled on the man. And when my mother told the story, she focused on the part where my father jumped in after us, and how close his bravery brought him to death. For years, I too would focus on the men in the story.

It's only now that I'm telling the story the way I experienced it. Not as a story about men but of women. It's hard for me to say for sure who came for us. The men, while certainly heroes, are a blur of sea and arms. I never saw their faces. It is my mother that is most central to the story I lived that day. It was she who held me as those waves tried to drag us under. She who reminded me each time we came up for air to call for help. She who held on to some faith that help would come, and that until it did, she would not let go.

PART II
THE SAINT

*A thing is mighty big when time
and distance cannot shrink it.*

ZORA NEALE HURSTON

APOLONIA

In 1612, a girl we will come to know simply as Apolonia climbs a hill. She is searching for her mother, a woman whose own name will become lost in the telling and retelling of this story. What we know is that the mother is one of the enslaved women who work the copper mines that give El Cobre its name. The rest we can imagine because we know what it means to be a mother. That it is she who has taught Apolonia how to find her way through the hazards of a town known for scorching sun and copper mining, slavery and contraband. How to sew and plant. Where to find the herbs that heal and how to tell them from the ones that poison. The *monte* held as many gifts as it did dangers—benevolent gods who ruled its rivers and forests. Ancestors who appeared before their beloved as praying mantises and birds. But there were malevolent spirits too: monsters too terrible to behold, with heads like spiders and feet growing from their ears.

Now the mother is dead, leaving Apolonia to find her way alone. It's impossible to grasp such a loss. She sees her mother everywhere. There, in the swath of dirt that cuts through the Sierra Maestra, carrying the line of miners with pickaxes and cloth sacks in and out of the ground.

And there, where the women gather by the river, sifting for ore that washes from the veins of the mines. Maybe one of the women lifts her head, smiles, and as she does there is the mother again. But when the girl looks again, she finds only an egret pulling its head from the stream, its white feathers mirrored in blue-green water. The two watch each other, bird and girl, for what might be seconds or hours before the egret shakes its bill and picks its way downstream.

It's then that Apolonia sees a burst of lights showering the hill above the mines. Later, the whole town will say they saw the lights too. But Apolonia is the one who chases after them. She knows the path from memory, has walked it a thousand times at the side of her mother, the two of them scanning its curves for flashes of copper they trade for soap and sugar in Santiago's markets and, when there is enough, a bit of ribbon for her hair or silver lace for Apolonia's Sunday-best skirts.

The girl half expects to find the mother waiting at the top of the hill, calling after her to stop moving like such a chameleon, that legendary slowpoke who took so long to deliver the news of eternal life to the world that the lizard sent to spread the word of death beat him to it.

"Hurry up!" she hears her mother call. But when Apolonia reaches the summit, she finds only bare rock. Her knees give way. She falls to the ground. Beats her fists against red earth. Cries out for her mamá.

When she stands, she finds the space left by her mother's absence no longer empty. In its place there is a presence she feels more than sees. Years from now, artists and storytellers tasked with articulating Apolonia's vision will render a living, breathing version of the icon found by the three miners in the Bay of Nipe—a larger, more corporeal Madonna dressed in blue and gold they'll embellish with angels and puffy clouds.

But I imagine Apolonia's vision is not so literal. There is no clearly delineated figure. Only the shaking of the ground beneath Apolonia's feet. The sense of being gathered in the arms of that sound. A warmth she feels as if it were radiating from her own solar plexus. A resplendence that bathes the valley in an amphitheater of light. And yet Apolonia too will swear someone was there. How else to explain the sound of a voice calling out her name?

11

PIRATES & THE MOTHER SAINT

Four hundred miles southeast of Havana lies the Cuban region known as *el oriente*. It's a short plane ride down the slender belly of the island and when you arrive, you're closer to Haiti than Miami. It feels distinct from Havana. The lowlands of the west are replaced by the mountains of the Sierra Maestra, their jagged peaks furred with trees.

This is frontier country. It is on these eastern shores that the Spanish first dropped their anchors. The city of Santiago where they built Cuba's first capital. The nearby town of El Cobre where they founded the copper mines that would supply ammunitions for their cannons and where they would meet the resistance of the men and women they enslaved in their mines. And it was here in the east—among *piratas* and *conquistadores*, rebels and slaves—that Our Lady of Charity chose to announce herself, appearing in the Bay of Nipe before the men known as the three Juanes and again before the young girl named Apolonia.

I catch my first glimpse of the east through the open windows of the Lada sent to drive me from Santiago's airport to the bed-and-breakfast where I'll stay. Soviet motorcycles tear through narrow streets, beeping their horns. Buildings ravaged by Hurricane Sandy, their roofs and windows torn from their bones, await the materials necessary to remake them. Even the street dogs look rougher and hungrier than those I'd seen in Havana. And then there's the famed heat. The Sierra Maestra hold the city of Santiago like the arms of a forge. The sun pins my dress to my chest and legs, to the upholstery of the car. My driver for this leg of my journey is Tomás, and every few minutes his cell phone rings as the owner of the bed-and-breakfast—an Ochún priestess with whom I've been corresponding—asks for an update on our arrival.

I'd been all but discouraged from coming to the eastern side of the island, warned that Ochún—who arrived in the songs and prayers of the Yoruba enslaved in the western part of the island—was almost nowhere to be found among Santiago's descendants of Bantu and other tribes. Here it was all about Our Lady of Charity. Her El Cobre sanctuary lies just twelve miles to the west of Santiago. Her feast days are now less than two weeks away.

I hear Zunilda and Generoso, Daniel and Miriela tell me, "Ochún is Our Lady, and Our Lady is Ochún," and wonder if here Our Lady is simply Our Lady. But if anyone could help me connect the dots between the two figures, it would be the anthropologist-priestess Maruchi who agreed in our email exchanges to serve as my guide to both Ochún and Our Lady.

The reviews I'd read about Maruchi's bed-and-breakfast had been mixed. Its convenient location, within walking distance of Parque Céspedes and Casa de la Trova, were noted by all. From there the reviews diverged into two camps, depending on the guest's attitude toward staying in a house of Santería. There were those who called the bed-and-breakfast a Garden of Eden, an oasis filled with parrots and hanging gardens and "dolls and statues" that made them feel like they were living in a religious museum. Others found the museum less quaint, reporting trouble sleeping while sacrificial goats cried outside their door.

The reports about the woman who owned the bed-and-breakfast were equally divided. Some found Maruchi helpful and warm. Others found her unfriendly and aloof. Even though we hadn't met yet, I'd formed my own opinions about the Ochún priestess. I imagined both her voice and figure as ebullient as the goddess she adored, my expectations bolstered by the emails she's sent, written in all caps and signed with strings of x's and o's.

Where I'd expected warmth and curves, the Maruchi who opens the door is cool angles and lines. Her red hair is cropped short, her dress boxy and matter-of-fact. Absent are the flourishes of kisses and *maravillas* that had filled her emails. The hug she offers now is perfunctory, followed by a kiss on each cheek.

But if Ochún isn't evident in Maruchi's demeanor, she is clearly in residence here. A lush altar to her—stacked with pumpkins and sunflowers and brass bells—presides over the parlor. She flutters in the white curtains of the patio, with its white lacquered chairs and greenery. Orange-and-black fish dart in an aquarium, and at the center of the patio a four-foot fountain carved in the shape of a mother goddess burbles, the deity's voluminous lap opening onto a small pond filled with turtles.

Maruchi ushers me through each room, acquainting me with the people and animals who populate them. Her introductions are quick and to the point. Unlike Miriam with her soft eyes and voice, Maruchi is all about business. And unlike Miriam's, where she and her elderly mother and I were its only occupants, Maruchi's house hums with activity. In the TV room, her daughter Narjhara nurses her infant while Lucas, the family basset hound, watches from the sofa. Maruchi's staff bustle in the open-air kitchen: Ernesto, the Rasta handyman reworking grout between bricks while Tatica and Mabel stir pots at the stove. A parrot named Kuky squawks from a cage above them. A gray tabby named Changó prowls for crumbs on the tiled floor.

Maruchi shows me up a set of steps to my guestroom, which sits on the roof amid wind chimes and orchids and potted ferns. Outside, there's an iron table and chair where I'll eat breakfast each morning. Inside is a single room with an adjoining bath tiled in rose. The bed is covered in crocheted lace—another assurance, I think, that Ochún resides in this house. After Maruchi leaves, I turn on the air conditioner and crawl under the coverlet. The cool air rushes through its open weave, a reprieve from the heat.

I close my eyes and focus on the feel of lace and air against my skin, the respite of muscle and bone against the mattress that supports them.

I think of how quickly and fully I'd made my room at Miriam's a home. I'd lined my personal belongings along the windowsill, laid my maps and books on the bed next to mine, traced my plans for each day across their pages. Now I was starting out in a new house with a new bed to break in and a fresh itinerary that shimmered with its own promises.

Over the next two weeks, Maruchi will invite me to join her on the patio for a series of *pláticas* about Ochún and Our Lady she'll refer to as our work. She has also arranged for me to meet with a number of people who she believes will be helpful as I prepare for Our Lady's pilgrimage. There are the historians: Julio Corbea, who is the official keeper of El Cobre's town history, and Olga Portuondo, who has written what many consider to be the definitive text on Our Lady of Charity. There is the El Cobre Spiritist named Madelaine who is known for his ability to channel the dead. And there is Maruchi's neighbor Roberto, a television producer who will double as my guide and videographer during Our Lady's feast days.

As I lie on the bed that first afternoon, I take in that there are just thirteen days—less than two weeks—separating me from those celebrations, Our Lady's sanctuary just twelve miles away. In Havana I'd seen how the eyes of her devotees lit up when they prayed before Our Lady of Charity's replica, the altar beneath her heaped with candles and sunflowers. Now that I'm this close to Our Lady's El Cobre sanctuary, I wonder: If a surrogate could instill such reverence, what would I feel in the presence of the actual icon?

I trace Our Lady's shape in the air before me: the barest suggestion of a triangle that gains weight and substance as I trace her again and again. There she is appearing before the three Juanes, their faces ecstatic, hands lifted in prayer. And there before Apolonia, illuminating the hill of the mines. And there again—only twelve miles from where I am—she stands at her altar, her hands lifted to receive those who come to kneel before her.

Twelve miles.

Thirteen days.

I stretch my fingers in the direction of Our Lady's sanctuary and imagine a line connecting my fingertips to hers.

Thirteen days.

What would I feel when I got to El Cobre? Would I feel what those three Juanes felt in that moment they saw Our Lady floating on the sea, her robes dry amidst those stormy waters alerting them that they were witnessing an honest-to-God miracle? Something both of and out of this world?

Would I let myself fall, as Apolonia had, to my knees? Cry out before the mother? Admit that I was here not just for Our Lady but for my own mother, Mimi Meyers Huntman? That I hoped to find her among those glittering bits of copper; feel her presence among the hush of Our Lady's sanctuary; glimpse her shape among those pilgrims who flock to her feast days. Hear her voice among theirs.

Or would I approach quietly, hug the walls as I had in Regla, and pretend I was here simply to document a faith I was still too timid to claim as my own?

THE TOWN

JUAN MORENO IS TEN years old when he sets out with the Joyos brothers to find salt for the mines. His name has not yet been abbreviated from Juan Moreno to Juan. He is not yet a symbol of the nation. He's simply a boy lost in a storm. When those waters turn choppy, sending great beasts of waves that beat against the side of their small boat, he turns his eyes to the heavens, presses his hands together the way the priests of the mines have taught him. It's this gesture that will be caught forever in the engravings that commemorate what happens next: a boy's hands lifted in prayer.

I like to think that what he remembers best is not the storm but the silence that follows. It's in that silence that they spot what might be a bird bobbing on the sea. No, not a bird. A statue. Just under a foot-and-a-half tall, her torso fashioned from strips of wood, she floats on a wooden tablet. Her blue and gold robes are untouched by the waters. The baby Jesus is cradled safely in her arms. The words etched into the tablet at her feet announce that she is their Lady of Charity. Over the next days and weeks, the boy will help carry her first to Barajagua and then to El Cobre where she will lay claim to a hill over the mines, showering it with lights that draw in the girl named Apolonia.

Each of the townspeople of El Cobre would later claim that they had seen the lights. Every greeting and conversation revolved around the sighting and what that person had been doing in the precise moment when the lights flashed over Miners' Hill.

The parish priest had been polishing the effigy of Santiago the Apostle when he saw the burst of illumination outside the church window. He'd thought it must be some act of *hechicería*. The town was filled with *curanderos* who professed their love for the saints before him, then went home to kneel before their own gods.

María Enbote was in that very moment marking her threshold with palm oil so the ancestors might feel more welcome in her home.

Lucía, *mujer* de Alejandro, was at the river searching for copper trailings while her husband was working in the mines. The men underground didn't see the lights so much as they felt them shaking the earth.

Chino was stepping out of his thatched hut to check on the storage house and Manuel Catungue, who called himself King of Angola, had stopped to talk with the blacksmith.

Elena, the carpenter's wife, was hoeing manioc in the *conuco* behind the house, and the soldier Francisco was cutting firewood with his machete.

The hermit Mathías de Olivera was filling the oil lamp he kept lit before Our Lady of Guidance, who he called Mother of God.

Two creole children were playing hide and seek under the shade of a royal palm. Bartolomé the smelter passed them on his way to the Big House where he was to meet with the captain, Don Francisco Sánchez de Moya, about the Spanish artillery's latest copper contracts.

The captain was waiting for him at his desk, passing the time in self-congratulation over his acquisition of the newly-discovered Madonna figure he'd ordered to be brought from Barajagua.

And the Joyos brothers were in the middle of recounting for the thousandth time the story of how they'd been with Moreno the day they found her floating in the Bay of Nipe. She'd refused to stay put in the hermitage they built for her in Barajagua, disappearing from her altar each night only to appear the next day as if she'd never been missing at all.

Some said the lights were colored like rainbows.
Others said they were white as fire.
They showered the mountains
Like comets.
Like fish jumping from the river.
Like sunflowers turning their faces
To follow the sun.

They were the act of gods or witches
Having something to do or not to do
With the mother who refused to stay put,
Appearing and disappearing from altar and sea.

The only thing they could agree upon was that they had all seen the lights. They had seen Apolonia too as she came running down the hill, had heard her shouts sweeping them up in the conviction of her pronouncements. The mother was alive. She had come to tell them she wanted her sanctuary built on the hill overlooking their mines so that she might bless them and bless their children and their children's children for generations to come.

12

BLOOD

When Portuguese explorers encountered Yoruba cities and kingdoms in the fifteenth century, they called the religious objects they came across fetishes—from the Portuguese word *feitico*, something "formed" or "made up." They called the people who believed in the magic of those holy objects heathens, their worship of them barbarous. They deemed the Yoruban people superstitious because they refused to peddle the sacred as commodity, profane because their symbols did not look like their own.

In the Americas, European colonizers sought to supplant what they thought of as worthless primitive objects with authentically valuable ones, planting crosses in place of ceiba trees, doling out rosaries and pictures of Catholic saints to replace totems of African and Indigenous gods.

Some of the greatest violence came in the language that accompanied these actions. The worship of non-Christian images was branded as idolatrous and their devotees labeled as witches. Even more violent than the words were the ideas they contained. The notion that one set of practices was real and the other made up.

Maruchi invites me to spend my first day in Santiago observing a Santería initiation that will take place on her patio. A high priest in the religion of Ifá, a babalawo who has yet to receive the primary oricha, will receive them all in one day—the warriors Eleggua and Ogún, Ochosi, and Osun; the sky god Obatalá and the thunder god Changó; the mothers Yemayá and Oyá and Ochún. There will be sacrifices to each of them, and their fundamental stones and tools will be baptized in prayers and blood.

I spend the morning unpacking my own fundamentos: the warriors and sacred stones I received from Daniel in Havana along with their tools and crowns. I'd picked them up at the pink house just two days before and wrapped them in paper for the trip to Santiago. Now I relish the satisfaction of rediscovering each item. These talismans had been made sacred with the pulse of breath and song: prayers spoken over the fall of coconuts and the ringing of bells. My parents' names evoked alongside Jorge Luís's and Daniel's, Yolersi's and Aristides's. The blood of the birds I'd held between my hands. Hadn't I yearned for an object—a gravestone, an urn, an image or story—that might serve as a crossroads, a nexus through which I might connect with my mother?

When I'd first received these objects, they'd shimmered with the promise of all that aché. But they'd come also with reminders of the sacrifices that had given them life. Bits of blood still stuck to the edges of Eleggua's stone head, and a few feathers remained at the feet of Ogún's cauldron. Daniel had provided lengthy instructions about the care they'd continue to require—which offerings each of the oricha liked best: cigars and candies and rum for Eleggua; honey and flowers for Ochún. On which days to light each of their candles. Which to clean with palm oil and which with coconut water. They weren't just magical, consecrated totems; they were objects for which I'd accepted the responsibility of care.

Now, as I make a provisional home for them at Maruchi's, I worry I might not be up to the task. I have a history of jumping from interest to interest, leaving artifacts in my wake—abandoned embroidery projects and sports equipment; half-read spiritual recovery manuals. Even those paper cranes we'd folded for my mother eventually went the way of all discarded projects. Would these articles that felt so precious and fresh in my hands fare any better?

I follow Daniel's instructions, freeing warriors from paper wrappers and placing them where they can watch over me: Eleggua by the door; Ogún's cauldron inside a wood cabinet at the foot of my bed. The metal rooster that represents Osun goes on a top shelf near the door. I create a makeshift sopera for Ochún from two bowls, arranging her stones in a circle inside the first, then crowning them with the cowrie shells through which the river goddess speaks, and laying the oars she needs to row from the spirit world on top.

My upbringing in the Congregational Church had led me to think of religion as something without much need for adornment. This was true even of its stories. The narrative it espoused was a simple one, with one father and, when we remembered to speak of her, one mother. But I couldn't help wonder about the way these intermediary saints I was coming to know, with their rituals and beads, seemed to open doors to mysteries that abstractions such as Father and Mother couldn't fully capture.

I think of the world Apolonia walked—a world in which every stone and tree vibrated with the breath of the gods. Every object holy, not because it pointed to a semblance of a deity outside itself, but because it was itself made of holy things. Each stone beneath Apolonia's feet was a receptacle of power, an actualization of a force it held inside its own skin. Each animal she passed an incarnation of an ancestor or a god.

Daniel and Miriela had shown me there were those who still held this understanding. The provisional sopera before me was not merely a pair of bowls but a universe. The river stones they held were made from the stuff of the gods. These shelves-turned-altar the meeting place between the living and the spirits. The beads a way to yoke my story to theirs.

As I pour fresh water over Ochún's river stones—parched and porous after their travels wrapped in cloth—I can almost feel the gratitude with which they receive the liquid that gives them life. I place the second bowl, upside down, over the first and cover it with Ochún's gold handkerchief, adding her five-pointed crown on top. I ring her brass bell and listen as the room fills with sound.

The rest of the morning passes in minutes and hours as we wait for the initiations to begin. Lucumí priests and priestesses arrive one by one, falling into chairs around the patio. The babalawo who will receive the oricha is dressed from head to toe in white; the obá who will lead the initiations wears a pink T-shirt and jeans. Maruchi's godmother Maritza—an Ochún priestess trained in reading her oracle—sits with them in a purple headscarf and yellow beads, smoking and telling jokes. Seated nearby, a young apprentice named Angel tears leafy herbs into bowls.

Maruchi's cooks dart back and forth between the kitchen and the patio. Tatica and Mabel bring out coffee, and Leonides prepares the outdoor stove. I sit at a table in the shade near the priests with my journal and books. A pair of Italian tourists check in to a guestroom off the patio, and I listen as Maruchi answers their questions about things to see and do in the neighborhood and wonder what they will make of the day's activities.

From time to time, Tatica checks in on me. Since I arrived at Maruchi's, both she and Mabel have adopted me, taking frequent breaks from their work to ask about my life in Ohio and tell me about their own. Mabel is petite, a bright-eyed Ochún devotee who is saving money to pay for the asiento ceremony that will crown her as Ochún's spiritual daughter. Tatica is older—a wide-lapped grandmother; an espiritista who draws on various spiritual traditions and who seems to delight in sharing her wisdom with me.

Today she wants to make sure I understand what we are about to see. The sacrifices will be on behalf of the man who we refer to simply as "the man dressed in white." Maruchi's son and son-in-law, both of whom are trained in the butchery rites of the babalawo, will be in charge of the *matanzas*. And since the man in white is receiving all the saints at once, the sacrifices will be many.

It's mid-morning when the ceremonies begin. The offerings to the egún are first. I join the circle of priests and cooks before a brick fireplace in reciting the names of the ancestors while the obá asks their permission to continue the day's rituals. One by one we pass before the priest, turning in a circle as he touches our forehead and torso and arms with the dove that will be sacrificed. Some of the women hold their hands over their breasts as they turn. "These are women who have children," Tatica whispers. "They cover their breasts as a sign of protection."

Tatica shows me how to take handfuls of something that looks like salt from a bowl. How to cleanse myself by moving my hands over my head, my shoulders, my arms, and finally my legs, as if pulling on a pair of pants.

Near my feet a turtle works its way from the fountain into a slice of shade. I watch it toddle between the legs of chairs and tables and question the wisdom of its venturing onto this part of the patio. At Daniel's, the animals to be sacrificed had remained hidden from view until the last moment. But here they remain in plain sight. Through the open bathroom door, I count more than a dozen-and-a-half birds and four goats—two brown, two white. The fifth, I'm told, is yet to arrive.

Over the next hours, I'll force myself to walk over to the bathroom and visit with the animals there. Notice the singularities among them, their unique markings, the precise tone of each of their cries.

For now, I watch the turtle weave between the legs of a nearby chair and wonder about the trust it seems to place in all of us. How vulnerable its soft body is under its shell: one unlucky stab of a chair leg and it would be pierced in an instant.

And then we wait. For more priests. For the fifth goat. The day grows hot and sticky. Mabel brings out more coffee and then lunch. I try to focus on the book in my lap, the famous historian Olga Portuondo's account of Our Lady's place in Cuban culture. I want to prepare myself for the interview Maruchi has promised to arrange with Portuondo. But the academic Spanish bunches up on the page, forming a wall too thick to work through in the heat. I drift off to the sounds of the morning as it turns to afternoon: the burble of the fountain and the chanting from the nearby room where the priests have gone to conduct the parts of the ceremony that only they can know.

When I wake, a little homesick after being away for two weeks, I slip a packet of photos from my journal to sneak a look at Rick. One is a shot I took while we were on vacation in Maine. I call it Movie Star Rick for the way his sunglasses are perched on top of his head. Then there's the tender one that captures him just as he is waking, his head and chest framed by golden sheets.

"He's in love with you," a friend announced when I showed her the photo. She sounded as surprised as I was that I'd finally let someone in.

In a third photograph, the two of us smile from our seats at a Clippers baseball game. Around my neck I wear the silver egret pendant Rick asked a jeweler to make for our first Christmas together, its lacy wings spread in flight. From the beginning, the present felt immense. More than just a gift, it was an acknowledgement of who I was and what was important to me. That, while Rick might not believe in the power of image and story—that an egret and bison might be destined to find one another—he knew I did and was willing to commemorate that.

Accordingly, in the photo I am wearing a baseball cap, a thing I'd sworn I wouldn't do for anyone. I was not a woman who wore a baseball cap, nor was I a woman who went to baseball games. At least not until I met Rick. And yet there I am sitting at a game with a baseball cap on my head. The arm of my baseball-loving partner thrown around my shoulder. The silver egret resting near my throat.

How far away that woman feels now! The egret replaced with Ochún's yellow beads. The woman who wears them capless, her copper hair curling under the Santiago humidity. The man who holds her over 1400 miles away. What would he make of the woman who sits among priests and priestesses waiting for a day of blood sacrifices to commence?

Tatica interrupts the waiting to tell me I have a visitor. Maruchi's neighbor Roberto, a thirty-nine-year-old television producer and documentary filmmaker, is here to see how he can help me with Our Lady's upcoming feast days. I take an immediate liking to him. He reminds me of a Boy Scout or a Marine—his hair is cut short and his chest and arms are wide and strong, his demeanor both formal and sincere.

We sit in the shade drinking espresso Mabel brings out to us on a porcelain tray. Unlike Maruchi, Roberto is an atheist, a lover of Our Lady's history more than her religious cult. And yet he can't help but venerate her. He shares his birthday with hers, the September 8th date the Catholic Church associates with the birth of the Mother Mary and the day the island celebrates as Our Lady's feast day. By sharing his birthday with Our Lady, Roberto is her child.

At 5:40, the sacrifices begin. I see the tail first as Maruchi's son and son-in-law struggle to extract the first animal from a white cloth bag. Fat and rubbery like a rat's, but certainly too large to be any kind of rat I've ever seen. Later, Maruchi will tell me the animal is the *jutía*, native to Cuba and Eleggua's favorite food. Whatever it is, its claws cling to the sides of the sack, resisting the men's efforts. Finally, the thing emerges, its teeth bucked like a beaver, its fur bristled and thick. I wince when I see it, not only because the animal is to be sacrificed but because it is so ugly. Not an animal but a beast.

There is a mercy to each of the killings. The smaller animals are kept in their cloth bags until the moment of sacrifice, the larger ones in the bathroom so they won't have to witness the death of their comrades. The movements of the babalawos' hands as they move the knife are certain, trained like those of a rabbi, to ensure a quick death. There is a reverence in how each part of the animal is utilized. Its meat, blessed by the babalawos so that it carries the spirituality of the sacrifice, is shared among humans. The inner organs, which hold the vital life force, the aché, of the animal even more than the blood, is cooked and presented as a gift to the oricha.

When I ask Maruchi about the sacrifices, she reminds me that life feeds on life. Animals feed on other animals and plants. Humans feed on the same. The spirits are no different; they need to eat in order to live in the physical world. The sacrifices we make to them are our way of thanking them for their part in organizing the world for us and helping us to live and prosper within it. Still, it is difficult to watch. Without a role to play, as I had with Daniel and Yolersi, I find myself on the outside of the narrative, stuck with the inescapable physicality of the rites.

I watch as the babalawos hold each chicken upside down, tug at a few feathers, jerk its head twice toward the floor, then twist. Over in a flash. With the doves, the killing is a simple pulling of feathers and then the snap of their head. With the larger animals, the rituals become more elaborate. The men speak prayers over each goat, feed it green herbs. The man in white presses his forehead to the animal's. In low tones he asks the goat to lend its aché to the oricha. The two are now in agreement, this occasion to give and feed physicality to the oricha a shared contract between animal and man.

I watch again as the babalawos cover the goat's eye with one ear so it won't see what's to come, test its throat with the knife before plunging it through one side and out the other. The blood that will feed the oricha pours, thick and red. Too red to be real. And so much of it. This is the moment when Heaven and Earth meet. The transcendental return to the beginning of the world when oricha and human enter into their first communion, this letting of blood a renewal of that first covenant between Earth and Sky.

After each matanza comes the *limpieza*. The man in white on hands and knees ceremoniously wipes up feathers and blood, sweeping them toward the fundamentos of the oricha. One of Maruchi's helpers, a young girl who waits on the sidelines until we're ready for her, mops any last bits of blood and sinew across the red brick of the patio and into the drain, wringing the mop rag into a bucket of water that turns first crimson and then dark red and then brown.

I watch, both fascinated and repulsed by the swirl of feathers and blood. I wonder how much of my aversion is fueled by a religious upbringing that shielded me from the physicality of blood while celebrating its virtue. The Judeo-Christian sacrificial letting of blood traced its lineage from Abraham and Moses to Jesus, who died so that we might have life and that we might have it more abundantly. How inured we'd become to that scriptural violence! The word "covenant"—mentioned almost 280 times in the Old Testament, its root meaning both "to eat" and "to cut"—so much more civilized sounding than the word "sacrifice." Yet, no matter what the religion, a covenant involved an exchange, and that exchange came at a price.

Over the next hours, Maruchi's patio locks into an assembly line where everyone knows their place. The babalawos are in charge of killing and butchering, carrying quartered parts first to the room where priests work secretly behind closed doors and then to Maruchi's godmother Maritza, who stands at the chopping block cutting them into pieces. Beside her, the obá dips chickens into pots of boiling water before passing them to Tatica, who plucks feathers and claws from their steaming corpses. In the kitchen, Leonides works to prepare the *aché de santo*, arranging those parts of the animals that will be fed to the oricha in plastic tubs and labeling them with the names of their recipients: Obatalá, Changó, Ochún.

Day turns to night. Lucas the basset hound watches, bored and hot, from the kitchen. The parrot Kuky peers down from a brick ledge. Mabel weaves through the assembly line, bringing out trays with delicate espresso cups for the priests and dinner for the Italian tourists, who are eating on my rooftop so they might be spared dining amidst the carnage.

The faces of those at work grow increasingly weary. The tabby named after Changó rubs his neck against a chair. Mabel mutters under her breath that she never thought she'd be going home this late. Still, the matanzas continue.

The turtle to be sacrificed for Yemayá is the hardest to watch, perhaps because, as with the jutía, I don't see it coming until the men pull it from its cloth sack. They work for several minutes to coax the animal's head from the protection of its armor. When they finally have it, they force it backward against its shell in the hopes the neck will snap. But the neck refuses. The men try a second and then a third time before one of them grabs a stone from the ground and begins beating it against the turtle's neck. Blow after blow, until all that remains of the head is a mash of blood and pulp.

The men lower the body of the now-headless turtle and place it, neck first, on the ground. Still the turtle moves, its legs waving in the absence of any brain to coordinate them. One leg floats up while the other floats down. And then in reverse. Slow motion but continuous. Rhythmic. Almost beautiful. All those parts mysteriously in sync, like a metronome.

It's 9:30 when I pick my way through bits of goat and bird up the stairs and to my room. My ears are ringing, my stomach churning. It's all I can do to undress and shower. I stand under the stream of water and try to wash the smell of blood and sinew that clings, like the claws of that jutía, to my skin. When Rick calls, there are no words to communicate what I've witnessed. How to separate everything that has happened from the languages in which I've experienced them: the recitation of ancestors in Spanish and Lucumí tongues; the singing over herbs; the vernacular of blood and water spilling onto floors and drains. Those turtle legs danc-ing, perfectly timed, one side rising as the other fell.

How to tell him that I'd found the image both grotesque and inviting, as if those legs had been waving me to press past everything I thought I knew about the finality of death and behold the grotesque, the illogical, and yes, the beautiful, stunning even, resoluteness of those legs?

How to articulate such a thing to Rick as he sits in his living room in Columbus? I picture him, surrounded by the familiar trappings of the living—his rat terrier Skip stretched behind him on the ledge of the couch, the muted television turned to Law & Order or ESPN. The sound of Rick's voice fills the distance between us as he tells me he loves me. The sound of my own voice responds in kind. Why then do I feel as if I'm keeping something from him?

TESTIMONY

IT'S IMPORTANT TO NOTE that Juan Moreno's name appears, along with those of the Joyos brothers, in the 1608 personnel inventory of the mines. Again, in the notarized depositions he offers eighty years later when—now an old man—he describes his childhood encounter with Our Lady for the official record.

These particulars are less vital to the oral record. Moreno's last name becomes dropped in the telling and retelling of his story as he becomes remembered in the collective memory as Juan de la Caridad or simply, along with the Joyos brothers, as one of the three Juanes. And perhaps this is all well and good. The name Moreno, certainly lent him not by his African parents but by a Spanish landowner, is its own kind of fiction. Still, his possession of a last name anchors him in testimonies and inventories. The dates that accompany the name further corroborate his existence. If he's real, then perhaps the story he tells—the one about the miraculous copper-skinned mother who appears to those in need—is just as real.

Of Apolonia, there is no such historical anchoring. There are no Apolonias recorded in the mine inventories, only a Polonia in 1620, and two more in 1647. Whether the inability to locate the girl's name is due to a simple misspelling, or because her name was not recorded—either because during this period young enslaved girls were not assigned last names or because she's a figment of someone's imagination, a trope added to flesh out the role of young seer girl in Our Lady's story—we cannot know. What we have of her is an oral history handed down word-of-mouth, its details changing along the way like a game of telephone.

Apolonia's story first enters the written record in 1703 when the chaplain Father Don Onofre Fonseca de la Caridad pens his version of Our Lady's first miracles. And while Fonseca draws his account from oral history contemporaneous with Moreno's own testimony, Moreno himself does not mention the girl.

It could be that Apolonia, like many details of Moreno's life, simply slipped through the cracks of memory. He's well over eighty when he offers his report of what happened to him as a boy for the official record. Perhaps, after so long, he was offering not the whole picture, but the bits that shone brightest to him.

Am I not also offering my own sort of testimony? Like Moreno, there are more bits missing than present as I try to root these stories onto the page.

What I know is this: There was a mother. A bright sparkling mother who spun cloth from her fingertips and stories from her tongue. A mother who baked her family's birthday cakes and Christmas cookies and tucked her children into bed each night. A mother like so many mothers, which is to say she was both ordinary and extraordinary.

She had a daughter who climbed a hill. There were no bursts of light. No angels. Just a quiet breaking inside the daughter's chest. A crack so small it could hardly be detected from the outside.

[13]

WHEN GOD HAD A WIFE

I AWAKEN TO FIND the iron bones of my rooftop breakfast table set with a bright tablecloth. Soon Mabel will climb the stairs with trays of mango and pineapple, carafes of coffee and guayaba juice, an omelet stuffed with cheese and ham. In the meantime, I watch a pair of geckos climb among orchids and vines, the tabby Changó hammocking on the swath of cloth that shades the patio below it. When I go downstairs, all signs of the matanzas will be swept away.

Later today, when I try to describe these first days at Maruchi's in an email to a friend back home, I'll spend many lines trying to capture how I feel both exhilarated and unnerved by what I'm experiencing here. I mention too the pleasure and guilt I feel at being waited on by the women of the house. My friend's response will come immediately and in one line: Hadn't I always wanted to be a goddess on a rooftop with attendants and festivals?

She's referring to the part of me that has always wanted to live large—the dancer who painted *Move into the fullness of your being* across the walls of her studio; the choreographer who felt most at home among accolades and applause. I'd thought my aspirations were an additive process. But the older I become, the more I think they might be more subtractive, requiring me to let go of façades and expectations, dig past titles and résumés to uncover whatever raw, primal stuff I am truly made of.

Like Inanna, the Sumerian goddess of Heaven and Earth who divested herself of clothes and jewels, even skin, as she descended to the underworld where she hung naked on a hook, waiting to be remade. Or

Salvador's painting *El Secreto de Ochún*, in which the artist captures the mystery that is Ochún, showing us not her face but rather her substance, those strong waters that both give and take life.

Was there a first mother? A primordial matrix from which we were all made? And if so, why didn't we talk more about her? These were questions I shared with Rick before I left for Cuba. I told him about scholars who argued that the God of the Bible had a wife and that she'd been purposefully edited out of it. I also told him of the handful of inscriptions that offered proof of her existence: Bronze Age texts discovered in northern Syria that tell of a father god named El and his consort, the Lady Athirat. A rock shelter at Sinai's Kuntillet Ajrud whose walls and storage jars depict a female deity seated on a throne along with a written appeal for blessings from "Jhwh and his Asherah."

"How could something so big be kept a secret?" Rick had asked. "If something like this were true, don't you think we'd have heard about it?"

Scholars have argued that we've known about Asherah for centuries. The Phoenicians had called her Astarte and the Akkadians Ishtar. She was Inanna of Mesopotamia and Isis of Egypt. The Aphrodite of Cyprus. The Venus of Rome. Whereas those officially sanctioned Judeo-Christian religious texts that pointed to the stories of a male god were widely considered eternal truths, the stories that recorded these feminine names were filed under that suspicious genre known as mythology, so often translated as "legend" or "false belief."

But before the Queen of Heaven and Earth fell from grace, the Canaanites had called her Qaniyatu Elima, or "She who gives birth to the gods." The Sumerians had called her Ashnan, meaning "strength of all things." Others knew her as Lady of Heaven and Queen of Gods, or simply Holiness. The Cubans knew her as Ochún; the Yoruba as Ọ̀ṣun.

Rick had listened as I rolled off names and attributes. As a Catholic, it's unconventional—sacrilegious even—for him to imagine those stories that might have been left out of the Biblical canon when those men charged with its assembly chose the names and stories that would stand in for all of us.

"Why is this so important to you?" he'd asked. And he hadn't meant just Asherah, but the whole question of a mother spirit.

I didn't know how to convey to him that I'm familiar with her excision from the culture not just as a cerebral puzzle but as something I experience through my own body. As a child I'd wandered the thicket behind our house searching for Jesus's cross. At night I'd kneeled by my bed praying to whatever father god looked over me. Nowhere had I been looking for a woman—a feminine source I carried *inside* myself. A power that had to do with intuition and mystery. An earthly intelligence that could be accessed through the body itself.

The Old Testament translates Asherah as "grove," after the Hebrew custom of worshipping her in nature where they built *asherim on every high hill and beneath every luxuriant tree*. Some of these asherim took the form of living trees; others were consecrated poles carved to look like trees or to resemble the Goddess.

In northern Babylonia they knew her as their Divine Lady of Eden. In the Kabbalah she is both the Tree of Life and the Shekinah surrounding it, the dwelling place or feminine principle of God who is Mother, Daughter, Sister, and Holy Spirit.

The violence it took to break such matriarchal worship is well documented. The Old Testament's authors detail God's hostility toward kings who worshipped Asherah's groves, championing those reforming priests who destroyed her symbols by chopping and burning her trees and poles.

Break down their altars, write the authors of Exodus.

Smash their sacred pillars and burn up their Asherah poles, instructs the book of Deuteronomy, tacking on a directive to not only *cut down the idols* but to *wipe out their names from every place.*

In Ezekiel: *And they will know that I am the Lord, when their people lie slain among their idols ... on every high hill and on all the mountaintops, under every spreading tree and every leafy oak.*

I think of all the figures that have been maligned and misrepresented, omitted, erased—Mary Magdalene and Eve demonized for their sensuality. Others like Asherah and Ochún so lost to the Western canon that even as I type their names my editing software fails to recognize them, launching into autocorrect mode that turns Asherah into *Dasher* and Ochún into *Ocher*. I fight to spell them back into existence. After two tries, auto edit gives up trying to correct me, underlining them in red to let me know I've made an error and must continue at my own peril.

It wasn't just my mother I'd lost but a larger sense of the mother. I wasn't alone. My whole country seemed to have lost her. We were surrounded by images of the feminine—pop icons and underwear models, feminists and porn stars, soccer moms and saints—all of them flashing large but pointing in different directions, unglued from whatever architecture might give them a coherent narrative. A blueprint that might hold us through the waters of our deepest anxieties. A guide who might answer those questions I'd been exploring throughout the years in journal entry after journal entry: *Who am I? Am I part of something larger than my own life? And if so, how do I fit within it?*

When I'd come to Cuba, I'd expected the mother to present herself in grand, showy gestures. But here on Maruchi's roof I notice her in the humblest of details. She is there in the care with which Mabel and Tatica prepare my breakfast, arranging fruit on my plate like flower petals the way my mother used to. And there in the chinkle of wind chimes and the flutter of laundry from rooftop lines—brightly colored skirts and blouses waving like flags as far as the eye can see. Again, in the plants and flowers that populate every inch of Maruchi's rooftop and patio—sumptuous vines with golden blooms that open like wine cups; hanging baskets cascading with bougainvillea; clay pots shaped like goddess heads filled with ginger lilies and hibiscus. Spiky bromeliads that grow like space creatures. Begonias that remind me of the ones my mother grew as annuals in her garden on Marvilla Lane. These nods toward femininity that could be written off as decorative root me to that primal, potent, fertile place that is not just pretty, but powerful.

From the patio below, I hear Maruchi talking on the telephone with one of the many initiates who make up her spiritual household. Nearby, her daughter Narjhara fusses over her infant. Unlike the homes in the U.S. where outside and inside are clearly delineated, in Cuba the outside is not only incorporated into the home, it is central to it. The rooms of Maruchi's house branch from a central patio with its goddess fountain and turtles and fish. It is there, among banana trees and heliconia, that the women of the house drink their morning coffee and tourists check in and out for their stay. It is there that Ernesto tends to brickwork and Tatica feeds the turtles in the fountain. There that priests prepare offerings to the gods and initiates receive their blessings. And it is there each day, after the bustle of the house finally settles, that Maruchi and I meet for our evening pláticas.

It is during these talks that Maruchi's Ochún-ness—which I'd found difficult to locate during our first meetings—begins to reveal itself. Maruchi's pathway to Ochún is not the ebullient, coquettish one of Ochún Aña or Ochún Yeye Moró. Hers is the path of Ochún Ibu Yumu, the serious one who holds dominion over serpents and wasps. If her manner is matter-of-fact, it is because she has things to do. Not only does she run a household and a business, but she also runs a house of worship, an *ile* where she initiates and guides the Santería practitioners who call her their godmother.

She is generous—not in the luxuriant way I'd expected—but in the practical way she offers her assistance to colleagues and neighbors, children and godchildren, tourists, and spiritual supplicants like myself. And if I'd expected that generosity to clothe itself in softness, the way it had with Miriam, Maruchi again reminds me that there is more than one path to the feminine. For if Miriam had spoken about Our Lady and Ochún in hushed tones, as if talking about them were a secret, Maruchi claims the goddess not as a secret but as a self-evident truth.

She tells me about the spiritual lineage—the godmothers and

godmothers of godmothers who connect her with the women and hills of Nigeria. The burble from her fountain, she explains, connects this house to the Òṣun River where the goddess first pressed her feet into the earth. The lush vines and potted plants that populate her home echo the ancient groves of the Yoruba, who cleared space between town and bush to erect their outdoor cathedrals to the gods.

It was in the groves outside the town of Osogbo where Ochún's first devotees had danced—surrounded by parrots and river ferns, antelope and crocodile—beneath a canopy of coconut trees and palms, summoning the goddess in the sacred space that sits between the known and the unknown.

As I listen, I remember how it was there at the edge of our yard where I'd often find my mother—in the space before the acre that delineated our property dropped off into wild prairie—her face smudged with dirt, planting petunias and irises in her garden.

"Put a glass of clear water out for your mother," Daniel's drumming assistant Jorge Luís had told me during a break between lessons when I'd explained how hopelessly faraway she felt. "Fill it with your mother's favorite flowers. Write her name on a piece of paper and place it beneath the glass. Talk to her."

It's not just Ochún who presides at Maruchi's. In the parlor an ornate statue of Our Lady of Charity stands watch over the house, the three Juanes praying at her feet reminding all who pass by that she is only a prayer away. From my spot on Maruchi's roof I again have the sensation I could almost reach out and touch her at the altar of her sanctuary, twelve miles to the west; extend a hand and dip it in the Bay of Nipe where she first appeared fifty miles to the north.

If I close my eyes, I can hear the hush as the three Juanes enter that cove of black sand and mangroves, with nothing but the sound of waves and the cry of birds. Our Lady's effigy floats pristine and perfect, untouched by salt or sand, before them. Not yet a patron saint crowned in jewels from the Pope, her story not yet braided into the canon, her wig and rouge not yet touched and retouched by the restoration artists who will be commissioned to keep her looking her part. She has not yet read her script—that to be feminine means to be submissive and to be holy to be filled with tenderness and grace; that to be female is to suffer; to be pure to renounce all connection with earthly things.

In so many of her incarnations, the Madonna had been bleached, stripped of her undomesticated aspects of wisdom and sexuality, her dominion over life and death. But Madonnas like Our Lady of Charity were worshipped for the very qualities that tie them to the earth. Venerated not just in Cuba but in Spain and France, Switzerland, and Russia—in Mexico's Guadalupe and Bavaria's Our Lady of Altötting, in Italy's Our Lady of Oropa and Poland's Madonna of Częstochowa—Black Madonnas have been discovered in jungles and mountaintops, underground and in caves. Their features darkened by earth or by time, by the materials they were made of, or—depending on who you asked—either the sins or soot of those who lit their candles before them.

Great miracles have been attributed to these images—repelling armies; manifesting roses in winter; reviving drowned children from the dead. And it is before these icons that men and women continue to flock to be reminded of a power that is protective and nurturing, unceasing and transformative.

In ancient Jerusalem, priestesses at Yahweh's Temple wove ritual textiles in honor of their Asherah, the tree of life who spins all living things from her own body. In Greece, the Fates held the thread of life between their collective hands, spinning, weaving, and cutting the measure of each life. The goddess Aphrodite—called by Pausanias the oldest of the Fates—was not just a divinity of love but also of death, portrayed at times with a spindle in her hand or with arms and hands raised in the eurhythmic spinning position.

From Nigeria to Cuba, the goddess whose name means both source and all that is generated by that source could be found at the banks of her river, dyeing and weaving the cloth of our lives, plaiting our destinies through our hair. The threads she wove at the beginning of the world are what hold our stories in place, her steps that form the rivers of our days.

The cloth Ochún's Nigerian town of Osogbo is famous for is called *adire*—from the root word *adi*, meaning "to put something together" and *re*, "to soak or dye." In this form of tie-dye, strips of raffia are tied around sections of cloth to resist the stain of indigo. And so it's the parts we don't see—what is concealed from the dye—that are crucial to what we will eventually see; those parts that are hidden inside the textile that render the eventual pattern of the cloth. Like the child birthed from the womb, it is the invisible made visible by the shape that holds it.

The mother Mary is an heiress to this aspect of the feminine. The Madonna of the Pietá shown holding the son in her lap is inseparable from those Medieval paintings that show her spinning the thread of his life, already marked with the moment of his death even as she spins it from her fingertips.

An incarnation of both Mary and Ochún, Our Lady of Charity carries the thread to Cuba where she stands guard over the mines of El Cobre. In her arms is the child who holds the world in his hands. Her copper skin ties her both to her ancient, fertile roots and to the mines and town of El Cobre whose people she watches over.

LOST IN EL COBRE

Since my arrival in the east, Maruchi has been encouraging me to visit El Cobre to see how the town prepares for Our Lady's upcoming pilgrimages. And each day I circle the idea of visiting while putting off the trip itself. I tell myself I want to savor the anticipation. Tuck it, like Zunilda's copper, close to my chest. But if I'm honest, there is more to my postponement. An apprehension envelops the balloon of all that anticipation. A fear that the experience of Our Lady's pilgrimages might not live up to the hopes and plans I'm breathing into them.

For months, I've been tracking the countdown to Our Lady's feast days in my notebook. Imagining the tens of thousands who will follow Apolonia's footsteps as they climb toward Our Lady's sanctuary. Luxuriating in the anticipation of marching alongside them, discovering what it feels like to be part of such a grand celebration for the mother.

Now, with those pilgrimages only nine days away, Roberto and I throw ourselves into finalizing our plans and preparations. Each night, Roberto knocks on my door on his way home from work. He brings me the 24-hour schedule of masses that commemorate Our Lady's September 8th birthday, beginning at midnight on the 7th and continuing every few hours through the evening of the 8th. Reports on the car we'll rent to take us to and from the sanctuary. The size and power of the camera equipment he'll use to document the pilgrimages. His plans to bring his father Luís, a former television producer like Roberto, to help. The images both he and I hope they'll capture: waves of Our Lady's pilgrims arriving by bus and by foot, on hand and on knee, their faces gleaming with piety and devotion.

These scenes had seemed impossibly remote when I'd first imagined them from the distance of an Ohio library. My questions about Our Lady—how a small icon might be both capacious enough to embody the chaste Madonna and the sensuous river goddess, and miraculous enough to inspire multitudes to kneel before her—had belonged to a realm of intellectual curiosity rather than a physical experience I might touch with my hands and heart. Now that her pilgrimages are less than ten days away, I feel shy and strangely apprehensive.

And so, I busy myself in the more comfortable realm of research and facts. In the afternoons I meet with Our Lady's famed biographer, Olga Portuondo. A small but mighty academic, she invites me to her house where we sit among stacks of books and art as she recounts the historical evidence that roots Our Lady of Charity in her fantastic mythology. I meet, too, with El Cobre's town historian Julio Corbea, a tall man with wire-rimmed glasses and warm brown eyes who talks to me about the history of the mines and town and the spirits that still haunt them—ghosts of Spanish conquistadores and the Taíno and Bantu people they enslaved.

Between rounds of visits and interviews, I stop for lunch at the Hotel Casa Granda. Not because the food is good—it's not—but because its shaded terrace overlooks the historic Parque Céspedes, providing a cool and interesting respite from errands and heat. In April 1940, American monk Thomas Merton stopped after visiting Our Lady's sanctuary to compose his poem "Song for Our Lady of Charity." As I sit here, I'm aware of taking in the same view Merton once did—the Sierra Maestra, framed in blue sky and perfect clouds, winking at me from between El Ayuntamiento, where Fidel Castro announced victory in 1959, and the 1511 home of Cuba's first governor, Diego Velásquez: Spanish colonizer. Conqueror. Hero in the textbooks of my youth.

I remember how those books chose the conquest as the moment when American history began. The Europeans who arrived had been portrayed as discovering the land rather than appropriating it from those who'd been living on it for centuries: Christopher Columbus, who planted the cross of the Spanish king in these parts. Diego Velásquez, who followed soon after, founding Spanish settlements in Baracoa and

Santiago de Cuba and then Havana. What those textbooks didn't mention were the atrocities that flowed from that conquest's rush toward riches: the use of fellow human beings, first Indigenous, then African, to extract the precious ores that would enrich and defend the Crown.

Before lunch, I wander the rooms of Governor Velásquez's house-turned-museum, feeling my way through the heavy cadence of its architecture. Its stone walls were erected by Taíno slaves. Its cedar ceilings designed by naval carpenters to mimic the hulls of ships turned upside down. The windows are shuttered with heavy Moorish lattices carved from mahogany. They let light in but not out. A portrait of Velásquez painted in dark oils broods on a wall.

I imagine those first colonizers making plans for the gold they'll ship back to Spain from the refuge of these well-appointed rooms. I can almost hear the hooves of Spanish horses as they ride into the carriage space. The clang of iron bells, low and heavy—that tolling call for the enslaved men and women who live here too to report to work and to church.

Nearly a century after they exhausted their search for gold, the Spanish sent an artillery captain named Don Francisco Sánchez de Moya to found the copper mines at Santiago del Prado y Real de Minas de Cobre, now known as the town of El Cobre. While he was at it, the captain had orders to erect a small church on a hill near the mine so that soldiers and slaves—both Indigenous and African—might pray to the gods and saints of the king. Because the captain was from the town of Illescas, in Toledo, Spain, and had grown up a devotee of its patroness, Our Lady of Illescas, it was her image that presided over that first humble sanctuary.

In the decades after, Our Lady of Illescas's presence would fade, her station at the central altar replaced by the copper-skinned effigy of Our Lady of Charity. The new icon's ascendancy brought to the fore a different sort of mother, her narrative spun not by conquerors but by the people themselves: the Indian brothers Rodrígo and Juan de Joyos and

the African creole children Juan Moreno and Apolonia at the center
of the events that forever link Our Lady with the fight to end slavery.
Under Our Lady's watch, the royal slaves of El Cobre took on the king
of Spain, carrying Our Lady's effigy with them as they fled to the mountains to build their *palenques*. From there, they fought for land and for
freedom, and they attributed each victory in their struggle to the small
but miraculous virgin mother who guided them. It would be decades
before enslaved men and women throughout the rest of Cuba would win
their freedom too.

On my fourth day in Santiago, the anticipation is too much. Regardless
of any trepidation I might have, I want to see the miraculous mother
before her crowds of pilgrims arrive. And so, as the town of El Cobre
quietly prepares for Our Lady's feast days, I ask Maruchi's driver Tomás
to take me there. It's a thirty-minute ride. The stretch of road leading
from Cuba's central highway into El Cobre is marked by a gas station
that doubles as a restaurant-bar. There we turn off the highway, and
then it's a mile and a quarter of dirt road that winds its way through a
countryside dotted with chickens and oxen. An occasional farmhouse. A
mule. Every hundred yards or so we pass a wooden stand where vendors
sell bouquets of sunflowers and souvenirs to the pilgrims who pass this
way on their way to visit Our Lady. Then it's up the hill and around a
bend where the world opens to a view of her sanctuary, its red cupolas
and yellow plaster walls outlined crisply against a cerulean sky.

From her perch on high ground, Our Lady watches over the River
Cobre Valley and the 11,000 inhabitants—great-grandchildren of both
the enslaved and the landowners once brought to extract copper from
this red earth—that make up the modern town of El Cobre. And from
a second hill, opposite Our Lady's sanctuary, the monument called El
Cimarrón rises as an homage to the runaway slaves who escaped the El
Cobre mines to build their palenques in these mountains.

It is this sculpture where Tomás and I make our first stop. For days,

Maruchi and Julio have been talking about the monument and its relevance to Our Lady's narrative. As it happens, years after the ten-year-old Juan Moreno encountered Our Lady's effigy, he grew up to become one of those freedom fighters who took their name from the word *cimarronaje*, meaning flight.

Tomás stops the Lada before a set of stone steps that lead to the sculpture. I survey the ascent, wondering what exactly I'll find at the top. Just then a stocky man stands from the shade of a tree and introduces himself as my guide, Salvador. He's here, he announces, to safeguard me—whether from the steep steps or from sliding rocks or from intrusive animals or spirits, I'm not sure.

"There are three hundred steps," Salvador says as we begin our climb, then glances my way to see if this number daunts me. But I'm busy scanning the ground for flecks of copper my friends in Havana had said I should look for. The ground was littered with them, the drummer Jorge Luís had promised. But the path we climb holds only red dirt and common rock. The afternoon sun beats down on our shoulders and necks. My sundress clings to my sweaty flesh. From time to time, Salvador stops to wipe his brow.

Just as I decide the stairs will never end, we turn a bend and the iron sculpture known as El Cimarrón rises from the summit. Created by renowned Santiago artist Alberto Lescay, the monument is not a literal representation of a slave in flight but the artist's abstract interpretation: an arm, its palm pressed toward the sky. A face. A wing. Seeing it, I'm reminded of the winged Nike that caught my attention months before at the library—the goddess's figure poised as if ready to land or take off, her garments rippling in a long past breeze, her missing parts still tethered to her in the viewer's mind by some invisible presence. Certainly, the setting and context of the two figures could hardly be more different: the goddess spiraling, triumphant, from the prow of a Greek ship; El Cimarrón rising from scorched rock. But they both spoke of containment and flight. About finding one's place between worlds, and about the mysterious forces that help us find our way.

At the base of his sculpture, the artist constructed an iron cauldron. Known as a *nganga,* this element is a nod to the Kongo, those first Africans brought to work the mines of El Cobre, who dedicated their ritual pots to the *mpungu* or spirits they held at the center of their beliefs.

I ask Salvador to lift me so I can stand on its lip. Below my feet the enormous bowl of the nganga yawns like an inverted bell, revealing a collection of bones large enough to have come from cattle or oxen. I ask if they are just for show or the remnants of actual offerings. Salvador shrugs.

Only later will I learn that the El Cobre Spiritist Madelaine acts as custodian and caretaker of these offerings. It's not an official role; it's a stewardship he's taken on. For the past few days Maruchi has been on the telephone working to arrange a meeting for me to see the famed Spiritist. She and Roberto, Olga and Julio have all told me how the people of El Cobre trusted Madelaine to heal their physical and mental ailments, and to help them speak with their departed loved ones. When they spoke of him, it was always with the same phrase attached: Madelaine was "the real deal."

They also told me how he relied upon a spirit he calls El Cimarrón to help him cross between worlds. But it isn't until now that I connect the dots and realize how before Madelaine's Cimarrón was a spirit he was an actual cimarrón, one of a group of men and women who took flight to the mountains where I now stand before the statue that stands in their place. The vestiges of the copper mines that once defined their lives are tattooed into terraced steps of red rock below. A quarry pit, over a half mile in length and 200 feet deep, once filled with rich ore, now holds a trillion gallons of sparkling blue waters too toxic with heavy metals to drink or swim in or even touch.

I imagine those first cimarrones risking everything to take to the freedom of these green hills. Stories tell that as they took off in the cover of darkness, using their knowledge of the local terrain to leave the mines behind them, they carried their beloved Madonna in their arms. Standing on the nganga, I look out at the lush monte. The red rock of the mountains is framed by banana trees and royal palms, the air still and clear. From their separate hilltops, Our Lady's sanctuary and the monument to El Cimarrón bookend the history of this mountain amphitheater. Between them rises a third hill, the one a young enslaved girl once climbed in search of her mother. An egret circles above and I can almost hear the beating of wings.

Four centuries have passed since Apolonia first climbed Miners' Hill and Our Lady signaled she wanted her temple built at its summit. Since then, that first shrine has suffered landslides and earthquakes, been built and rebuilt, moved from its original hill to the one where her sanctuary now stands. Once Salvador delivers me safely back to Tomás, I ask him to leave me at its base so I can climb on foot. I want to take my time, relish my moment alone with the mother before her pilgrims arrive in the thousands for her feast days.

The road uphill is flanked with vendors selling souvenirs, and the quiet of the monte Apolonia once navigated is now filled with the cacophony of their calls. They vie for my attention, pressing souvenir stamps of Our Lady into my hands. "*Un regalo*," they tell me as they hurry me toward their stalls to show me there's more to buy: bits of copper scavenged from the closed mines; key chains and rosaries inscribed with Our Lady's image; carved wooden virgencitas that remind me of the ones Miriam's brother brought back from his own pilgrimages to El Cobre. Their presence before me is a tangible sign that I've arrived. I run my eyes over vendors' shelves, noting the variations in size and shape, in craftsmanship and embellishment.

No matter how many ways the artisans of El Cobre find to craft her image, always Our Lady's figure begins with the triangle. Her crowned head forms the point at the top, the edges of her robed hem the bottom two.

From there, her artists fill in the details, drawing in those symbols that from the beginning have rooted Our Lady in the two religions that claim her as their mother. The rosary in her right hand, the baby Jesus in her left, identify her as the Marian Madonna. Her copper skin and the inverted half-moon on which she stands link her with the fertile mysteries of Ochún.

Determined not to arrive empty-handed before such a mighty figure, I purchase a bouquet of sunflowers from an old man in aviator glasses and cradle them in my arms as I continue up the hill.

An iron gate marks the threshold between town and church. Beyond it are a final set of stairs. As I look up, I feel a sudden urge to kneel, to surrender to whatever mystery awaits me at the top. I look around to see if anyone else has dropped to their knees, but the few who climb do so as politely and unremarkably as if they were on their way to any church. I follow after them just as modestly.

Inside, the sanctuary is high-ceilinged and bright. Light pours through arched doorways, flashes off marble and gold, streams through windows cut from stained glass. Both the architecture and the splendor draw my eye to the front of the sanctuary where Our Lady presides over visitors who trickle in and out to light a candle or leave a bouquet.

Nuns, stationed like museum guards, guide us in the correct order of worship. The first stop is the Chapel of Miracles. The room is an homage to centuries of devotion to the great mother. Its walls and glass cases are filled with ex-votos and crutches, soccer trophies and war medals. The alleged remains of the wood tablet on which Our Lady was found have been framed and hung between stained-glass windows. A line of *retablos* depicts Our Lady's story: the first miracle where she appeared floating on that tablet before the three Juanes, her dry robes untouched by stormy seas. A second where she continued her marvels, disappearing each night from her altar only to return the next morning as if she'd never been missing at all. Her robes not dry—as they had been in her first miracle—but wet from her midnight swims.

In Juan Moreno's depositions, he testified that he'd heard Mathías de Olivera, the hermit appointed to watch over Our Lady's first shrine, on more than one occasion chastising the icon for the way she came and went as she pleased. "Where do you go at night?" the old hermit asked. "How can you leave me here so alone? And why do you come back with your clothes so wet and dirty when you know you don't have any others or money to buy them?"

By the middle of the eighteenth century, Our Lady's sanctuary had become the richest and most frequented on the island. The more miracles Our Lady performed, the more donors she attracted. A silver lamp was donated after the Virgin expelled three bladder stones from the cantor of the Cathedral of Santiago; months of handiwork promised after she helped a master carpenter recover his sight, and another after she cured him of syphilis.

By the twentieth century, Our Lady's miracles had earned her the titles of Supreme Mother, Guardian of the Lost. Her fans included the humble and the famous. She'd inspired enslaved miners to fight for their freedom. Independence heroes and popes to kneel before her, the first to receive her blessing before heading into battle, the second to proclaim her patron saint of the island. It is said that Fidel Castro's mother visited Our Lady to pray for her son's victory. Ernest Hemingway left his Nobel Prize at her feet, the spot which he called the safest in Cuba.

I find Our Lady standing high above me at the central altar, encased in glass and crowned in jewels. The dress she wears is not the original Mathías de Olivera once fretted she'd get too wet and dirty. Spun from gold threads and hand-sewn by Spanish nuns, it is just one of a collection of gowns the church is rumored to keep in a wardrobe. The 14-karat rays of her crown spark off shafts of light that stream through stained glass to frame her blessed figure. The marble altar on which she stands is arrayed with vases of roses and gladiolas. And filling the vast space around her is the sound of "Ave Maria"; the rustling of bodies in pews; the footsteps of visitors lighting a candle or leaving a prayer.

But for all Our Lady's splendor, there is a smallness, an ordinariness about her. Just under a foot and a half tall, her dainty head painted and fitted with a wig, the body under her robes constructed from strips of wood—she presents herself as decidedly doll-like, more object than divine matriarch.

What disappoints me most is not the Madonna's size, but the distance from the glass case in which she presides to the pews where her devotees gather. What a different vessel she is from the nganga I've just come from. I think about how I'd danced on its rim, stared into its jaws. How high by contrast Our Lady hangs, a remote mother encrusted in jewels and gold.

Until recently, priests regularly rotated the case to face a back room where visitors could climb a staircase and kneel before her. This access has been closed off, a protective measure to safeguard the fragile relic. The church employs restoration artists to repaint her delicate features and remake her wigs. Still her head, made from four-hundred-year-old vegetable paste, continues to deteriorate, her hair to rot. Signs throughout the church advise visitors to refrain from photographing Our Lady from too close a distance, and to leave their offerings on the ground below her altar or in the Chapel of Miracles. I follow their instructions, placing my sunflowers in one of the designated buckets on the floor before taking my seat in a front pew.

Yo sé que tú me comprendes porque sabes mirar con el corazón, the prayer at Our Lady's altar—the one I recite before offering my flowers—reads. Now, seated before her, I copy the line in my journal, relishing both the words—*I know you understand me because you see from the heart*—and the pages in which I write them. This is the same journal I'd crafted when I was still in Ohio, pasting Our Lady's image on its cover, building her triangular form through collage and paint. Adding those shells my therapist had given me. 'Something to slip in your pocket," she'd told me. A tactile reminder, like a bit of copper tucked inside the lining of a bra, of who I was and might be.

Now, as I rest my hand on its cover, I feel the raised image of Our Lady meet my fingertips. Who was this presence who understood me, not through her mind but through her heart? Did she know just how fragile and alone I felt? My life fractured, ever-changing and in flux after the death of my mother, two divorces, a move to an unfamiliar city. A geographic break from Alex. A new career and relationship. Could she see how hard I'd struggled to be a mother in the absence of my own? How harshly I'd judged myself every time I'd fallen short of the expectations I set for myself. How harshly I was judging her even as I sat before her.

I'd hoped to feel Our Lady's presence. Hear her voice as Moreno testified the hermit Mathías de Olivera once did and as Apolonia must have. I'd wanted angels to appear as they did in those early images that show Our Lady's apparition before the three Juanes. But she stood, unblinking, at her altar, looking small and unremarkable and impossibly far away.

Was Our Lady merely an effigy, a doll made of wood and paste? A story repeated so many times it had taken on a life of its own? Its narrative of the mother who appears to those who need her just another way for me to mitigate the grief of losing my own mother? Or was there something real and enduring to her presence—a miraculous mother who held vast mysteries beneath those triangular robes?

I will return to the sanctuary several times before Our Lady's pilgrimages commence. Each time I will study her shape, tracing and retracing her lines and angles as I try to figure out what they add up to. The triangle emerges as a robed mother. An inverted heart. A mountain—both the one Apolonia climbed and the metaphorical one I'd been trying not to fall short of my whole life. No matter how lavish her trappings, the path to Our Lady remained the same. There was a hill to climb, and a daughter hoping to find salvation at its crest.

In most of the versions of Apolonia's story, the girl who climbs the hill is looking for a living mother who works in the mines. But the version I've written, the one I keep circling, is the one in which Apolonia climbs the hill not to meet with a living mother but to grieve the death of the mother she's lost. This version, which was told to me by one of the priests who watches over Our Lady's sanctuary, I trust because I know this act of looking for a place to deposit one's grief, this yearning to find a spot that might either mark or fill the absence of the thing lost. I know the shape and sound of the bereft Apolonia as she falls to the ground, beats her fists against the earth, shouts until her grief fills the sky.

But the part that resonates most deeply—not because I'm familiar with it but because I yearn for it—is the part that happens next. This is the point in the story when, the daughter breaking open on the ground, the mother appears before her. And how after that visitation, Apolonia makes her way back down the hill, no longer crying from the loss of her biological parent but with the joy of having found her spiritual root.

I hear the voice of Julio, the El Cobre historian, in my head, telling me that miracles appear to those who believe in them; the voices of storekeepers and taxi drivers telling me, "Without faith, we have nothing."

And, "Whether or not we are religious, we believe in Our Lady."

Our Lady was an icon, no larger than a doll, who was also a miraculous patron saint. She was the protectress, defender, benefactress of an entire island. A *patrona*—from the same root as "pattern." Those wooden staves that give Our Lady her shape flare at the base like a bell. The child she carries is another bell ringing in her arms. Its sound announces the presence of the mother who is both alive and dead, constant and ever-changing. Mother. Daughter. Spirit. A most holy trinity.

Turn the bell on its head and Our Lady becomes the nganga of the Kongo. Both a literal artifact—the sacred cauldron dedicated to their spirits—and a universal symbol the artist leaves to remind us of the great African womb that holds all our stories.

For the last four centuries, pilgrims have been making their way to her, traveling from Holguín and Havana, from Camagüey and Granma, from Piñar del Río and Santa Clara and Sancti Spíritus and Bayamo.

They arrive by bus and by car, on foot and on knee, leaving their offerings in her Chapel of Miracles—sports medals from victorious teams, and keys from cars whose owners inexplicably stepped away from fatal accidents; graduation diplomas from those who've passed their medical exams. The first woman in Cuba to earn her black belt leaves her karate certificate. A mother whose premature infant survives against all odds leaves the dress the child wore when she was discharged from the hospital. One whose child is cured of cancer leaves a lock of hair.

Accompanying each offering are thank-you notes written on the back of requisition forms and menus, lined school paper and hotel stationery. Some are laminated, others illustrated with photos or drawings of children and grandchildren, nephews and uncles who Our Lady has blessed.

A tí, madre, each note begins. Never the formal form of the second person pronoun *Ud.*, but the familiar form reserved for family and friends. Querída Virgencita. Cachita. Santísima Virgen de la Caridad. Nuestra Señora. Beloved mother. Our Lady.

When I return from the sanctuary, I find Maruchi on the patio entertaining a pair of French filmmakers who've come to interview her for a documentary they're making about Our Lady's pilgrimages. Dressed in a tunic printed with Ochún's peacock feathers, her made-up face animated as she fields their questions, this is a different Maruchi than the one I see each day directing the business of running a family and bed-and-breakfast in a housedress and sandals. Different too from the priestess who almost faded into the background during the sacrifices she hosted just a few feet from where she now sits, as if on a throne. This is the Maruchi who is a trusted expert: a priestess who is also a scholar; an anthropologist who straddles the worlds of religion and academia; a mentor who knows how to speak the language of miracle in a way that sounds not fantastical but learned and wise.

I swell with pride as I listen from the table next to theirs. Like her guardian oricha, Maruchi is a rock star. Earthy and self-possessed, she's a woman who commands the room through both her intellect and her charm. She waves her fan as she relives Our Lady's miraculous apparition in the Bay of Nipe and the French couple hang on every word. How fortunate I feel to have found my way into Maruchi's house. Grateful for our nightly sessions where she shares with me her knowledge of Ochún and Our Lady.

The filmmakers explain they hope to hire Maruchi to be their guide and narrator as they make their way to the Bay of Nipe where Our Lady's story begins. They want for her to translate as they interview the people who live closest to that most sacred spot, to help them track those pilgrims among them who will set out in a few days to retrace Our Lady's steps from that first encounter to her sanctuary in El Cobre.

Maruchi considers their proposal, negotiating for the price she knows will make the trip worth her time. When she says she'll accompany them, I feel the ground give way beneath me. What will happen to me if Maruchi leaves? If Maruchi becomes their guide, who will be mine?

"Can I come?" I hear my voice, small, a child clinging to her mother's skirts.

It's not Maruchi but the Frenchman who answers. "There's no room," he explains. Not in the car they've rented to drive to the bay. Not in the houses where they've arranged to stay. No, I cannot come.

"I'll be back on the eighth," Maruchi assures me. "We can continue our work then." But the air between us is already shrinking. The eighth will be too late. I return to Ohio on the tenth. By the eighth I'll know just about all I'll be able to know on this trip. Without Maruchi, I'm on my own to discover it.

I'm making too much of this, I tell myself. I'm just tired. But something about Maruchi's departure feels seismic. Our Lady had felt distant at the sanctuary. And now Maruchi, the closest I had to a mother here in the oriente, was leaving too.

I climb the stairs to my room to look for my journal. I want to sort out my feelings on the page. And not just any page. I want to sort them out on the pages of that treasured notebook, its covers layered with shells from my therapist, those twin images of Ochún and Our Lady protecting my most intimate thoughts and prayers.

But my journal is nowhere to be found. I look in my purse, then my suitcase. I look under the bed. I call Tomás to see if I've left it inside the Lada. He tells me to hold on while he searches, then returns to the line to tell me he's found nothing.

"Did you look under the seat?" I ask. "All the seats?"

But the notebook is not under the seats. And just as suddenly as Our Lady once appeared before three miners lost at sea, my journal devoted to her disappears.

It's not the loss of my notes I find myself mourning—I'd copied most of them onto my laptop—but the feel of the notebook in my hands. The collaged covers that bridged the self who began this journey in Ohio with the one who now curls in a fetal position under the crocheted lace of Maruchi's bedspread. The photos of Rick and Alex I'd tucked between its pages. Those notations, fashioned in my own handwriting, that documented my dreams and blueprints for this trip. Those first drawings of Ochún and Our Lady when they were little more than a circle and a triangle. My name written inside the front cover back before I'd written anything else and those pages were nothing but a promise.

I'd been keeping journals since I was nine, the first of them a small leather book with a gold lock and key, each entry dutifully beginning "Dear Diary." Over the decades, I'd moved on to composition notebooks and mass-produced hardcover journals. Only recently to collaged artist sketch-books like the one I'd made for the trip. No matter how much the outer shape changed, the musings inside them stayed the same.

Who am I? I pondered as I fretted about how I fit into groups of friends and social orders, romantic partnerships and schools, colleges and jobs.

How might I leave my mark on the world?
And:
Why do I feel so alone?

My mother kept her own diaries, penning her life to the pages of note-books and calendars, shopping lists and greeting cards. After I left for college, she sent letters filled with hand-drawn stick figures and news of the family's comings and goings: *Jon is planting beans at the farm.* Or *Vicki is visiting.* She wrote about dinner parties and brunch at the Mandarin House. About rugs she was hooking and curtains she planned to sew for my dorm room. Mostly, she reported on her treatment. She and my father were attending a macrobiotics conference in Boston. They were cracking open apricots at the kitchen table. She was swimming laps, noting how her energy improved with each milestone: first 12 laps, then 15, then 20.

Hooray! she wrote when she reached 40. *I can still do it.*

Later, after she began to spend more time at the Gerson Center in Mexico, she wrote about her faith in the doctors she believed would heal her. And toward the end of my freshman year of college, as I planned to spend what would be our last summer together: *I feel so far from you.* And: *I can't wait to see you, Becki. It's been awful missing you; I can tell you now.*

The last place I remembered holding my journal was in Our Lady's sanctuary. I'd taken it out of my bag to copy the prayer *I know you understand me because you see from the heart.*

Our Lady was the patroness of things lost and found: the three Juanes searching for salt for the mines; Apolonia calling out for her mother. If spirit needed a material place to manifest, then perhaps part of my spirit was in that notebook, my leaving it at Our Lady's feet no accident.

Before I left, I'd slipped among a group of women praying before flickering candles in the Chapel of Miracles. I'd read the placard mounted to the wall suggesting that the candle I leave be the light that illuminates my path. That it transform itself into a fire that might burn all egoism, pride, and impurity. That it be a flame that warmed my heart. And, since I couldn't stay long, that with this candle I might leave a part of myself.

Had Our Lady, who'd seemed so unreachable when I'd sat before her, been guiding me to leave a piece of myself there at her altar?

Had she taken the entries inside my journal for some sort of offering, a *promesa* I might fulfill if she came to my aid and restored me to wholeness? What would she make of those bits of myself I'd left within its pages? In what image might I be remade?

I fall asleep and dream of watery things: the three Juanes lost in a storm, their lifted hands manifesting the aqueous mother who appears and disappears. My mother's name written in the pages of a journal collaged in paper the colors of the sea. Her image takes root in the movement of my pen across its pages as I feel my way back to the stories where the mother still holds the daughter. There, at the Gerson Center, where she sits on the edge of my bed waiting for me to return from my dinner with her doctor and his friends, her fingers curled around her pen, her letters rising like waves across the page. *Because I love you always, Mother.*

And before: the two of us searching for seashells on a beach in Puerto Angel, Mexico.

"Let those shells speak to you," I hear my therapist telling me. "Remind you of those parts of yourself you need to remember."

Always, a promise.

The date and place written at the top of every page of our journals a manifesto: *I am here.*

Dear Becki, my mother began her last letter to me, the date—June 17, 1983—proof that she was still alive, the warp and weft of her life anchored firmly in the ink and pulp of the page.

The tide reaching for our ankles, pulling us out to sea.

Because I love you.
Always.

It is August of 1983 when she writes those words, *I love you* and *always*—the blue ink of her pen washing over the page. In October she'll be gone.

[*15*]

THE SPIRITS SPEAK

I WAKE STILL GRIEVING the loss of my journal and Maruchi's impending departure. I listen for sounds of her presence and am relieved when I hear her talking in the kitchen with Tatica and Narjhara. The sound of her voice reassures me that she is still connected to the comings and goings of the house—the whoosh of running water and the clang of pots and pans in the sink. The squawks of the parrot. The clatter of espresso cups. Among them, I try to feel my way back to the sounds and shape of my own mother—the fall of her steps in the hallway as she moved throughout her day. The boom of her operatic voice filling the house with scales and arpeggios. That same voice forming the shape of my name.

At a quarter till three, Maruchi's driver Tomás and I make our way to El Cobre to find the man I hoped might reconnect me with that voice. A man I'd been told lived in a house painted in murals. An espiritista who was said to channel the dead. I first heard of Madelaine when I was still in Ohio. I'd pictured him, cross-legged in his colorful temple, surrounded by smoke and bones. Written his name in my journal, planting the seed that I might find him once I got to El Cobre, ask if he could help me speak with my mother.

"The real deal," the people of El Cobre called him. Before I left for Cuba, he'd become part of Rick's and my pillow talk, a way for me to share the anticipation of my trip with him. "If I were going," Rick told me, "I'd try to find a way to trick him, find out if he was real or not."

"That's the difference between us," I'd told Rick. "I don't want to trick him. I want to find out what he might have to offer me."

Later I'd added, "I'll know if he's real or not. I'll feel it in my bones."

When we reach El Cobre, Tomás stops to ask where we might find the home of the Spiritist. Everyone knows the house and the man who lives inside it. They direct us past the police station and down a street where we find Madelaine's tucked among a row of square, concrete homes.

The house is just as we'd been told. Its blue façade is covered with murals that root the house in the imagery of the spirit world. African deities dance before mountains. Their symbols guard windows and doors. An inscription on the side of the house reads *Templo al Cimarrón*, a nod to the eighteenth-century Maroon who speaks through Madelaine in trance. A gold key painted on the front door reminds all who enter that Eleggua guards this home, that it is he who decides who will enter.

"A resource," Julio, the historian, had called Madelaine when we'd met at his office. I liked the sound of the word: resource, not quackery—a way of knowing and seeing that not everyone shared; an intelligence to be utilized and treasured and protected. It wasn't just through his role as El Cobre's town historian that Julio knew of Madelaine. The two men had been friends since childhood. Julio had watched firsthand as Madelaine crossed the threshold between worlds, summoning first the spirit of El Cimarrón, and through him the spirits of loved ones his clients came to speak with.

"How much do I pay him?" I'd asked.

"Leave whatever you want when you're finished," he'd answered. "He doesn't do it for the money."

Now Tomás and I find Julio waiting for us on Madelaine's porch, seated next to a short, dark-skinned man in a striped T-shirt and shorts and a cigarette dangling from his mouth. Julio introduces him as Juan.

And then Tomás leaves, with instructions to return for me in a couple of hours.

I follow Julio and Juan through the gold-keyed door into a room painted with more murals. From floor to ceiling, the mountains of El Cobre provide a backdrop to the scenes that play across them—a white horse, its rider brandishing a machete; Our Lady and child floating ethereally above Ochún's waterfall; a nganga filled with bones. In a corner, a mural shows Eleggua urinating, his exposed penis marking this territory as his own, while on an opposite wall Jesus and Saint Lazarus preside over a table strewn with coconuts and candles, herbs and rum. A banner above them reads *La paz sea con vosotros*. Peace be with you.

"They're interpretations of my dreams," Juan tells me, waving through cigarette smoke at the four walls. "An artist friend painted them for me."

I trip over his words, wondering why Juan would ask someone to paint *his* dreams on *Madelaine's* walls. I have yet to make the connection between the man before me—in his striped shirt and with his deep sparkling eyes and neat mustache—and the Spiritist I'd imagined I'd be meeting: an old man muttering to spirits before smoke and bones.

As if sensing my confusion, Juan tells me, "I'm Madelaine. Madelaine, and also Juan."

The name is only the beginning of my confusion. "I will feel it in my bones," I'd told Rick. But now that I was here—before the man named Juan who was also Madelaine and who I hoped, over the course of the next hours, would channel El Cimarrón so that he could connect me with my mother—I wasn't sure what I wanted to feel.

What if I discovered Madelaine wasn't, as the people of El Cobre claimed, the "real deal"? That the idea of connecting with my mother was a foolish one? That she was dead, gone, lost. Any thought that she might be within reach simply the hallucination of a grief-stricken daughter.

Even more unnerving was the idea that the stories about the Spiritist might be true. That Madelaine might actually reach through that curtain between worlds and touch the other side. What would I do with the knowledge that such a thing was possible? That my mother wasn't gone?

That she was there, on the other side of that scrim, waiting for me to speak to her.

I'd been able to summon my mother on two occasions. The first was when I walked home from a winter college exam and felt her hand solid in mine, the illumination through the stained-glass windows of Alice Millar Chapel lighting our way as we walked. The second had come two decades later at a yoga studio where I'd started taking classes in my forties. The instructor encouraged us to think of our body like the skin of a drum, every part of our being alive and ready to be awakened. In classes we'd tap our fingers along our chest and ribs. Chant and stretch. Count our breaths. Coax invisible balls of energy to life between our hands. But my favorite classes were the ones they held on Friday nights when we got to dance. The music, heavy on drums, rooted my body—another drum. The absence of mirrors and choreography and the fact that no one was watching was also freeing. I moved—an arm, a foot, and I was flying: a spinning top. A dervish weaving between bodies both separate and not separate from my own.

"I can see atoms!" I'd told my best friend when we were nine, the two of us gleeful that we saw things grown-ups needed a microscope to see. Now I was dancing with those particles, my breath and sweat ribboning out into the room, every speck of skin and muscle belonging both to me and to every other molecule of space.

When we finished dancing, we'd stretch face up across the floor, close our eyes, and pound our backsides against the ground—the sound of our buttocks hitting the linoleum another drum.

I hadn't been thinking of my mother when she materialized on the mat next to mine, dressed in one of her homemade aprons with the bric-a-brac sewn around the edges, and thumping her bottom against the floor like the rest of us. The two of us giggled as we remembered the mat she'd kept on the floor of her bathroom before she died, the rubber bag she used to administer her daily regimen of coffee enemas draped around the doorknob, the tube she stuck inside her rectum dangling in plain sight. The indignity of it all, which suddenly seemed funny to us both—the great, animal reality of ourselves. The absurdity of being in a body in the world. We laughed about that enema bag and about the wheatgrass she and my father grew in the windowsill. Smiled as we remembered how devoted he became in those last months. How thoroughly he committed to their shared conviction that they could beat the cancer if only they believed hard enough, cracking apricots to extract laetrile, attending to the preparation of cleansing elixirs that would make her whole again. We smiled and then we laughed, our bodies ringing with the joy of being alive. And then we began crying. Crying that it took my mother's dying for my father to show a love like that, that it took her dying for any of us to realize how irreplaceable she was. And then, just like that she was gone again.

"You're in good hands," Julio tells me when he says his goodbyes. I follow Madelaine to a room off the living room that doubles as his bedroom and work room. Every inch of it is dedicated to the tools and symbols of the spirits he works with. Wide-eyed gods and saints peer from posters and statues; *jícara* cups made from hollowed-out gourds nest near plastic soda bottles filled with soda and rum; a set of machetes is pinned to the wall. Above his bed, flanked by drums, hang portraits of Jesus and the Madonna. An altar on a bureau is filled with candles and photographs of the dead.

"Make yourself at home," Madelaine tells me, gesturing toward a wooden chair. While we wait for his wife Záhilys to come home from her job at the post office, he opens a wooden box and produces a business card. Aside from the artist Generoso and the owners of bed-and-breakfasts, this is the first business card I've seen since I arrived in Cuba. *Juan Gonzáles Pérez (Madelaine)*, it reads. *Espiritista cruzado, Muertero.*

Espiritista cruzado because the work he does crosses religions. He works with Catholics and Santeros, with practitioners of Palo Monte and Vodú. *Muertero* because his work centers around channeling the spirits of the dead.

Underneath these first titles, his card offers another: *El Cimarrón.*

"What have you come for?" Madelaine asks once Záhilys arrives. The three of us face each other in wooden chairs and the negative space between our bodies forms a perfect triangle.

"I want to talk with my mother," I answer. It's been thirty years since I've heard her voice—not just in dreams and apparitions but as an actual, physical sound. "Can we do it?"

Madelaine explains that it would be easier if we had some object of my mother's that held her aché. A ring. A photograph. Without them he'll try his best. And so we begin. For the next hour and a half I watch the El Cobre Spiritist who is both Juan and Madelaine weave the magic he hopes will entice my mother into the room—fumbling through piles of candles and saints for a slip of paper on which he asks me to write my mother's name; dropping it into a goblet filled with water made holy from smoke and prayers; blessing himself and Záhilys and me with the sharp perfume water he promises will protect us from nefarious souls who might try to latch onto us if we succeed in making contact with the spirit world.

Madelaine and Záhilys pray and sing, and their hymns sound like church. Madelaine's gravelly voice sings *Misericordia,* that strange sounding word for pity that fills the room with a sound that might break the very air in two. Záhilys' rises between his: *Oh Mother—hear my voice.* A reprieve.

The two of them exhort me to join in, insisting that without my voice their efforts to stir my mother will fail.

I search the inventory of my religious background for any practice that might strengthen the energy we are building. I shut my eyes, turn my palms up in my lap, but Madelaine chastises me for trying too hard.

"Piensa; piensa en tu mamá," Záhilys tells me. *Think of your mother.*
I close my eyes and sift through a river of images I know as much
from photographs as from memory. I see my mother kneeling over a
garden filled with jonquils. Everything in the image comes at me in
Kodachrome—the lush grass; the trumpet of the flower in pale, buttery
hues; the calyx just turning papery brown. My mother's hair is a brilliant
halo and her skirt fans around her in a cotton print that mimics the
scenery.

Another in which I join her outside our house in the Illinois countryside. A two-year-old naked except for a pair of white briefs, I lie on
my stomach before a blue and white metal swing set. This is before my
parents move the family to the St. Louis suburbs so my brother and sisters and I can attend private schools, move among more refined circles,
make something of ourselves. In this photo no one is trying hard. Both
my mother and I are simply playing the roles we occupy in the world:
she as Mother. I as Center of Her Universe.

The light streams over my mother's right shoulder, illuminating the
child in front of her. My golden hair curls around my face. I stare into the
lens of my father's camera. Neither self-conscious nor unaware of myself,
I am simply there, a child planted in her environment. Palms and knees
connected to the earth, I push my torso off the ground, the sole of one
foot kicking into the air as if to announce that at any moment I might
crawl out of the picture frame.

My mother is smiling, looking not at the camera but at me. And I
was mistaken about the direction of the light. It is not falling over her
shoulder but sliding past my own to illuminate *her.*

I have no idea what happens after the shutter clicks. It is only this
pose I hold onto: my mother watching over me, radiant in this brief
moment before I push off the ground and set out on my own.

"Say your mother's name," Záhilys tells me and motions for me to stand.
"It's time to call her into the room."

Mimi Meyers Huntman, I speak. Softly at first. Then more loudly. Finally, as if my life depends on it.

Mimi Meyers Huntman. The sound of my voice braids through the others in the room.

Mimi Meyers Huntman.

Oh Mother—hear my voice.

Hear my voice, Mother—hear my voice.

The air swells with the amplitude of our song. And then it isn't just our voices that fill the space between us but something else. An element new to the room breaks through as first Madelaine's body and then his eyes and then voice give way to El Cimarrón's. The Maroon bobs in his chair as he orients himself to the strangeness of Madelaine's bones and skin. Blinks as if trying to locate the thing he's come for. His eyes narrow as he settles on me. When he speaks, it is no longer Madelaine's voice but another, his words clipped and strange.

El Cimarrón brings a jícara to his lips to drink, gestures with his hands for Záhilys to light his cigar, widens his eyes in a way I recognize as the expression now familiar to me from the dancers I saw with Lourdes and in Regla.

"What does she want?" El Cimarrón asks Záhilys. His voice sounds either drunk or simply like that of a man caught between gravity and humor. His repetition of the question Madelaine and I began with almost two hours ago is a reminder that El Cimarrón is new to the conversation.

"She wants to talk with her mother," Záhilys answers. El Cimarrón takes in her words slowly as if to measure their weight, then he begins to cry. Not in the shamed way of grown men but in the unedited way of a child. His tears stream down his face. He dips his fingers into water and makes the sign of the cross on my forehead. He'll repeat these three gestures—tears, water, cross—every time any of us mentions my mother, and each time he does a look of great pain will come over his face, as if my pain is his. Later, Madelaine will tell me how El Cimarrón had to leave his wife and child in order to flee to the mountain palenques where he joined the fight to end slavery. All these years later, he cries for the loved ones he had to leave behind.

"You've come from far away," El Cimarrón announces in a manner that is also a question. "Are you a witch?" I smile as I think of Dorothy and the Wizard of Oz, and how some mistook her setting out from home as a form of witchcraft. I think about how removed I'd kept myself at every step of my own trip—from blood and from birds. From the dancers in Regla. Mostly from the one person with whom I most wanted contact.

"No, I'm not a witch," I tell El Cimarrón. As I say it, I am disappointed with my answer. I feel even now impossibly distant from my mother. No matter how hard I concentrate or how many times I say her name, her memory has faded every time I reach for her, the sound of her voice as distorted as the glass records she recorded seventy years before. The name she called me, Becki, just as distant. Since she'd died, I'd changed my name to Rebecca and then Rebe. No one called me Becki anymore. That first name floated in a faraway realm, as if it belonged not to me but to someone else, a girl who had had a mother.

"I'm going to help you," El Cimarrón announces. He turns his attention to a bowl filled with pebbles, picking over them until he's satisfied with the four in his hand, then releases them into the glass where Madelaine dropped the slip of paper with my mother's name. *Mimi Meyers Huntman*. It had been hours since I'd formed those letters with Madelaine's pencil. Hours since Madelaine had tried to read them, stumbling over the strangeness of the foreign name.

When El Cimarrón speaks again, his words come in a thick mix of Spanish and Bozal.

"El Cimarrón wants something of yours," Záhilys translates, "so he can call your mother into the room. A *prenda*," she adds. "A hair ornament. A piece of jewelry."

I touch my hands to my head and then my throat, and my fingers settle on the silver pendant I bought in Havana. I smile as I trace the raised image of Our Lady of Charity, her triangular form still holding the child who holds the world, loosen the black string for the first time since I first tied it around my neck, and hand the necklace to El Cimarrón. He prays over its silk and metal, washes both pendant and cord with cologne water, then slides them into the goblet—first silver, then cord disappearing, like the tail of a fish, under water. There the necklace joins the four stones that signal the opening of Eleggua's path and the paper that holds my mother's name, Our Lady's pendant resting alongside the other two. Stone and paper and silver tangle together in their own sort of holy trinity. The water that holds them has become the medium through which El Cimarrón hopes to communicate with my mother.

El Cimarrón turns his attention to the goblet before him. His brow furrows as he concentrates on calling my mother's spirit into the room. He clasps his head with his hands. I close my eyes and focus on my mother: the shape of her genuflecting before a garden filled with jonquils. A photograph where she watches over a toddler in briefs, taking note of each move as the child tries herself out. And there—sitting at the edge of my bed as she reads a bedtime story to me, her fingertips tracing the words she reads across my arms and back, the sound of her voice whispering "Have a sweet dream, Becki" before she turns out the light.

When I open my eyes, El Cimarrón is sitting straight in his chair. His eyes widen as if lit with a presence that wasn't there before. His hands cast about as if to unwrap something that lies in the air between us. His mouth works to form a sound: a stutter that with rehearsal becomes a name, strange and awkward as it takes shape for the first time in his mouth.

"Becki?" he speaks in a voice that comes through El Cimarrón but is my mother's.

It will be days before I cry. But it is here, with the speaking of my name, Becki—the only name my mother called me by, that girlish nickname she used before she died and I grew into Rebecca and then Rebe. A name that neither Madelaine nor El Cimarrón, so removed from any familiarity with American nicknames could possibly know—that I feel something. Not tears, but the thing that makes way for them. A crack. An opening. What I imagine Apolonia must have felt when Our Lady of Charity appeared before her on Miners' Hill. A presence she felt with her whole body. A voice ringing through her like a bell, letting her know she was not alone. The utterance of those two syllables feels just as impossible.

Becki.

"When your mother died, others were far away," El Cimarrón breaks through my reverie. I nod as I remember how my father and brother tried to protect my sisters and me from the reality that my mother was dying. How, sensing something wasn't right, I'd hopped into my car to drive from my college dorm room in Chicago to my mother's St. Louis hospital bed, arriving just in time for her to tell me, "My children are coming. My children are coming from Phoenix." How she died before my sisters, far away in Arizona, even knew to come.

"But you were there," El Cimarrón says. Again, I nod, remembering how awkward I'd felt in that hospital room. My mother seemed a stranger to me—a near skeleton pretending to be my mother. There is a particular light when I recall this scene, a haziness that is either hers or mine: my mother's hair askew; the seeming madness with which she grasped at thoughts and images invisible to the rest of us; a reluctance on my part to look head-on at what was happening. There was so much I still needed from my mother. And so, I'd searched the room for solid points, things that weren't dying, on which to fix my gaze. I'd focused on her rings, the one part of her that hadn't changed. A telephone next to her bed I told her reminded me of the one in my dorm room, that chance object the last image I'd held before I left the room.

I didn't stay to witness her dying. I raced back to my parents' house, nested myself among those things that still vibrated with her touch: her aprons still folded in the kitchen drawer; her winter boots waiting in the hall closet for her to step into.

"Your father helped your mother," El Cimarrón announces. And I think again of how devoted he was to her through her final months. That last night, the nurses had found him sitting at the edge of her hospital bed. In spite of all his experience in the funeral business, he'd faced even those last moments of my mother's death with all the hope and naïveté of a novice—holding her hand long after the woman it belonged to stopped breathing.

"Everything changed for you when your mother died," El Cimarrón offers, bobbing between great plumes of cigar smoke.

"Yes," I answer. "Everything changed." I remember the pain of her loss filling every breath, every motion of hand and foot and throat. And yet there at the end, in that hospital room when I still had her there before me—wavering, yes, but still there—it had been impossible for me to look directly at her. How to look at such a thing? The thing we work so hard to pretend doesn't happen happening right there in front of us. The body, once so firmly tethered to the life it holds, unspooling before our very eyes. The realization that it isn't just the mother who will soon be gone, but that we too will follow.

"When your mother died, you felt like you had to struggle alone," El Cimarrón continues. I nod as I think about how I'd pitted myself against the world: a grieving daughter fighting to prove she could make a life for herself. A single mother striving to raise a son. How alone I'd felt through it all.

"You're not alone," El Cimarrón tells me. "Our Lady is on your right illuminating you.

"Do you know who Our Lady is?" he asks, as if we're in the middle of a game show instead of a séance.

"Yes," I tell him, a child pleased to show off she knows the answer.

"Do you know who Ochún is?" El Cimarrón asks, pointing to the dresser-turned-altar where her figure—ebony black and naked to the waist—presides. Her gaze is directed across the room at a print of Our Lady of Charity framed modestly on the wall. The spot at her feet is strewn with the sunflowers that link the two mothers.

"Nature holds many mysteries," El Cimarrón tells me, puffing on the cigar clamped between his lips, its smoke filling the space between the two mothers who bookend the room.

Something lay at the juncture between them: Ochún and Our Lady's dark skin and sunflowers linking them with the fertile mysteries of the earth. The inverted moon beneath Our Lady's feet a nod to the mother's power over life and death—her ability to invert the order of things. To defy expectations. Appear and disappear.

A magic the girl named Becki had believed in without questioning—scanning the curves of the neighborhood creek for fossils I carried home in my pockets. Watching atoms dance in the air of my own backyard.

Just this morning, I'd set out after breakfast to buy flowers for the provisional boveda Jorge Luís suggested I make for my mother: a tangible shrine where I could talk with her, call her presence into the room. I'd followed Tatica's directions to an avenue of small stands where I'd deliberated over possibilities, settling on pink-red roses whose bright color made me think of her.

I'd set them in my window near Ochún's brass bell, hoping the sight of them might remind me to talk with my mother. The water in the goblet that held them a medium to summon her spirit. Her name—*Mimi Meyers Huntman*—written on a card to identify the spirit being called. Below it, the word *Mother*.

El Cimarrón motions for Záhilys to pick through the flowers at

Ochún's feet, bring the one that looks like it's folded from silver foil gum wrappers to him.

"This flower is from Ochún," he tells me. "Take it home with you and take care of it like you would a child."

"Of course," I answer. I finger its silvery petals, thrilled to have a piece of this room to call my own.

"You're a cimarrón," he tells me, pointing to a line of machetes that adorn the wall. Their crescent blades make me think both of Our Lady's half-moon and of Ogún, the hunter-blacksmith who uses his machete to cut through any obstacle in our way.

What did it mean to be the kind of woman who might yield such a knife? For the past thirty years, I'd thought I had to choose between tears or strength, grief or sanity. Between keeping my mother at a distance or succumbing to the pain that came with inviting her in. I'd believed that to give in to my tears would be to be engulfed by them, to drown in a pool of crazy from which I might never return.

Here with El Cimarrón—this warrior who'd taken to the hills with his machete, who was not afraid to feel the pain of all he'd left behind— another door opened. A kind of sanity that was inclusive enough to embrace both the machete and the tears. A way to hold my mother close without losing my way.

"I'll take care of your camino," El Cimarrón assures me, his head bobbing. "Do you want me to take care of your path?"

"Sí," I answer.

"Sí, Señor," he corrects, and he blows smoke in a way that makes it difficult to know if he is being stern or comical. He dips his fingers into the water with my mother's name and paints the sign of the cross with it on my forehead.

"El Cimarrón takes care of all," he announces. "God accompanies you. Our Lady accompanies you. El Cimarrón accompanies you. Whenever you're in doubt over something, don't lose your head but call on the spirits."

A change in the room. The air thins as Madelaine returns to his body and El Cimarrón slips away. No longer does the man before me bob and sway. The Spiritist sits straight in his chair. His eyes settle first on Záhilys, then me, then the goblet.

It is the goblet that holds his attention. Something new in the arrangement of pendant and paper and stone.

"What do you see?" he asks, waving for Záhilys and me to look from his vantage point.

"I don't see anything," Záhilys answers.

Madelaine shakes his head, disappointed. "What do you see?" he asks, turning to me.

I stare at the water, narrowing my eyes until I see what he sees. There, where the cord from Our Lady's pendant floats above my mother's name, it has formed two perfect loops.

"The letter M," I tell him. "M for Mimi. For Madre. For Mother."

I move through the afternoon like a woman who holds a secret too precious to speak out loud, smiling each time I replay the last hours with Madelaine in my head—the loops of Our Lady's necklace settling at the bottom of his glass to form the letter M; the sound of my mother's name and then my own filling the room.

In spite of not having any of my mother's possessions with me, in spite of my lack of familiarity with the Spiritist misa or my shyness about singing, Madelaine had succeeded in reaching through the membrane between worlds. He'd touched the other side, made contact with my mother. She had spoken to me, let me know she looked out for me. She remembered my name.

But as afternoon turns to night, I feel a sort of ennui settle over me like a damp rag. I go to bed without waiting for dinner and wake several hours later to a room filled with shadows and a distinct sense of another presence, hostile and cold, in the room. Pinpricks raise the hair on my arms and neck. A chill curls along my spine. Across my body I feel the needling sensation of something boring into my skin and teeth.

El Cobre was a haunted town, Julio had told me. Its streets and homes swirled with the spirits of those who'd come to work or administer its mines. When Madelaine had first met Záhilys, she'd told him that when she looked in her mirror, she sometimes saw a man with bloodshot eyes staring back at her. When Madelaine called on the spirits who'd occupied the house to ask why this man was haunting Záhilys, they told him there were unholy objects buried under the patio. Until those things were removed, the man in Záhilys's mirror would continue to haunt her. And when Madelaine dug under the patio, it was exactly as the spirits had said. He found the cursed bones and offerings that needed to be excavated so the spirits could stop their haunting.

"Are you all right?" Rick had asked in the months before I'd left for Cuba. He worried as he watched me immerse myself in the activity of digging up my own past—scouring my mother's journals and calendars, listening to the glass records that held her operatic voice, searching for any bit of my mother she might have left behind in their grooves.

"Is this healthy?" he'd asked when he saw how much I was living between worlds, dreaming night and day of a mother who'd been dead nearly thirty years. I'd reacted defensively, unsure if my attempts to resurrect my mother were healthy or not, only knowing it was something I needed to do.

I'd gone to Madelaine's this afternoon to summon her; had joined in song and prayer; searched my own religious repertoire for ways to strengthen our efforts, turning my palms upward to invite the spirits I was familiar with to join the force field we were creating together in the room.

What else had we stirred in the process? Since I'd arrived in Cuba, I'd been reminded—by Daniel and Maruchi, and now Madelaine—that life feeds on life. It was the blood of animals that gave sustenance to the oricha so they could join us in the physical world, the breath of our utterances that called the spirits forth. Not all those spirits were benevolent. And in that house filled with bones and bells, Madelaine had opened a doorway between worlds, creating a fissure through which spirits of all types might fly.

"I'll feel it in my bones," I'd told Rick when we'd first spoken of Madelaine. Were the entities I now felt part of my imagination, or were they as real as they felt?

I grew up in a house that did not acknowledge its hauntings. An oppressive weight hung over our family—especially the women—to be perfect. Masculinity wound its way through the house like a threat, taking shape in my father's criticism and lists, his affairs, his guns. His favorite oil painting, which he'd bought at auction and hung over the den couch, depicted a masked robber forcing another man at gunpoint to empty his pockets. It was enough to put all who passed before it on alert. The painting I think of as my mother's hung on the opposite wall and showcased a vase spilling over with bright sunflowers in various stages of bloom and decay. Any message of those flowers' agency was mitigated by the pressure my mother felt to follow someone else's sun: to be the perfect wife and mother; the perfect seamstress and cook, hostess, storyteller. Perfect even in her dying. Apologetic to the end for the way her body failed her.

After my mother died, my father swore she haunted him, but not in the reassuring way she came to me. She fucked with my father—rearranging dishes in the pantry. Switching the way the toilet paper unrolled, not from the underside as my father had always insisted on its being set, but from the top, as if finally in death she might take back some power. But the way my mother really got my father's attention was at night when she quaked the hallway that led to their bedroom. My father swore she shook those walls so fiercely that the family photographs we'd hung there came crashing down. Among them, all those carefully curated portraits he'd had my mother pose for—chin here, shoulders there, don't forget to smile—their pieces re-arranging themselves as they hit the floor. The most daring among them fell into the shards of frames that held another mother, my father's mother Antonia.

My grandmother Antonia was our family's greatest ghost. We never spoke about the fact that she'd been mentally ill—a woman so out of sorts, so unable to control her emotions, so *hysterical,* that first her husband and then her son, my father, had institutionalized her for months at a time. Nor did we talk about the final act in which she took her life, shooting herself in the chest with a .22 Sentinel one day before her 75th birthday. The only story we told about Antonia was a heavily edited one. We cooked her ravioli, hung her picture in the hallway where her fashionable suits and ostrich-plumed hats testified to the kind of decorum we all might aspire to.

That Antonia had the power to break through the frames that held her messy bits, to come crashing off the walls, seemed as terrifying as anything else I knew about her. For no matter how much I resisted the idea of a neat and ordered life, I counted myself among those who strove to conform to its norms. My own failures to do so loomed larger even than my predecessors': two divorces; a thousand ways I felt myself come up short as I tried to parent my son alone.

Stoking these moments of self-flagellation was a broader aggression that met me in both my waking hours and my sleep. It had begun when I was a girl when in my nightmares the masked robber of my father's painting would step out of the frame and force me at gunpoint to kneel at his feet. The threat of violence had carried on to the flawed men I'd dated and married as well as those I barely knew. Strangers who, uninvited, forced their hands and mouths on me. The first among them the man in Puerto Angel who'd shadowed me, mere hours after my mother had held me in those threatening waters, down the hill from the hotel.

A feeling of heaviness had assaulted me since I'd arrived in Santiago.

It came from Soviet motorcycles tearing through narrow streets, announcing themselves with a blare of horns but never slowing. It was there in the violent history that permeated Parque Céspedes, which held the home of Governor Diego Velásquez, its stone walls built by slaves and its corner furnace burning with ill-gotten riches. It was in the sun that held the city like a forge. Baking somewhere at its white-hot center were my fears that the spiritual beliefs and practices I was opening up to in Cuba might land me in the same boat with Antonia—that I'd be branded as too outside the established norms. A crazy woman. A witch.

I could feel the weight of all those things pressing in on me. Taunting me from every corner of the room. Swinging from the ceiling. Dangling from walls. I could sense them closing in on me—parasites clinging to my scalp and nails, feeding on my flesh.

For the second time today, I search the inventory of my religious experience for any shield that might protect me from the specters in the room. I sift through Buddhist meditations and Congregational prayers before landing on the fierce invocations I'd learned at the Pentecostal church I'd briefly attended almost a decade ago.

"Demons be gone!" I shout.

If I weren't so frightened, I might find the words melodramatic, even comical. But I'm terrified. I utter the words slowly and deliberately the way I was taught, focusing on what both Pentecostal preachers and Santería priests had wanted me to understand—that I was the head and not the tail. Madelaine had called me a cimarrón. Told me I was not alone. That I was not to lose my mind but call on the spirits.

"In the name of Christ!" I shout, still in Pentecostal mode, into a room thick with shadows. "You're not welcome here!"

And then: "In the name of Eleggua, Guardian of the Threshold!

"And in the name of Obatalá, Prince of Light.

"In the name of Our Lady, Nuestra Señora de la Caridad, and in the name of Ochún," I continue, my supplications gaining strength with each refrain.

"In the name of Mimi Meyers Huntman," I add, remembering that it is not just the gods but the ancestors who protect us.

"In the name of my mother's mother Josephine Grubel and her mother Lillian Horn."

And, as if I might rescue us both from the shadows, I add, "In the name of Antonia," the strength of my voice filling the darkness until whatever demons lurk there begin to loosen their hold.

[*16*]

GOD LIVES

I WAKE TO SUNLIGHT streaming through the open shutters of my room, washing away the last of my nightmares and reminding me that today is a new day. The documentary filmmaker Roberto has suggested we take a break from all things Virgin and Mother for a day of sightseeing before Our Lady's pilgrimages begin. We've arranged for Tomás to take us, with stops at the Gran Piedra and its neighboring coffee plantation, Cafetal Isabélica.

The trick is getting there. Located on the southeast edge of Santiago de Cuba, the 63,000-ton boulder known as the Big Rock teeters from its mountain perch, like something straight out of a Dr. Seuss book. Its origin has been attributed to everything from ancient geological shifts and underwater volcano eruptions to the strike of a meteorite. Regardless of how it came into being, the resulting landscape forms a convenient plateau. Set high over a panorama of mountains and coastline, it's an inviting destination for the tourists and hikers who dare risk the climb. On a clear night, Roberto tells me, one can see the gleam of lights coming all the way from Haiti.

The first leg up the mountain is a steep drive. The scenery along the way is filled with orchids and pines, the air with mist. We pass the occasional herd of sheep grazing at the side of the road. A man on horseback. A pig. A sign cut into rock above a stream that reads "God Lives." But otherwise, it feels bare of human presence.

When we finish the paved part of the climb, Tomás lets Roberto and I out of the Lada. We continue on foot, following the red dirt path to the 452 stone steps that lead up the face of the great rock. I don't tell

Roberto I'm terrified of heights. Nor do I tell him how those fears are inextricably woven into an even greater fear, the mountain a metaphor for all the warnings my parents instilled in me about failing to live up to my potential and falling onto the jagged rocks of mediocrity.

Fueled in equal parts by my desire to take in the majesty of the place and my fear of missing out—another form of failure—I will myself to keep going. I cling to the iron railing that supports us during the final and steepest steps, and then we emerge onto a shelf of rock to find a sky dotted with clouds, both the coastline and the Sierra Maestra laid at our feet.

With a pair of binoculars, one might trace an entire history in that view. The stone walls of El Morro, the Spanish fortress built by enslaved men, juts from the cliffs that flank the Santiago Bay. Its cannons, still poised to ward off pirates who once patrolled these waters, rust under sea air. Roberto, who grew up in Santiago, laughs as he recounts the rough beginnings that shaped the city, even though much of it is grisly. Lured by gold they'd seen adorning the necks and wrists of the native population, the Spanish had made their first capital here in the east, recruiting the Taíno to bring them gold, cutting off their hands if they brought less than what was required, unleashing dogs on those who tried to escape. After exhausting the shallow supplies of one ore, the Spanish turned their sights toward the silver of Mexico, moving their Cuban capital to Havana to establish a port more strategically proximate to their new center of wealth.

Everything I know about Santiago supports this image of a city left to fend for itself: its merciless heat and congested streets; the wreckage left from Hurricane Sandy, which included Roberto's house. When I'd gone to visit, I'd found its roof gone and most of the second floor destroyed. Without it, Roberto and his elderly parents had relocated their sleeping quarters to the living room where they camped on cots.

And yet it was here in the oriente—among cannons and hurricanes, pirates and thieves—that Our Lady first appeared. And here in the east that the mother claimed her place over the copper mines of El Cobre. Under her vigil that miners and revolutionaries fought and won their wars against those who tried to subjugate them.

Our second destination takes us downhill over red dirt and rock. The vegetation on either side of our path is dense with banana trees and birds of paradise. Through its greenery the Cafetal Isabélica materializes like a mirage from the monte.

Built in 1812 by a French landowner who fled the Haitian slave revolution, the coffee plantation has been roughly restored, if not to its previous glory, then to an approximation of how it once might have looked. A young guide in a blazer and heels appears, like a second mirage, from one of the outbuildings. Roberto and I are the only visitors. Still, she takes her time with us, showing us the stone slabs where coffee beans were once laid to dry; the cramped stone quarters that housed the humans responsible for the labor to grow and harvest and process those beans. An iron bell, hung from porch rafters, still holds the memory of its former clamor: one cadence to ring the start of the workday, another to pronounce its end. A third, more insistent, to sound the alarm of a runaway slave. An arched doorway at the side of the house, covered in lichen, leads to tunnels where dogs trained to hunt those cimarrones were kept.

Even the interior of the home feels aggressive. Its parlor is filled with stiff tables and cane-backed rockers. A lace tablecloth and a piano in the corner provide a veneer of civility to a system based on keeping by force those who yearned not to be kept. But it isn't until the guide leads us to an outer workshop—its walls lined with shackles and machetes, an impression carved into the center of its floor, deep and round—that I feel the fuller force of the horror that happened here.

"The purpose of the hole," the guide tells us, "was to accommodate the prone belly of a pregnant slave, so she could be whipped without causing damage to the future property of the plantation.

"And why might she be punished?" the guide asks, as if reciting from a script, then continues without pausing for our answer.

She points to the iron instruments that line the walls. "For attempting to escape so that her child might not be a slave."

For being a woman, I whisper to myself. I think about the women who were made to lower their belly into the hole before me. Not belly, I correct myself, but womb—that watery home in which we are first given shape; that most holy of vessels where, even as she bent before her master and laid herself into this hole, a woman was creating life.

I do not pretend to know what it's like to kneel before a hole like the one I see carved in the floor before me. I am not a nineteenth-century enslaved woman in Cuba. My ancestors were not shackled and forced onto the boats that brought them to America. They crossed the Atlantic willingly, their eyes lit with excitement for the lives they would build and the children they would raise. And so I do not know what it's like to literally not own my body. This is a level in the hierarchy of patriarchal power that I—as a middle-class white North American woman—cannot know.

What I know is not the depth of the hole before me but its shape—both the shape of the woman who bends before it and the man who stands over her. This understanding has come to me through thousands of messages, small and large, silent and spoken, delivered through movies and television ads, glossy fashion magazines and pulp fiction romance novels—their heroines in turn impossibly thin or voluptuous, childlike or profane. The impossible lists my father felt no shame reciting before my mother and sisters and me, each item ticked off his tongue reminding us that as women our bodies were not fully ours to control. The very word "woman"—from the Old English *wimman*, literally "woman-man,

an altered form of *wifman*," meaning "woman, female servant," a com-
pound of *wif* "woman" + *man*—its own kind of vivisection.

Like my mother before me and her mother before her, I learned that
the arrangement of my body was not solely mine to decide. I absorbed
the knowledge that the various parts that made up our figures were as
malleable as those Barbies I once twisted into preposterous configura-
tions, our limbs and torsos a thing to curate so we might appear more
agreeable—as in careful not to offend (smile, be polite); and impress
(look, how pretty!). Our bodies were a prize to be cinched and adorned,
embellished with paint and gold. A thing that with just the right measure might achieve an artistry that might stir the heart, elevate all of
humankind.

But the body was also a thing to rein in. The mouth not an instrument of expression but of agreement. Its ideal shape an *O*. Its sound a
great moan. Still, it was important never to appear as if we were asking
for something, even—or especially—if it was something we wanted. We
were to make ourselves small—as in, soft voice and hands. As in, willing
and kind. As in, careful not to spill over our own edges, appear to be too
much. As in, don't take up too much space.

I watched my mother pin dress patterns to the gridlines of her cardboard sewing board. Cover the neck my father found unsightly with turtlenecks and scarves. Fill her dresser drawers with garters and girdles, her
body a thing she must literally gird herself against. Still, she expanded
beyond her borders, losing and gaining the same forty pounds over and
over. Stuffing her feelings only to have them explode in front of unsus-
pecting store clerks and family members.

"Control yourself," I'd heard my father tell my mother whenever
her voice grew too loud. As in, keep it together. As in, be cool. Don't go
flying off the handle. Whatever you do, don't become hysterical—from
the Greek *hystera,* meaning womb. Originally defined as a neurotic con-
dition peculiar to women and thought to be caused by a dysfunction of
the uterus, the word "hysteria" was coined to describe a general sense of
excess emotion or excitement.

"Stop being hysterical," my father told my mother when she railed
against his affairs.

"What will the neighbors think?" when her protests got so loud they seeped beyond the borders of house and yard.

This problem of containing the body got handed from mother to daughter. My mother and I giggled with equal parts of glee and shame as we licked cake frosting or cookie batter off the spoon, aware without ever naming them of the unspoken pacts that governed our lives—that to eat was both a treat and a sin. This having a body, the flesh and curves of it, was a thing to moderate, an object to be fed and starved in turns.

The practice of these postures was so familiar many of us had forgotten to question them. Either from habit or indoctrination, we'd bought into their messages. We'd tweezed and plucked our unruly bits, suctioned our fat and our emotions. Sacrificed whole parts of ourselves as we conformed to another's specifications, adopted their templates as our own. We were daughters and wives with fathers and husbands we were not to disappoint. But the largest demands were reserved for the mother. She was to be selfless and chaste. Empty herself of all but her devotion and compassion. Feed the world from her breast.

How much pressure my mother must have felt to live up to such lofty expectations! The pressure my own stories about her only added to their weight, placing on her the additional demand that she be the great shining mother, the one who holds us all. What about those times she didn't fit the mold? The times I hated her—for frightening me, as my grandmother Antonia had, her unpredictable emotions threatening to undo us all. For disappointing me whenever she fell short of the impossible expectations we placed on her, not least among them our demand that she live forever.

I'd felt a similar constricting pressure raising Alex. I'd persecuted myself every step of the way. Internalized judgments offered by strangers and loved ones alike—that I was in turns too attentive or too self-absorbed, my mothering either too strong or too weak.

Again, and again—as mothers and wives and daughters and sisters, neighbors and coworkers—our bodies failed to live up to the demands stacked against them. We were too fat or too thin; too present or too aloof. Too meek. Too bold. Too selfish. Too spineless. Too easy. Too uptight.

Our punishments were as numerous as our crimes. We were under-estimated and undervalued, dismissed and pitied, patted and underpaid. Both our flesh and spirit had been fetishized and commodified, while the life-giving powers of our womb were demonized, made pornographic or into a cartoon, a joke: the vulva no longer the sacred gateway of the ancients but a pussy with teeth.

Our personhood was rebuked for not getting the joke, not knowing how to play the game (not being better sports about it). Our stories edited to fit someone else's narrative, those unredacted parts that held our last unbroken bits maligned, beaten, stalked, raped, bartered and traded, sold and enslaved.

And here before me! This dark gaping hole where the mother had been made to kneel again and again before the master. I imagine the man who stood over her—arm raised, eyes flashing with a hatred that masked the fear beneath it. Fear that this vessel beneath his feet, this woman with the power to generate life from the void, was not his to own.

With every step to the car, I feel the heaviness of the cafetal mixing with the nightmares from the night before—the masked robber who stepped out of my father's painting; the curly-haired man who stalked a ten-year-old in a swimsuit striped and starred like a flag. All of it collapses into that giant hole. And still the abyss threatened to swallow more: the harsh masculinity surrounding Governor Diego Velásquez's home, its furnace stoked by the fiercest violence—both against the men and women forced to excavate its ore and the ground they stripped it from. Like the crater from the El Cobre mines filled with water too toxic to touch, the crimes against the mother were also crimes against the Earth.

"You hate men," Rick tells me whenever he detects in my tirades a particular mix of fear and anger, and his voice is both sad and matter-of-fact. Most times I protest that I love men, even if it's hard to separate my love from my anger. My father had been critical and disappointing. His affairs and perfectionist views about women left permanent marks on my mother, sisters, and me. But he had also been creative and generous. A selfless father who had dived into the ocean to save a drowning wife and daughter. A devoted husband who dedicated the last months of his wife's life to her care. He had good politics, waved to strangers, could dance a mean jitterbug. It was he who'd encouraged me to learn Spanish, who'd taught me to be curious about the world and unafraid to venture into it. In spite of his flaws, he had been my one and only father.

Meanwhile, Rick helped me remember that not all men were so complicated. Rick was a man who leaned into his responsibilities. A bison. There wasn't anything he wouldn't do for either of his children, now in their twenties, or his dog Skip. I was coming to believe there wasn't much he wouldn't do for me.

Walking at my side was another good man. Roberto worked tirelessly to provide for his family and to help his parents rebuild their house. He'd given this day to show me the sights, and in only two days would accompany me to Our Lady's pilgrimage. We hardly speak as we follow the path back to the car but I feel his presence at my side—the firm set of his shoulders, the vigilance with which he scours the path for potential dangers. Both the strength and tenderness of these gestures remind me that in the Yoruba cosmos nothing is just one thing. Even attributes like masculine and feminine are not relegated to gender. Mothers and warriors alike could be both sweet and strong. Ochún used her waters to give and take life. The warrior-blacksmith Ogún used the power of his forge to make both weapons and tools. Eleggua used his position as gatekeeper to open as well as shut the doors along our path.

"I've got you," Roberto tells me, a flesh-and-blood Eleggua volunteering his arm each time we hit a patch of loose rocks in a sign of protection that nods not toward possession but partnership.

After years of living on our own, it was this notion of partnership that Rick and I were reaching toward. The most powerful gift he offered me was his insistence that I show up before him unedited and whole. Let him see exactly who I was. No man had ever asked such a thing of me, nor had I asked it of myself. After years of censoring my messy bits—costuming myself in postures and garments to show off my best angles, always striving to frame myself in the best light—the idea of such honesty felt both liberating and terrifying.

Rick offered no promises that he would like what he saw, or that he would stay no matter what my nakedness revealed. Only that he would stand just as honestly before me. That if we were going to have a shot together, we had to show each other what we were made of.

Now, with Roberto, I hold out my palms to receive the breath of the mountain as I focus on my own breath, that simple, life-affirming act that so many spiritual masters have called attention to. The breath a way to center the mind in meditation. A reminder to pause and revel in the feel of one's self inside its skin. I make my way slowly, noticing the way my feet press into the red earth—heel to toe, each step anchoring me for a moment before moving on. At my sides, butterflies flutter through birds of paradise. Overhead I hear the flicker of carpenter birds and royal thrushes, wild pigeons and tocororos.

God lives, someone thought to carve into the rock below us. Underfoot, mimosa blossoms spring open and shut. How miraculous, I think, that these wondrous flowers can grow so close to the remains of such a wicked place.

17

OUR LADY

WE LEAVE EARLY IN the morning for Our Lady's festivities, Roberto and his father Luís in the front seat of a rented Hyundai, me in the back. The gearshift is inlaid with the image of Our Lady. "A sign," Roberto says, grinning. I grin back at him, and my whole body rings with anticipation. This is the day. The one that has marked my calendar since I first read about Our Lady. All the plans for the trip, all the rituals I'd taken part in, have led to this day when I might witness what devotion to the mother looked like when it showed up in the tens of thousands.

I am not alone in my enthusiasm. Luís fills the car with talk about the priests he knows at the sanctuary and the pilgrimages he's attended in the past. Roberto reminds us that he shares this day with Our Lady. At midnight, the candle he lights will honor both his birthday and hers. I look from father to son. Roberto's hair is clipped short, his face smooth and clean-shaven. By contrast, his father is wiry and wild, his blue eyes framed by a ramble of orange and white hair, the rest of his face all eyebrows and mustache. Still, there is a similarity between them. They are proud men—proud of the work they do as cameramen, of the way they look out for family and friends. They've signed on to accompany me to Our Lady's celebrations not just as cameramen but companions.

Our car is packed with overnight bags, cameras and tripods. Our itinerary is carefully planned and ambitious. The seven o'clock parade from El Cobre's Parque Antolín Cebreco to the sanctuary will launch a twenty-four-hour cycle of masses in honor of Our Lady. Before the activities get underway, we'll stop to check into the home where we've arranged to stay, then go to film Our Lady's sanctuary before the crowds begin to arrive. From there, we'll visit Madelaine.

"Come back in a couple of days," the Spiritist had told me. He'd wanted me to leave Our Lady's pendant to marinate in whatever magic had congregated in the waters of the goblet that held it. Now it was time to return, and not just for the pendant. Madelaine had prepared something else for me. "Something," he'd told me, "so your mother will be with you wherever you go."

Our hosts are waiting on the porch of their farmhouse when we arrive. They are the children and grandchildren of the doctor who built this home in the countryside near El Cobre. The family matriarch Alina is the first to welcome us. In her sixties, with brown hair and motherly eyes, she guides me by the arm through the property, pointing out the yard where goats and chickens graze among laundry lines and fruit trees. The farmhouse was built in the 1950s, and the surrounding acreage is used by the family to grow lettuce and ocher. The renting of rooms to Our Lady's pilgrims is just one of the many ways the family cobbles together a living.

Alina pats my arm as she shows me the makeshift suite of rooms at the side of the house that will serve as our home base during the festival: an air-conditioned room with a private bath where I can rest between masses, and an adjoining room where we can take our meals. There's a second bedroom inside the main part of the house for Roberto and his father.

Less than a mile away, separated by fields of lettuce and mango groves, lies Our Lady's sanctuary. Its red cupolas and yellow walls are visible through the tree branches of Alina's yard.

"When my mother lived here," she tells me, "these trees weren't planted yet, and she had a clear view of the sanctuary from the porch.

"She told me this spot was blessed," Alina adds, "and that we were blessed to live here."

As I stand with Alina, her arm still linked with mine, the blessing her mother spoke of feels almost palpable. Its promise hangs like a blanket of protection over the family's livestock and fields. It glimmers over the dogs I see chasing each other through the yard. In the dirt beneath our feet, red with the copper that inundates this place, a reminder of the miners and cimarrones to whom the Virgin first showed herself. It was here, just beyond these trees, that Our Lady announced she wanted her temple to be built. The image she left so bright, so mysterious, it lit the skies. And she was right there still, waiting on the other side of these branches.

Both the sanctuary and the inn that adjoins it are humming when we arrive. In the snack shop workers are busy making ham and cheese sandwiches to sell to hungry pilgrims. The glass cases of a souvenir shop gleam with statues and rosaries, key chains and posters, stickers and T-shirts printed with last year's slogan: *La Caridad Nos Une 1612-2012,* a celebration of four hundred years of unity under Our Lady's watch.

On the sanctuary steps two men carrying digital cameras and a portable mini printer, their baseball hats outfitted with hand-lettered signs that read *fotos al momento,* ask if we'd like our picture taken for a souvenir photo. But we're here to make a different kind of recording. I have shared my hopes for these days with both Roberto and Luís—that I've come to discover what devotion for the mother looks like when it's enacted by multitudes; that I'd like, too, to better know the mother who could inspire such an outpouring—and I've seen the flush of excitement on the faces of both father and son at the prospect of capturing such a thing on film.

Now Luís and I fan out among the handful of pilgrims who've begun to gather before the mother. Our cameras catch the lighting of a candle; the movement of hands and lips in prayer; the face of a child turned to peer at us from her mother's lap. Near the altar, Roberto searches for the best angles to film the Virgin herself, zooming in through his telescopic lens to catch a softness in her features, a spark in her eye, that are not perceptible from the ground.

When we finish, we head to Madelaine's. There is handshaking and a professing on all sides about how much this meeting means to everyone involved. Then Madelaine leaves the two men to entertain themselves in the parlor and leads me to his workroom. The goblet of water that holds Our Lady's pendant is still on the dresser where we left it. Madelaine and I seat ourselves before it and it feels like I'm sitting across from an old friend.

Madelaine reaches for an object that I hadn't seen on my last visit: a *güiro*, the dried round hollowed fruit of the calabash tree used to make drinking cups and maracas. The one Madelaine holds is mounted onto a wooden base like a trophy. Its outsides are polished to bring out patterns of brown and gray that remind me of a turtle's shell. Crowning its top is a carved statuette of Our Lady that Madelaine has glued there. Across its front he has painted *Mimi Meyers Huntman* in red, the letters of my mother's name still sticky to the touch.

"I've never made anything like this for anyone," Madelaine tells me. "But there was something about your need to have your mother with you that told me I needed to do this for you." He shakes the güiro so it rattles, names the plants and grains he's placed inside. "Basil and maravilla to open your path and light your way." Other plants too secret to name.

"More important than the herbs," Madelaine tells me, "is the thing I've added just for you.

"The depths of your mother's heart are inside," he announces, tapping the sides of the güiro so I might hear their sound.

Madelaine passes the precious object to me. I shake it, listening for my mother's voice in its rattle before cradling it in my lap. *I will never let you go*, I think, the same promise my mother made to me all those years ago, and that I had made to Alex when he was young.

Next, Madelaine reaches for the water goblet. He holds it to the light so I can see how both pendant and cord have settled at the bottom of the glass, forming not just the letter M we saw the other day but also, how the outer lines of the M meet to complete the shape of a heart.

He dips his fingers into the water to retrieve the necklace. Sprinkles it with perfume and prayers, pats it dry, then loops the cord around my neck. I feel the weight of silver as Our Lady's image settles at my collarbone, her triangular robes held within the circle that echoes the shape of the güiro I hold in my lap. Both of those spheres reference the gourd that once housed the two halves of the world. And when I think about how snugly those two halves held one another, it reminds me of that familiar church refrain: *As above, so below.*

Madelaine marks my hands and forehead with a cross he makes with cascarilla, sprinkles perfume on my palms and brow.

"Your mother's spirit is with you now," he tells me. "Any time you want to talk with her, you only need to give the güiro a shake and you will feel her with you.

"And she is here in your pendant whenever you wear it.

"Wherever you go, you have her with you.

"Your mother is with you. Our Lady is with you." He points to where he's glued Our Lady's figure above my mother's name.

"Ochún is with you.

"El Cimarrón is with you."

The table at Alina's is piled with lunch when we return—plates of roasted chicken and homegrown avocado, mango and plantain. While we eat, Luís entertains us with stories about his latest efforts to rebuild their second floor. He notices me marveling over the food and pauses, his blue eyes twinkling under wiry eyebrows. He's curious about what we eat in the United States. Specifically, he wants to know about McDonald's. "Is it good?"

I hesitate before answering, mulling over the difference between tasty and nourishing. I look at the chicken on our plates, caught fresh from the yard outside our door, and wonder if anything could be stranger in this place than the thought of a McDonald's nugget, the bird that gave its life for it processed to the point of unrecognizability.

"Millions of Americans love McDonald's," I tell Luís, "but it isn't good like this food is good. There's nothing subtle about it. Its flavor relies on grease and sugar and salt. Certainly, it isn't good for you."

Roberto and Luís don't say a word and I worry I've offended them. I think of the two men camping on cots in the living room while they wait for supplies to rebuild all they lost in the hurricane. How easy it is for me to romanticize this island that makes so much from so little. And yet there is an abundance here that surpasses anything I see in my own country—a generosity in the way people open their homes and hearts to one another; a luxury in the way time slows down and allows you to savor the moment. Even today, with so much ahead of us, we've taken time to sit together and enjoy this meal, every bite of it organic and fresh and whole. The sun warms our skin. The scent of the perfume water Madelaine blessed me with wafts from my neck and hands. The weight of Our Lady's pendant at my throat reminds me of the fullness of the world.

"We have so much in our country," I say, "and we don't always appreciate what we have. We're too busy thinking about the next best, next biggest thing. So that, even when we're surrounded by more than enough, we want more."

It's not lost on me that what I've just said about racing to the next thing personifies the three of us as we leave the lunch table to rush, full of anticipation and expectation, toward the next leg of our day. Our plan is for Roberto to drive Luís back to Santiago so he can film a group of pilgrims as they begin their twelve-mile march on foot from their home church in Santiago to Our Lady's sanctuary in El Cobre. But the two of them are barely out of Alina's driveway before I am imagining what it will feel like to witness those pilgrims as they arrive before Our Lady.

It is this march of the faithful that had sparked my desire to come to Cuba. I'd pictured them arriving, as I'd read, in the thousands——many on their hands and knees—and wondered what kind of devotion, what kind of piety for the mother, could inspire such reverence.

Before dawn, Roberto and I will return for Luís so the three of us can welcome the pilgrims as they near the sanctuary. In the meantime, Roberto and I plan to focus on El Cobre, beginning with the 7 p.m. motorcade that will carry Our Lady's twin effigy, the Virgen Mambisa, from the square to the sanctuary to kick off twenty-four hours of masses and celebration.

Normally on display at a cathedral in Santiago, the Virgen Mambisa acts as a stand-in at festivals and parades for Our Lady, who is too precious to leave her glass case. Dressed in Our Lady's hand-me-down dresses and jewels, the Mambisa has twice toured the nation, the first time in 1951. The same year marked the lead up to the fiftieth anniversary of the pre-Castro Cuban Republic, and, as it happens, the fifth wedding anniversary that brought my parents to Havana.

I doubt if my parents were aware of Our Lady's cross-country procession when they booked their trip to Cuba, but I like to think they might have run across her. The celebrations were prodigious, with speeches, postage stamps, and parades to commemorate the republic. The year-long tour of the Mambisa was a crowning piece of the spectacle. As her motorcade took the streets, her golden dress and nimbus sparkled against a backdrop of gambling casinos and mob-run hotels. The three Juanes at her feet were a reminder to all who gazed at her of her miraculous apparition at the Bay of Nipe. Proof that this land was a blessed one. Her jeweled rosary was in her right hand. In her left, the child who will wash the world of its sins.

It's 6:30 when Roberto and I arrive at the square, where we find the first of Our Lady's devotees gathering in the dusk. A handful of nuns huddle under umbrellas to escape the light rain that has begun. Families congregate under the overhang of roofs. A group of altar boys stand in the open, their white tunics draped like knapsacks over their shoulders, as if they're on a field trip rather than a holy assignment. Once the archbishop arrives with the motorcade van, these boys will throw their tunics over their heads and pick up the crucifix at their feet. Their expressions will turn solemn as they transform from town boys to leaders of Our Lady's procession. But until then, they are just boys, filling the space between them with jokes and pranks. And until the archbishop arrives, the town of El Cobre is just a town. Groups of men smoke cigarettes in shorts and flip-flops, their backs pressed against the walls of the police station. Women with their heads wrapped in curlers and headscarves hold babies in their arms. Others watch over small children who pull at their hands and legs. Among the crowd I spot a few familiar faces. I see Madelaine and Záhilys, who look oddly pedestrian away from the context of their painted house, and the historian Julio wearing a red baseball cap and talking animatedly with a friend.

Above us the sky darkens with storm clouds. A mother calls for her daughter to watch out when crossing the street. A dog laps water from a gutter. And then the van arrives, Our Lady's Mambisa twin, jeweled and resplendent inside a glass case mounted to its roof.

A pair of speakers statics the air with a call to fall in line. The altar boys rush to take their position at the head of the motorcade. The tallest one hoists their cross from the ground to his breast, and the rest come behind him with their lamps held at their waists. The crowd fills in the spaces at the sides and back of the van and we begin our march toward the sanctuary.

"*Señora de la Caridad del Cobre, ruega por nosotros!*" a voice booms from the speakers mounted to the van as the archbishop leads us in the first of many chants and songs.

"Our Lady of El Cobre, pray for us!

"*¡Un aplauso para la Madre de Dios!*"

My hands join hundreds more as we clap for the mother, and the intensity of our applause sweeps me up in a fervor I have no reference for. I've never seen an entire town come out for the mother. The closest I can recall were the small, private family gatherings held each year in honor of Mother's Day. And this isn't just any town, but the town where Juan Moreno and the Joyos brothers brought Our Lady to watch over them. These very hills were where she showed herself to the girl Apolonia. The descendants of those first cobreros march at my sides. Together, we sing her name. "*¡Que viva la Caridad del Cobre!*" we shout. Our applause grows more exuberant with each refrain. The clouds that have been knitting themselves overhead break, and the rain that falls on us only adds to the sense that we are part of something lush and electric and alive.

With each block more townspeople join the parade. Others gather on rooftops and porches or alongside the road to watch. The archbishop works the crowd, dipping his aspergillum in and out of holy water, its spray mixing with the rain drizzle that saturates the air, baptizing the crowd with its *bendiciones*. I angle to get close so that I might add the blessings of the archbishop's holy water to the cologne water Madelaine christened me with just hours before, layer myself in perfume and holy water and rain.

As we near the church steps, the sanctuary's clock glows yellow against the night sky, announcing it's almost time for the eight o'clock mass to begin. The lighted silhouette of Our Lady—not the twin strapped to the van at my side but the miraculous effigy too precious to leave her altar—shines through its doors, calling me to break from the procession and climb toward her.

Inside, the sanctuary buzzes with the arrival of Our Lady's first devotees. Some are dressed in the yellow and white of the observant, others in satin and sequins as if they were on their way to a prom. I find a seat in a middle pew. In front of me a row of nuns kneel in prayer, the backs of their T-shirts advertising both La Caridad and the name of their home church. Near the altar visitors jostle to take their photo with Our Lady. The flash of their cameras reminds me of the men we'd seen on the steps this morning with their souvenir *fotos al momento* sign and I feel a tinge of annoyance as I wonder if the people I'm witnessing have come to sightsee or to pray. Before I let the thought sink in, I shift my attention back to the row of nuns bowed in prayer before me, and when I look up again the cameras are gone. In their place a woman dressed head to toe in yellow leaves an offering of sunflowers at Our Lady's feet. Another holds her baby high above her head so she might touch or be touched by the great mother.

From the back of the church, altar boys and priests begin their procession toward the altar to begin the first mass. When the clergymen speak, Our Lady will become a supporting character, blessed not because of her own strengths and merits but because of her relation to the Father and the Son. Still, no matter how the priests' prayers seem to direct us away from her, all eyes are locked on the mother at the central altar whose name we hail: *Santa María, Madre de Dios; Saint Mary, Mother of God.*

When the time arrives to bless our fellow travelers with the sign of peace, I'm simultaneously struck by the beauty of this moment when the congregation is invited to break through the fourth wall of the mass, and overwhelmed by my own shyness at joining in. I shake hands with those nearest me. But it isn't until I spot our hostess Alina from across the aisle that I'm filled with the spirit of the thing. Here among a church of strangers is a person I know. I rush to join her and her family and am swept up in embraces.

Buoyed by their warmth, I greet everyone in my path—the beautiful white-haired woman seated behind Alina; the nun with the broad grin; the young girl dressed in yellow satin.

When I return to my seat, I feel myself renewed. No longer the shy outsider but the lady of exuberant kisses.

"An applause for our Virgin of El Cobre!" the priests call from the altar.

"*¡Que viva la Virgen de la Caridad del Cobre!*" we shout back, still standing. "*¡Que viva!*" Our bodies sway as if at a rock concert and we lift

our arms, waving them slowly and in unison—not unlike the turtle legs
I'd watched at Maruchi's—arcing left to right as if following an invisible
metronome.

Roberto and I spend the next hours toggling between masses and brief
rests at Alina's. With each mass, the vendors selling bits of copper and
sunflowers and virgencitas along the road to the sanctuary grow more
animated as they vie for business. The parking lot swells with buses and
taxis that bring Our Lady's pilgrims from every corner of the island, and
beyond. The church steps overflow with those waiting to enter: families
with children and grandchildren in tow; men and women in various
stages of romantic and religious vigil. Among them are still more familiar faces. Salvador, the guide who'd accompanied me to the cimarrón
monument, passes fistfuls of candles to friends to light in the Chapel of
Miracles. Maruchi sits with her husband and children—the matriarch
of the family just arrived from her pilgrimage with the French crew to
and from the Bay of Nipe; the daughter-priestess of Ochún, dressed
from head to toe in white, as regal as if she'd stepped straight from her
Nigerian river.

With each mass, the mood of those inside the church also changes.
Voices mount to make themselves heard over the throng. Even after the
service begins, the crowd doesn't settle down. A young couple dressed in
party clothes flirt in voices so loud I can barely hear the homily. Children
seated in parents' laps begin to squabble and no one asks them to quiet
down. For the second time tonight, I feel a tinge of annoyance as I
wonder if the crowds are here to commune with the mother or to have
a good time. All around me the pop and flash of cell phone cameras fill
the sanctuary as greater numbers compete to take a selfie with Our Lady.
Each click of their shutter taints the air with something that feels more
like tourism than devotion.

I scan the crowd for those true believers I'd hoped to find. But it
seems that much of this late-night crowd has gathered out of a social

obligation perhaps not much different from the one that once motivated my family to attend Easter and Christmas Eve services. Absent are the pious prayers, the tears of joy I'd imagined. Absent are the pilgrims I'd longed to see by the thousands on their knees. Even those who've journeyed from afar seem—now that they've arrived—just plain tired.

I am one of the weary. I'd come to Cuba to discover a faith that might eclipse anything I'd known at home. What would it mean if those I'd thought held the key to that faith were just as lost and ordinary as I was?

Exhausted and hot and disappointed, I leave the sanctuary. Roberto and I begin our drive back to Santiago to pick up Luís. For the last hours he has been filming pilgrims as they begin their twelve-mile march from Santiago to El Cobre. Now we are eager to catch up with them as they arrive before Our Lady.

As Roberto and I maneuver our way out of town, my mood continues to darken. In the hours since Our Lady's motorcade passed through El Cobre, the roads have turned from devotion to jubilee. In the park, vendors hawk roasted pig and ice-cream cones. Reggaeton music blasts from porches. Where there had been holy water, now there are bottles of rum. And where devotees had chanted Our Lady's name, now couples stagger down the center of the road cradling half-empty bottles in their arms.

"Look how pious the town is on the day of Our Lady's festival," Roberto says as he swerves to miss them.

"A carnival," he adds in a laugh that is also a cry, and I realize that it is not just me who is disappointed in the irreverence of the pilgrims.

It will be different, I tell myself, when we see those pilgrims who've chosen to walk all the way from Santiago.

It's three-thirty in the morning when Roberto, Luís, and I park in front of the restaurant-bar that marks the turnoff to El Cobre. Through its lighted windows we see a group of men pound their fists against a table as if drumming. Outside, a circle of young people pass a bottle of rum under a tree, and their voices mix with the merengue music that filters through the bar's open door.

On the car ride from Santiago, Luís has told us how the young pilgrims had been in good spirits as they prepared for their long march. Now he paces between parking lot and road, anxious not to miss the moment when they'll turn the bend. Roberto and I wait near the car, balancing our disappointment with what we've seen—the flash of selfies and souvenirs, the carousing, the bottles of rum—against our anticipation for what's yet to come. I can tell we're both hoping that the young people we wait for will climb the hill to Our Lady's sanctuary like Apolonia once did—devoted, illuminated by belief.

Our talk of pilgrims reminds Roberto of a friend who went to Israel to visit the Holy Land. "He came back with a vial of sacred earth for each of his friends," Roberto tells me. "Only he'd forgotten to bring enough for all of us. So he dug some dirt from his backyard, placed it in a tube, and told our friend David it was blessed.

"As it turned out, it was David who really treasured the gift. He strung it on a cord so he could wear it around his neck, swore it brought him all kinds of luck. The rest of us felt sorry for him, but we didn't have the heart to tell him it was just local dirt."

As Roberto finishes his story, the first of the young men and women Luís watched depart from Santiago round the bend. I scan their faces for the signs of reverence I've been waiting for. But they look weary, their faces not lit with the piety I'd expected of pilgrims but ordinary; their marching not devout but perfunctory. With less than a mile and a half left to the sanctuary, two of the young men veer off toward the bar. Their friends shout for them to rejoin their ranks but they wave them off, laughing.

"Where is Our Lady?" I ask Roberto. I'd traveled all this way to see what devotion looked like when it came out marching on foot and on its knees. I'd kept myself awake all these hours only to watch this unruly band straggle into town.

As we make our way back to the sanctuary, the vendors we pass seem as weary as the pilgrims we've left behind us. A few struggle off their chairs to wave us down, but others simply go through the motions of raising a bouquet or souvenir in our direction.

We find the lobby of the sanctuary's inn crammed with men and women stretched out on wooden benches to sleep off their journey. The man behind the reception desk that doubles as a souvenir counter is fast asleep, his face fallen onto his arms that are not as much crossed as splayed across his desk.

We've planned to take in two more masses: the 5 a.m. and the 9 a.m. But I'm suddenly either too tired or disappointed to power through. The excitement I'd woken up with nearly twenty-four hours before has been replaced by the fear that what I'd hoped to see and what I will see are not the same, the movie I'd invented in my head of saintly multitudes arriving on their knees replaced with real-life images of stragglers and drunkards.

At Alina's I head straight for the shower. The water heater has been turned off for the night and so I stand under a cold stream, shivering as I try to scrub away the images of the night: the flash of camera selfies and fotos al momento; vendors with their endless parade of souvenirs; the chants of the motorcade disintegrating into a carnival of roasted pig and rum. Roberto's story cycles alongside each of these images, that vial of backyard dirt his friend wore proudly around his neck as if it contained some great mystery contaminating the objects I've been holding most dearly: the güiro in which Madelaine had placed my mother's spirit; Our Lady's silver pendant he'd baptized in the waters of her name.

Suddenly all my experiences in Cuba carry the dirt of the day: sacred drums and dancers calling the oricha back to earth; my mother's voice speaking my name. The beloved new friends who'd opened up those worlds to me—Daniel and Yolersi, Maruchi and Madelaine—all caught up in the same taint of *vendedores* and *borrachos*. I'd come all this distance to witness an outpouring for the mother that might be called miraculous. But in the end, I wondered if it were all just one carnival. Was the güiro a portal to another world? Our Lady a miraculous mother? Or was a gourd just a gourd? The Virgin just a doll made from sticks and paste?

After a few hours of sleep, Roberto, Luís and I make our way back to Our Lady's sanctuary. Perhaps it is the sun warming her steps, or the way the light illuminates every inch of cupola and spire, but both my mood and the mood of those around me seem improved. The weary figures of the night have been replenished by a river of yellow and white as thousands of pilgrims climb the sanctuary steps for Our Lady's 9 a.m. mass. Beaded Santeros shade themselves under white umbrellas. Boys race each other up the stairs clutching wooden virgencitas in their fists. A pair of men in crisp white shirts cradle bouquets of sunflowers the size of faces. And yes! Among them are the true pilgrims I'd been waiting for. A mother and daughter climb barefoot, their sandals dangling from their fingertips. A man in sunglasses crawls on his hands and knees. The entire tableau is framed by a backdrop of mountains and blue sky, the iron figure of El Cimarrón rising from the Cerro de Cardenillo; Miners' Hill marking the spot where a girl named Apolonia once climbed to find her mother.

Inside the sanctuary, every pew and aisle fill as standing room gives way to breathing room. Old women, their faces creased with piety, clutch rosaries. Young girls cool themselves with lace-edged fans. Families line up to light their candles in the room of miracles. I try to navigate the narrow gaps between them only to be squeezed back onto the steps.

I'll see Our Lady next time, I think, then catch myself as I remember that this is it. In a matter of minutes Roberto and Luís and I will pack up our equipment, make our way downhill, and drive back to Santiago. I have one last chance to be with the miraculous mother, see if she might reveal what I'd come to find from her. But as I try to re-enter the church, I'm met with a press of people even more impenetrable than before. How to get close to Our Lady in such a crowd?

Days earlier when I'd had her to myself, I'd spent my time asking if she were not too small. Too distant. Now I wonder if it was Our Lady who had been distant, or if it was I. How easy to observe and judge. So many ways to circle a thing without committing. Always holding myself back, with one toe in the water, afraid to immerse myself fully.

With Madelaine and Záhilys, I'd held back my voice. With Daniel and Yolersi, my hands. I had a thousand excuses to keep myself on the sidelines. When it came to Ochún, I was not fully initiated in the Lucumí religion, not an oloricha. With Our Lady, I was not Catholic. Not Cuban.

On my first visit to her sanctuary, I'd felt caught between urgency and shyness, between wanting to drop to my knees, break open before her, and worry that the gesture didn't belong to me. But the word "pilgrim"—from the Latin *peregrinus*, meaning "foreign," by definition spoke of a relationship between the inner and the outer. Of the necessity of searching outside the familiar borders of the self to find the thing one yearned for.

I'd spent the night judging devotion from the outside, finding those who busied themselves with selfies and rum lacking. What about my own actions?

I look at the steps, now empty as the last service of the morning begins. Might I prostrate myself before Our Lady as I'd seen others do? The man in sunglasses who mounted the stairs on his knees. The mother who'd climbed barefoot with her daughter. Was I willing to stop half-stepping, stop talking about believing and believe?

Inside the sanctuary priests are talking—as they had throughout the night—about the Mother of God. Without hearing their voices, I know that they speak of her first and foremost in reference to the Father and the Son. And I know, without looking, that all eyes are on the Mother. How can they not? She stands at the central-most place in the sanctuary, her golden robes handspun by Spanish nuns, and the rays of her nimbus joining the sunlight that streams through the windows, framing her blessed shape.

All night I'd been rebuking her for not showing herself to me in large, showy displays. But she had been showing herself to me all along—in the parade of chants and holy water; in the flicker of candles; in the embraces of Alina and her family and the generosity of Roberto and Luís. In her very posture—the way she stood on her half-moon, its inverted form a nod to her ability to overturn our expectations. Shake the ground we thought we knew. Remake us.

She was a bell. A mountain. An inverted heart. A humble figure made from wood and paste who was also larger than life. She was a watery mother who defied our expectations; a shape shifter with the power to appear and disappear; a mother calling us to stop seeing things the way they were and see them as they might be. She had taken my journal to make sure I was paying attention.

I could feel something pushing past those places where I kept myself small and polite: that thing I'd felt beating inside my chest ever since I first read about Our Lady in an Ohio library. Something that had more to do with the language of gesture than word.

Before I can indulge more thoughts, my knees hit stone. I clasp my hands. I begin to *pedir*. Not in the half-hearted way I'd done with Yolersi when I'd still been afraid to articulate what I wanted. What that was now seemed suddenly both obvious and impossible to hold back. I wanted to break open. Put behind me all the ways I'd kept myself small by leading with the conjunction *or* instead of *and*. Thinking I had to choose between being perfect or lovable. An outsider or an insider. Polite or crazy. Grieving or sane.

Here before Our Lady, I ask to be broken so I might be remade in a larger image. To be both a stranger and an initiate. A tourist and a pilgrim. A North American who was both outside and inside the events unfolding before me. A daughter whose mother was both dead and alive. A forty-nine-year-old mother who understood she was dying even as she lived. An ancestor in the making. A child yet to be born.

18

RETURN

O̤N MY LAST MORNING in Santiago, I wrap Ochún's sacred stones, like Daniel showed me, in gold cloth, slip Our Lady's statue between dresses and socks. When I run out of room in my suitcase, I tuck the rest of my things in a cardboard box, nesting Eleggua's stone head and Ogún's cauldron between running shoes and books, a Che Guevara T-shirt I've bought for Alex, an Industriales baseball hat for Rick.

At the airport the box will draw attention from security dogs. Alerted perhaps by the scent of blood and feathers that still linger on the objects packed inside, they will circle it, sniffing at its edges.

"What's in the box?" a customs attendant will ask suspiciously, and I will struggle to remember the contents I am now packing with so much care.

"Some books and running shoes," I'll answer.

"Is that all?"

"And some souvenirs," I'll add, hoping to sound breezy, as if the box held nothing but a few mementos. Stand-ins for a vacation well spent.

Two flights separate me from the world of these objects and the world that is waiting for me—my job as a college writing teacher. My roles as Rick's partner and Alex's mother. My apartment, with its familiar art-work and writing chair. The three cats that consider my home theirs. Two times I pray for Eleggua to clear the way for the plane and for

Ochún and Our Lady to protect its passengers. Two times I watch the landscape below me rearrange itself, Cuba's royal palm trees growing smaller and smaller only to have their American cousins come into relief as we land in Miami. Those too vanishing as we leave Miami and make our way back to the Midwest.

It's not just the landscape that will change. The passengers on the plane to Miami, mostly Cuban, will know to applaud when we land, but on the flight to Columbus there will only be silence. Once I land in Ohio, I will be alone with the religions I'm coming to know. The beads that in Cuba are a language understood by everyone, each combination of colors a text identifying the person wearing them as a child of a particular god, will be just beads. The offerings I've grown accustomed to—candles lit before home altars and bovedas; the sound of batá drums rising from a threshold; the practice of animal sacrifice and talking with the dead not strange horrors but something that happens in the house next door—will feel as distant as the sound of palm trees tossing in a breeze.

How many atoms had I swapped out between the woman who'd set out thirty days earlier to look for her mother and the one who now returned? My hair has turned copper from the sun. My neck and arms are draped in beads, and Our Lady's pendant hangs from my throat. Even my posture has grown more regal, as if, strung with these objects, my very self now carries more weight.

I close my eyes and replay the last month. I see a newcomer arriving at a house on Calle Jesús María, my arms and throat bare, my suitcase not yet filled with the sacred objects I now carry home. An apprentice dancing in Miriela's kitchen, lifting my skirts as I mimic the rise and fall of Ochún's river, Zunilda's gold tooth flashing as she shows me how to embody her current. An initiate kneeling before the fall of cowrie shells as Yolersi teaches me to read the map of my life. A daughter invoking the ways of the goddess among the greenery of Maruchi's roof. A child joining my voice with Madelaine's and Záhilys's as we call my mother into the room. A pilgrim dropping to her knees on Our Lady's steps.

How would I talk about all I'd discovered in Cuba? How I'd come to see that the scrim between worlds was a porous one, the gods and ancestors within reach. Would the people at home who knew and loved me before I left—particularly Alex and Rick—think me charming or crazy? Did I have the courage to find out?

It was 11:00 at night, literally the eleventh hour, when I arrived, thirty years earlier, at St. Luke's Hospital to see my mother for the last time. For days, I'd noted the decline in her voice each time I called from my dorm room, until finally she didn't come to the phone at all. At no time did my father tell me she was dying. It was not our family's style to deal with things head-on but to edge around them. Why she couldn't come to the phone was for me to figure out.

Once I reached the hospital, I too found myself grasping for edges to hold onto. I fixed my gaze not on my mother but on the objects that still anchored her to her life: those rings on her hands, the telephone next to her bed. The rest of her visibly unspooling—her skeletal form too small for the hospital bed that held her; her milky eyes roaming the room. I'd felt a terrible urge to run, to vomit, to shit on the floor. Anything to expel the thing I felt welling up inside me—something feral and wild and much too large for its container. If I gave in, even to one tear, I would surely drown.

And so, I'd focused on the telephone next to my mother's bed. I told her it was the same model as the one in my dorm. I was aware that this was not what I wanted to be talking to her about and yet I couldn't seem to do any better.

I haven't yet grown into the forty-nine-year-old self I hope would not turn to the distraction of telephones but might sit at her side, meet her gaze, no matter how absent or wild. Ask if she is as scared as I am.

"My children are coming," my mother tells this nineteen-year-old version of me, and I wonder: Does she know I'm here?

Perhaps my mother knows something I have yet to learn. That I'm as much a ghost as she, too caught up in the narrative we've been spinning—that the mother, this great shining mother who holds us all in place, would always be there—to be present to what is happening right in front of me. Those frayed edges where the shining mother is unraveling won't be there if we don't speak about them.

The nineteen-year-old daughter can't look anymore. Not at the telephone next to her mother's hospital bed or at the rings on her fingers. Even these objects, so proximate to the woman disappearing among them, feel unreliable, and so the girl makes her excuses and leaves the room.

"You are so loving," my mother tells me before I leave, and I know I'm a fraud.

"Who is Our Lady?" I'd asked both Julio and Maruchi before I left. I'd hoped, as I did each time I asked the question, to elicit a definitive response, tie up my search with a neat bow. In his answer, Julio had reminded me of the many Cubans who associated Our Lady with the African mother Ochún, and those who linked her with the Catholic mother Mary. Others who thought of her first as a symbol of nationalism for whom her role as Mother of God took second place. But he also talked about his own mother, and how she'd made pilgrimages on foot each year to Our Lady of Charity to thank the great mother for looking out for the son sitting before me.

"Of course, it's hard to separate those threads," he'd said. "Our Lady is the maternal presence. All that is *mother.*" Such a potent word! For the past thirty days I'd been trying to dissect its power—drawing and diagraming her, studying her steps and prayers. Looking always for a single pattern that might hold her seemingly disparate parts. I'd puzzled over how Ochún, the African fertility goddess, and Our Lady, the Catholic virgin, could be thought of as one. How Our Lady, so small and distant, could also be both powerful and beloved. How both mothers could be both dulce and fuerte, both sweet and strong.

I'd been trying to solve a riddle of opposites, but the mother's paradoxes were not puzzles, they were doors. The mother's sweetness not to be conflated, as I had for so many years, with making oneself pleasing or reining oneself in, but rather with her willingness to open. Be vulnerable and tender. To see from the heart.

I'd been raised in a culture that privileged logic and intellect over emotion and intuition. I'd learned to apologize for my sensitivity, my gut feelings and instincts, clairvoyant insights, unknowable knowings.

In Cuba I'd seen those attributes upheld as a power not less than but different. An emotional and spiritual intelligence that flowed, like Ochún's waters—mighty in its messiness and wildness, in its ability to create and destroy. A strength that existed not in spite of the things that had been held against us—our intuition and heart, our connection with primal, earthy, magic things—but because of them.

"*La protectora*," Maruchi had said when I asked her what the mother meant to her. Protective first of the self and then of those she loved. She was compassionate and nurturing—not in the exhaustive, self-sacrificing way I'd seen in the women who raised me, but in the self-reflexive way that understood that to be strong meant to be sweet first to the self; to move into the wholeness of one's being. That to follow one's own inner map might be the most powerful thing we do.

The offerings we made to the mother weren't merely decorative or ornamental, as I'd grown up thinking. Not women's shit, as the professor had once told me, but potent. The healing, transformative power of flowers and plants were reminders of the fertile mysteries women carried inside our own bodies.

Goddess. Vulva. Womb. I lived in a country that could barely speak the words out loud, let alone acknowledge their power—the ability to bring life from the void. The mighty wonders of the umbilical cord that threads the living with the ancestors and the unborn.

For the last thirty years I'd thought I had to choose between keeping my mother at a distance or succumbing to the grief that came with letting her in. In Cuba I'd been learning to watch rather than look away. To use my voice to call the ancestors and listen for their answer. Exchange the numbed-out version of myself who thought she had to silence her grief to be sane for a different kind of sanity—one that did not try to pretty up its rough edges but planted itself both in life and in death.

How to carry all that home to a culture where the only sacrifice we know is the sacrifice of our own selves—the way we cede the complexity of life and death by surfacing over the messy, fertile ground of our feelings and our grief.

I don't remember the last thing I said to my mother, only the actions that accompanied it—the backing out of the room, the shutting of the door. Before it, the shutting of my eyes. I must have said something like "I'll see you tomorrow."

What would that nineteen-year-old girl have done if she knew there would be no mother in the morning? That in a few hours her brother would wake her from the bed where she has always had a mother and tell her their mother is gone?

But there I go telling this story in the third person, as if it were somehow someone else's. It's been easier to tell it this way, one step removed. The cocoon I've built around the loss is thirty years in the making, the ice block that holds it in place so solid in its construction it feels impossible to penetrate.

Now, as the plane hovers between Cuba and Ohio, I return to the moment when I stand at the threshold of my mother's hospital room and it is still before. Before I start talking about telephones and make excuses to leave the room. Before I have taught myself to look at this scene in third person. Before I freeze and go numb inside. There, in the moments before, when my mother hovers, wild-eyed, in that space between here and there. Skeletal. Near death. But still, beautifully, impossibly, there.

What might it look like not to turn away but to keep looking? Stop skirting the terror and enter it, draw it like a cloak around my shoulders, feel it from the inside out? Not as the nineteen-year-old who believes her mother can never die but as the 49-year-old who is coming to understand that life and death are a continuum that moves in both directions, the mother only dead if we forget to tell her story.

And so, as I give myself a do-over, this time I stop hugging the walls, step away from the door to sit at the edge of my mother's bed. This time I do not look at her telephone or her rings. I take her hand in mine. Allow myself to feel the knobs of her knuckles. Look into those eyes that dart around the room.

When she tells me, "My children are coming," I tell her, "I'm here."

"You are so loving," I hear her say, only this time I know it's true because I'm looking. When my tears come, I let her see how scared I am.

It doesn't matter that I'm surrounded by fellow passengers. I feel my tears hot against my cheeks. I don't wipe them away. Nor do I try to stifle the feral noises that accompany them. This is the moment I'd gone to Cuba for. More than the moment when I'd danced Ochún's steps or received her elekes. More than the moment when El Cimarrón had made contact with my mother. More than the moment I'd knelt on Our Lady's sanctuary steps. But this moment now when I break open, as Apolonia once had, and I feel my mother with me—not as a voice funneling through El Cimarrón, or as the shaking of seeds inside a güiro; not as a story about a girl who climbed a mountain to find her mother, but as something I carry inside—wild and alive, like wings beating against my ribs. They are sharp and painful, beautiful as glass. Like those stained windows I'd once walked toward with my mother after a college exam, each piece fitted to the next—sea and star and tree, woman and man and child—the whole of it held by some invisible force. My mother's hand, solid in mine, fitting precisely inside my own.

I reach for Our Lady's pendant and touch the watery mother who holds the child who holds the world, her triangular shape inscribed in the circle that might be Ochún's fertile calabash. That mighty womb that holds the two halves of the world reminds me of something I'd known as a child but either forgotten or been taught to apologize for along the way: that I could see atoms; that I believe in magic; that I miss my mother. I'd come to Cuba to find a way back to those things. Now that I've found them, I never want to give them away again.

In the weeks and months after I return from Cuba, my mother will come to me in memories that surface unexpectedly. In dreams. Sometimes as an actual presence. I will feel her wrapping her arms around my shoulders, will hear a voice calling me her Little Petunia, a nickname I'd forgotten for nearly three decades.

"Is it real?" I'll ask as I pass the güiro Madelaine prepared for me on the living-room mantel. Again, when I glimpse Our Lady's silver pendant flashing from my neck. Do beads and gourds and metal and stone hold the voices of the spirits? Or is it simply my belief in them, like the vial of dirt Roberto's friend strung around his neck, that gives them their power?

There will be a million reasons not to believe: the fear that the objects and rituals I've brought home with me won't fit into Rick's idea of who his partner should be. That they might appear to him, to others, even to myself, as foolish or naïve. So much women's shit.

Conversely, there's the fear that they are not mine to talk about. I will struggle with my place in this story, knowing there are those more qualified to talk about the religions I am just getting to know. I will do my best to render what I've learned as accurately as I can, returning again and again to Cuba—to immerse myself more fully in the Santería initiations that lead me closer to Ochún. Studying Our Lady from her front pew for so many hours I'll be invited to climb those closed-off back stairs and sit face to face with her. Each time, I will come home with more questions than answers, and a hunger to return for more.

I will not be the only one with questions. When I tell people I've gone to Cuba to find my mother, they inevitably ask if she or I are Cuban. And I will tell them what I tell you now. I am an outsider—born and raised, like my mother, in the Midwest—who found something in Cuba she hadn't been able to locate at home: an invitation to remember how the stones inside a soup tureen might carry the spirit of a river goddess. That the rattle of herbs and seeds inside a güiro might be the sound of a mother calling her daughter home.

In October, I will light candles to honor the thirtieth anniversary of my mother's death. First the candle to Eleggua, then three for Our Lady and five for Ochún. I will wash the insides of a sopera I'll order from a Miami botánica with coconut water and prepare it, as Daniel and Maruchi taught me, to become a permanent home for Ochún. "*Ay Madre, oye mi voz,*" I'll sing as I pour fresh water over her five river stones. I won't get the melody quite right nor will I be in the right key but still I will sing: "Oh Mother, hear my voice. *Oye mi voz. Oye mi voz.*"

Perhaps, as I talk to my mother, I'll be talking to thin air. After three decades of thinking I had to choose between keeping my mother at a distance or succumbing to the grief that came with letting her in, it will seem preferable to risk this craziness. If belief is a choice, I can be the woman who talks to thin air, or I can be the woman who ignores an air laden with spirits. How miraculous, I think, if after all these decades of believing my mother was gone, beyond reach, that she is now right there on the mantel, just a shake away. How grievous if she were there and, to avoid seeming crazy or wrong, I was to turn my back on her.

19

THE RIVER

T HEY SAY THAT EVERY river holds a piece of every other.

Twenty miles west of Columbus, the Big Darby Creek runs through three Ohio counties before emptying into the larger Scioto River where it joins with the Ohio and then the Mississippi, that great waterway that leads all the way to the Gulf of Mexico and to the Caribbean shores of Cuba. Continue east across the Atlantic to the Gulf of Guinea and you're in Ochún country, where the Lagos Lagoon receives the waters of the great river goddess who is both the source and all that flows from it.

Rick and I are lying in bed when I first tell him about Madelaine. I mention how, before we finished our session together, El Cimarrón had asked if I had a *pantalón*.

"Of course I do," I'd answered. The word pantalón, translated literally, means "pants."

"Do you love him?" El Cimarrón had asked, a question that sent me struggling to connect the dots between the words "love" and "pants."

It was Záhilys who'd rescued me, leaning close to explain. "Do you have a husband, a man—a pantalón?"

"Yes," I'd answered, smiling as I thought of Rick, as comfortable to me as a pair of pants I might slip over my skin. "Yes, I have a pantalón. And yes, I love him."

"Does he love you?" El Cimarrón wanted to know.

"Yes," I replied, pleased with my certainty.

Seemingly as satisfied as I with my answer, El Cimarrón had told me to find a river and go there with my pantalón. We were to look for a moving current and bathe each other in the name of Ochún; find five river stones for me and five more for my pantalón. In the cocoon of Madelaine's house, it had seemed almost plausible that Rick, the lover of logical, tangible things, might agree to such a baptism.

Now I lay next to Rick, my nose inches from his, as I translate El Cimarrón's instructions to ask Ochún, the great Afro-Cuban mother of love, to bless our partnership. "We're to find a river where we can bathe in honey and flowers," I tell him, skimming through the instructions that made so much sense when I was in Cuba. I laugh as though this foray were something I, too, might find frivolous. But Rick is listening.

"I know a river," he whispers as he nods off to sleep.

Rick has rules. When it comes to bathing in the river, his neck and face are fair game. Arms and legs if we have to, but there will be no stripping down to bathing suits and we will definitely not be getting naked. Nor will we think about attempting this ritual if anyone is watching.

I have my own rules. I'd returned from Cuba determined to stand strong in the convictions I'd worked out on the plane—that I wanted to hold onto the part of myself that was not only sweet but strong. Not only smart but magic. Before I'd unpacked a single item from my suitcase, I'd told Rick I'd come to believe things in Cuba I didn't expect him to believe. He was free to question the stories I'd tell him, but not out loud. The episode with Madelaine was something I particularly did not want touched by doubt. My mother had spoken to me. Had called me by my childhood name. Whatever rationale Rick's analytical brain might work out to explain how a Spiritist who lived in the remote town of El Cobre, who knew virtually no English, and who'd met so few Americans, could know my nickname was Becki, I didn't want to hear it.

Off limits too were the objects I'd brought home with me: the güiro

Madelaine had filled with my mother's aché; Our Lady's pendant he'd christened in the water goblet that held her name. Regardless of what Rick might or might not see in those bits of silver and gourd, I asked him to acknowledge how much meaning they held for me.

We're a couple who needs this level of communication. We come from separate molds. Rick is the bison who keeps me grounded. I, in turn, am the egret who challenges him to test his wings. Slowly, one step at a time, we navigate the world together. Take this moment now as we drive to the Darby River to follow the instructions of an El Cobre Spiritist. Rick, who is so good at getting from point A to point B, is behind the wheel. I'm in the passenger seat, dressed in the white dress I'd worn when I'd first received the warriors and Ochún. My elekes drape my neck; two copper stones from El Cobre are tucked inside the lining of my bra. My lap is filled with offerings—bottles of honey and coconut water still wrapped in plastic grocery bags; a bouquet of sunflowers. In my purse are a set of index cards on which I've copied El Cimarrón's instructions.

Rick wants me to know he is doing this only because he knows it is important to me. He loves me, and so he is here. Willing, if also anxious, about what's to come.

"There's a fine line and we're right on it," he tells me when I ask how he's doing, and we both know he's talking about the boundary between being open and being crazy.

From the backseat Skip whines, a reminder that he, too, is anxious about where we're headed. A rescue neglected and likely beaten by his first owner, Skip is high-strung and opinionated, often difficult to love. And yet Rick loves him unconditionally. Shortly after his divorce, Rick had driven from Ohio to Indiana to adopt Skip. He needed the dog as much as the dog needed him, he'd told me. I'd catch Rick talking to him before bed, the two of them nose to nose, the dog's ear cocked as Rick whispered the promise he never tired of repeating: They were best friends. Forever.

The three of us follow the river of highways and roads that lead to the Darby—through Columbus toward its unincorporated limits. Past a Loan Max and a Waffle House, a motel sign that advertises a $3 tan. And then we turn into farm country, where the edges of the city break into cornfields and split-rail fences. A bar and cemetery mark the last stretch before we turn off to the Darby.

Rick snaps Skip into his harness and leash while I gather our offerings and we're off, the three of us as odd a team as Dorothy and her own entourage. Here, there is no yellow brick road, only park signs that lead to the trails that follow the river. It's a perfect September day, the temperature in the seventies, neither too cool nor too hot. Excited to be in new territory, the dog sniffs at tall grasses and wildflowers, dives after smells we can't discern. Overhead, trees stretch to form a canopy, reminding me of the stories I've heard about el monte, and how the gods Apolonia and Juan Moreno knew were said to jump from canopy to canopy.

I close my eyes and call silently to the ancestors. I recite each name, beginning with my mother. I tell them we've arrived. Ask for their strength and their blessings. Thank them for granting permission to talk with the spirits. On the screen of my eyelids, a gate between our world and theirs swings open on its hinges, revealing another and another, like a hall of mirrors, each gate clicking in turn. I call to Eleggua and ask him to show us the right path—Eleggua who stands at every threshold, who brings together things that only appear to be separate: a bison and egret making our way to the river, our trusted terrier racing ahead, tugging at his leash. This forest another opening, the path we are on branching off to different sections of the river. Which to choose?

The first path we try opens onto occupied real estate with a young family wading in shallow waters, fishing poles slung over their shoulders. The second onto a slice of river that is unoccupied but static. Madelaine had been adamant that we were to find a spot where the current was moving. We can do better, we decide. But I can tell Rick is growing impatient. His shoulders are tensed, his steps deliberate, as if he were already counting how many he had left before we could go home. "Let's take the next opening," he says, "no matter what." He doesn't want to be wandering all day.

At the next turn we find the river fanning before us. Its current ripples, and the water at its edges is so clear I can see the river pebbles that line its bed.

Later, I will find a photograph of Ochún's river in southwestern Nigeria, and while it flows over six thousand miles from the Darby, its landscape is nearly identical to the one before me. A canopy of trees branch over moving water. Rocks jut like Ochún's sacred fish from its surface.

Even without the photograph for reference, I feel the presence of the river goddess. The sun, just starting to set, turns water and ground and tree to gold. A few leaves fall in slow motion, dropping soundlessly into the stream that carries them on a raft of light.

"Hello, Ochún," I say as I take in the movement of my own reflection.

I set our offerings among the roots of a large tree, arranging sunflowers and coconut over its knobs like a picnic while Rick searches for a place to tie the dog. He finds a slender tree facing the water, a good spot for Skip to enjoy the sun while still being out of our way. The dog strains at the leash and whines, letting us know he would rather be with us.

I'm ankle-deep in the river, opening a jar of honey and calling to Ochún when Rick catches up with me. "Let's make this quick," he says, worried someone will see us and get upset that we're throwing things in the river. Never mind that the offerings we've brought are organic, bio-degradable gifts for the river goddess to consume.

Later, Rick and I will laugh at how perfectly each of us is playing out our role within the relationship. "What a family we are!" he'll tell me. "There you are calling forth the river goddess and I'm worried we're somehow going to get into trouble. And then there's Skip, getting tangled in the brush."

I'll smile when I hear the word "family." Rick and I are family, not because we share rings or blood but because we've agreed to hold one another. It is a choice we renew again and again. A choice we are renewing right now as Rick stands beside me, fighting every voice that tells him what we're doing is crazy.

When we walk back to the car, he'll stop and turn to me, look at me in that way that lets me know the thing he's about to say will be the truest thing.

"I'm glad I love you this much," he'll say, his face and eyes bright, "and I'm glad that you open me up to do things like this. I know I don't act like it, but I'm glad we're here."

"I'm glad you love me this much, too," I'll say and I'll laugh, relieved beyond measure that he hasn't asked me to shrink from the magic of these rituals, to choose between being the woman who follows her heart and the woman who is loved.

"It's time to choose our stones," I tell Rick. We are wading at the river's edge, scanning the water beneath our feet for rocks that might hold the spirit of the river goddess. Five stones for each of us, El Cimarrón had said. Five, because it was Ochún's sacred number. River stones, because they were the ones that held her spirit. The subject of rocks is tricky territory. Rick and I had gotten into our first argument after I told him that my sister believed in the healing properties of crystals and that, while I was not as adamant about their powers, it made sense to me that something that held millions of years of history in such a compressed space might vibrate with an energy we might benefit from. Now, as we hunt for Ochún's stones, searching for the ones made smooth from centuries of the river goddess drumming her body against them, I feel my worlds collide—the woman who's come to seek the wisdom of African gods and the Ohio man she loves scanning for rocks in this river that could be the Òṣun River or the Río El Cobre. The canopy of Ohio trees that could be Ochún's grove or Apolonia's monte. Every stone and leaf, every molecule of water and honey either teeming with the sacred or static, dead things. Two lovers either receiving the blessings of the spirits or simply two people bathing in a stream.

Rick is not the only one who is out of his element. I too feel self-conscious as I attempt to make contact with the river goddess here in the middle of Ohio, with Rick as my witness. When I'd asked El Cimarrón why he was giving me these instructions, he'd given me that look that told me I'd asked an obvious question. "You said you loved him and that he loves you," he'd answered. "El Cimarrón wants to take care of you."

Rick and I wash our hands and faces with honey and coconut, bathe each other's arms and legs. Read the cards that ask the gods to look out for us so that our future might flow as easily as these waters.

As if in answer, I spot two heart-shaped stones and a handful of smaller, round pebbles.

"Take the heart and pick four of the others," I tell Rick, holding my palm out.

"What do we do with them?" he asks.

"I don't know," I laugh. I realize I didn't think to ask. How much I still had to learn!

Weeks before, I'd stood looking out over the Havana Harbor, searching for something I could barely name—a shape, both mighty and sweet, I'd first known through my own mother. My questions were just as vast. Who were Ochún and Our Lady? What thread connected them so that so many saw them as one? And why was I looking for both my mother and me, her daughter, within their contours?

Today I stood at the Big Darby. Not alone but with my pantalón. Our legs are rooted in water and our shoulders gently touch as we look out at the line where land meets sky. Following the last of our instructions, we loosen sunflowers from their wrapper and toss them into the stream. Our first offering is for Ochún; the second for my mother; a third for Rick and me. We watch as they drift downstream, like gold flitting across glass. Slowly, without sound, they stay within our vision until they hit a knot where the current pauses to catch its breath.

It is Rick who remarks how beautiful the flowers are. And it is Rick who wants to photograph them. Capture this moment when they bob in place before moving on, drifting farther and farther out toward that place where this river empties into another, and another, until—far from the landlocked Midwest—they all merge with the sea.

"Everything we can imagine, everything we are able to summon through image exists in the spiritual realm," Madelaine told me when I'd asked him about Our Lady. Was she a physical object? An effigy made of wood and paste? A story repeated so many times she only felt real? Or was there something irrefutable and alive, mighty even, beneath her stories and robes?

"Our Lady existed," Madelaine assured me. "She was a person named Mary. Not a construct but flesh and blood. A woman, like your mother, whose spirit might be summoned."

Madelaine had pointed to the güiro I held in my hands, bringing my attention to the statuette of Our Lady he'd glued to its top, her triangular form crudely carved and dusted in copper.

"You hold her image in your hands only because she exists as spirit in the spirit world. Ochún, too, has a spirit," Madelaine continued, beginning to circle the puzzle I'd been trying to solve ever since I first discovered Our Lady and Ochún's twin stories in the pages of a university library book and wondered how the Virgin and the River Goddess could be one and the same.

"The feminine comes to us not in one form but in many," Madelaine offered, his voice as matter-of-fact as if we were talking about analytical geometry. "She presents herself as Our Lady and as Ọchún. As Yemayá. As Oyá. And so on."

He'd then reached for a sheet of notebook paper and drawn a horizon line punctuated on each end by a dot. "Let's say this is where the mother originates," he said, pointing to the dot on the left. "And this is where she ends," he continued, pointing to the one on the right.

"But there's more than one way to get to her," he added, drawing a series of nested curved lines above and below the horizon line. Each of those arcs represented one of the many paths one might choose to travel from point to point. The resulting sphere had reminded me of the güiro I held in my lap, and of the gourd that holds the two halves of the world.

"No matter how different their external forms appear, the path to the mother begins and ends in the same place—that point that is constant and ever-changing. Omnipresent. Too vast for us to comprehend."

As I stand at the river, there are women all over the world who are feeling their way back to her. Daughters who still have their mothers, and daughters who've lost their mothers early or late in life; others who never knew their mothers but yearn for them like a phantom limb. Mothers who are giving birth to ideas and children and science and books. Farmers and foragers who plunge their hands into her fertile earth, hike the curves of her rivers and waterfalls. Witchy women who know food as medicine, who can name each of the plants and flowers that grow at her banks. Activists who fight against gun violence and racial inequality, against fracking and deforestation, who understand that aggression against any member of the planet is a type of self-violence. Poets and dancers who are raising their fists and pens against the censorship of their bodies, renouncing any norms that measure them by the size of their voices and waists. Women who are marching, chanting, *thundering* that our bodies are ours to govern. Each invocation of hand and foot, throat and tongue asserting that history is not always her story, and that mankind does not stand for humankind.

It's my own hunger to recover her that I'm feeling my way back to each time I fight to save her from the auto correct mode that turns Ochún to *Ocher*, and Asherah to *Dasher*. As I try to rescue her from the dictionaries that reduce "àjé" to "witch" and the assumptions that render the mother's power as a dangerous thing. This story is a part of the river that holds all her names: Ochún and Our Lady, María and Mami Wata, Kali and Kwan Yin. Mother and Matka, Mamá and Mère. Iya and Umama and Moeder and Mam, Mutter and Mater, Nne, Mum.

What would it look like to continue along the path I've started on? Slip the mother over my skin. Know myself as the river. Deep, as in layered and fertile. Bottomless. Both the source and the current it sets in motion. The water that comprises every cell of my body connects me to the one who birthed me: Mimi, who knew herself as Me-Me. And before her, Josephine, then Lillian. And before Lillian, Leah Josephine. Womb inside womb inside womb, like a river that flows back in time and place—from Missouri and Ohio to Germany and northern Europe. There, the paper trail of legal records ends, and still they continue to a single point on the horizon. For in the story of the world, we can all trace our origins back to a single place on earth and that place, from all the evidence we have to go by, is Africa. It is there that our stories that feel so separate—Záhilys's and Maruchi's, Marta's and Miriam's, yours and mine—converge in a single point: a first mother from whom we are all born. She who is ever-changing. Impossible to pin down. The creatrix who births herself again and again.

Our bodies aren't separate—no matter what stories we tell that make them seem that way—but interconnected. The conjunction that joins us is not *or* but *and*. Our hands connect like a line of paper dolls cut from a single sheet. Me *and* my mother *and* my grandmothers *and* the girl-women who will follow after us. Somewhere there in the middle I stand at the banks of a river, reaching my hand both forward and back as I birth myself again and again. I am Me. I am Me. Me. I am the mother.

AUTHOR'S NOTE ON LUCUMÍ SPELLINGS

Please note that there is no standardized spelling of Lucumí words and terms. Yoruba scholars use standard Yoruba spellings with all the necessary diacritical marks, while American scholars tend to Americanize spellings by leaving out accent marks. Those initiated in the Afro-Cuban worship known as Santería or Lucumí generally follow Spanish guidelines when adding diacritical marks to syllables; and even among those writers, the spellings of words can differ (such as Oshún or Ochún; Shangó or Changó; aché or ashé). To write about the oricha is to choose a framework from a variety of possible spellings, and in this work, I have chosen to use those I was originally taught by my teachers and guides in Cuba.

ACKNOWLEDGMENTS

Thank you, first and always, to the divine gatekeeper, Eleggua, for opening all the doors that made this book possible. Thank you to my agent, Leslie Meredith, and to my editor, Anne McGrath; I am the luckiest! To Grete Viddal, my flesh and blood Eleggua, for opening many of the first doors to this story, and for sticking around to fact check the final manuscript. To Lee Martin, Jim Phelan, Jen Schlueter, Jill Christman, Chelsey Clammer, and Carrie Frye, for helping me hone the first drafts of these pages. This book would not exist without you.

To Paul Cohen, Colin Rolfe, Sandra Capellaro, Dory Mayo, and the whole team at Monkfish. Thank you for championing literary and spiritual work, and thank you for choosing to champion mine. What you made happen is extraordinary!

To the brilliant friends in Cuba who opened their minds and hearts to me, with deep gratitude to Lourdes Tamayo Fernández, who first introduced me to Ochún; to María Isabel Berbes Ribeaux (Maruchi) for helping me decode her secrets; and to Juan Gonzáles Pérez (Madelaine) and Juana Chacón Pérez (Záhilys), for helping me find my way back to my mother.

To my beloved hosts, teachers, guides and companions—to Marta, Miriam, Daniel, Miriela, Zunilda, Yolersi, Aristedes, Jorge Luís, and Jordan in Havana; to Roberto, Luís, Rolando, Narjhara, Darío, Tomás, Mabel, and Tatica in Santiago de Cuba; and to Padre Eugenio, Padre Gustavo, and Hermana Martha Lee in El Cobre. I am forever in your debt.

Thank you to the many historians and anthropologists whose research informs my understanding of Cuban history and spiritual practices, with special thanks to Julio Corbea, Olga Portuondo Zuñiga, and the Casa del Caribe for sharing your historical knowledge of Our Lady and the Cuban oriente. And to María Elena Díaz, whose writings provided an invaluable resource as I worked to reconstruct the early lives of Juan Moreno and Apolonia.

To the artists Zaída del Río, Salvador González Escalona, Elías Aseff Alonso, Generoso Betancourt, Alicia Leal, and Alberto Lescay Merencio, whose artwork and interviews, while not physically included in these pages, shimmer just beneath their surface.

A very special thanks to Matanzas artist, Adrián Gómez Sancho, for granting permission to use "Anunciación, la gran ofrenda" for the book cover, and for creating artwork for the interior.

To The Ohio State University, whose funding made my travels to Cuba possible. And to the Ohio Arts Council, Greater Columbus Arts Council, Columbus College of Art & Design, PLAYA Artist Residency, Ragdale Foundation, The Porches, Virginia Center for Creative Arts, and Brush Creek Foundation, for giving me the space, time, and means to write.

Thank you to Brett Beach, Jaye Schlesinger, Annie McGreevy, Marjorie Gillette, Jenny Patton, and Merideth Hite Estevez for believing in this project when I needed it most. To Steve Brockman, for helping reconstruct my parents' tango showcase. To Cait Weiss Orcutt, for so brilliantly editing my book proposal. And to Sarah Russo, Laura Di Giovine, Laci Durham, and the team at Page One Media, for all your help getting this book into the world.

Thank you, forever and ever, to Jill—for holding my hand when I couldn't look. For keeping my mother alive in your heart. For holding the version of me who had a mother there beside her.

To Vicki, Susan, and Jon, for whom my mother is also your mother—thank you for corroborating memories and giving me access to your own. Special thanks to Vicki for sharing our mother's vocal recordings, and to Susan for granting me access to your vast archives of family movies, photographs, and diaries. So much gratitude!

To my El Cobre família: Alina, Milene, Indira, Jaime, Alinita, Eloy, and the entire Venzant Valls clan. Thank you for the 10,000 ways you've helped and cared for me, large and small.

To Ochún and Our Lady of Charity, who taught me that the Mother is too vast and mighty to be confined to any single body.

To my mother, Mimi Meyers Huntman, who first taught me to inhabit Her shape. And to my father, John William Huntman, who taught me to be curious about the world, and unafraid to venture out into it.

To my grandmothers Josephine, Antonia, Lillian, Anna Bertha, Wilhelmina, and Helena Margaretha, who connect me to that great river of mothers who sustain and animate each and every one of us.

To Rick, who is forever the bison to my egret. Your love and belief in this book mean everything.

And to Alejandro: I am so blessed to be your mother. You are my heart.

ABOUT THE AUTHOR

Rebe Huntman is a memoirist, essayist, dancer, teacher, and poet. For over a decade she directed Chicago's award-winning Danza Viva Center for World Dance, Art & Music and its dance company, One World Dance Theater. Rebe collaborates with native artists in Cuba and South America, has been featured in *Latina Magazine*, *Chicago Magazine*, and the *Chicago Tribune* and on Fox and ABC. The recipient of an Ohio Individual Excellence award, Rebe has received support for this book from The Ohio State University, Virginia Center for Creative Arts, Ragdale Foundation, PLAYA Artist Residency, Hambidge Center, and Brush Creek Foundation. She lives in Delaware, Ohio and San Miguel de Allende, Mexico. Both *e*'s in her name are long.